I was moved by Shanti Bannwart's passion to creativity, to art, to nature, and to life. Her questions to interesting artists, scientists, and entrepreneurs lead the reader to know and appreciate their work, their philosophy, and their daily life—and also to admire the talented author and her unusually varied experience, which enriches the book.
—Bill Broder, author of *The Sacred Hoop* and *Taking Care of Cleo*

Secrets of the Creative Life

Secrets of the Creative Life
A Book of Inspiration

Shanti Elke Bannwart

Golden Word Books
Santa Fe, NM

Also by Shanti Elke Bannwart
Dancing On One Foot: Growing Up In Nazi Germany, A Memoir

Cover Tapestry by Christine Fayon, France

Library of Congress Control Number 9781948749534

Secrets of the Creative Life. Copyright © 2020 by
Shanti Elke Bannwart
All rights reserved
Printed in the United States of America

No part of this book may be used or reproduced in any manner whatsoever without written permission except in the case of brief quotations embedded in critical articles and reviews. Send inquiries to Golden Word Books, 33 Alondra Road, Santa Fe, New Mexico 87508.

Published by Golden Word Books, Santa Fe, New Mexico.
www.GoldenWordBooks.com

ISBN 978-1-948749-53-4

This book is dedicated to the Muses.
Out of Chaos they create Art.

Contents

Foreword xi

Introduction 1

The Creatives: Their Bios 5
    Anya Achtenberg 6
    Cathy Aten 8
    Ruth Bamford 10
    Michael Broome 12
    Theodora Capaldo 14
    Tim Gosnell 16
    Vijali Hamilton 18
    Tony Juniper 20
    Esther Marion 22
    Amanda McPhail 24
    Peggy O'Kelly 26
    Chrissie Orr 28
    Elias Rivera 30
    Aaron Stern 32
    Uwe Walter-Nakajima 34
    Sara Warber 36
    Carole Watanabe 38
    Yael Weiss 40
    Jerry Wennstrom 42
    Wesley West 44

Chapter One. What is Creativity? 47
    A Web of Beauty 47
    I Want to Write About Creativity 51
    Fire in Water 52
    What Is Creativity?: The Interviews 53

Contents

Chapter Two. The Creative Process 71
   Perfection 75
   The Redemptive Power of Writing 78
   The Creative Process: The Interviews 81

Chapter Three. Encounters 105
   Aztec, A Love Story 105
   Facing the Mystery 107
   Encounter with Mark Rothko 109
   The Great Mother Thanacupe 111
   Encounters: The Interviews .117

Chapter Four. Place and Time 137
   The Intimate Substance of Time 137
   Angel in York 139
   A Creative Perspective on Time: The Vision Quest 141
   Place and Time: The Interviews: 142

Chapter Five. The Source of Creativity 163
   Contagion 163
   The Magic of Words 167
   Nothingness 170
   The Source of Creativity: The Interviews 172

Chapter Six. Darkness and Shadow 197
   Hiroshima 197
   Spring Equinox 200
   Clay, Fire, and Sake 201
   Darkness and Shadow: The Interviews 203

**Chapter Seven. Resistance. Procrastination,
and Suffering** 221
   Strangling the Flow: Writer's Block, Boredom, and
      Sacrifice 221
   Resistance, Procrastination, and Suffering:
      The Interviews 231

Chapter Eight. Community or Solitude 255
    The Artist and the Audience 255
    The Magic of Music 257
    Life at the Edge 260
    Community or Solitude: The Interviews 262

Chapter Nine. Money and Creativity 279
    The Maker and the Taker 279
    Money and Creativity: The Interviews 282

Chapter Ten. Science and Art: The Interviews 303

Chapter Eleven. Healing 313
    Creative Encounter 313
    Forgiveness—The Art of Relating 315

Chapter Twelve. Life as Art 317
    Broken 317
    Life's Longing for Itself: Birth 320
    Life as Art: The Interviews 327

The Interview Questions 379

About the Author 381

Foreword

Caress the Divine Details of your life.
—Vladimir Nabokov

Dragons and Unicorns

This is a down-to-earth and an up-in-the-sky book. It is deeply related to personal experience in daily life rather than theoretical contemplation. It follows my journey to find answers for my burning curiosity about the phenomenon of *Creativity*.

I wanted to know, and so I asked others. For this book, I interviewed twenty people who are creators, people who *actively live the creative life*. The interviews were conducted with artists and scientists and mothers and dancers and sculptors and environmental activists and painters and authors. They are people who feel passionate about writing, music, the environment, peace, medicine, pottery, dance, theater, science, and human relationships. I met these *Creatives* face to face in their homes, studios, and offices, or talked with them over the phone. I asked them questions about creativity and recorded their answers. I was deeply touched by their ruminations and discoveries and by their devotion to their art. I see us—including you, dear reader—as seekers, like a group of pilgrims on the road to some promising land where creativity is honored and known as a shaping force of this amazing universe.

My own thoughts and musings introduce each chapter in the form of stories or essays. As in any engaged discussion and encounter of kindred spirits, we will get to know each other over time. As you listen to personal revelations, and your own insights and opinions will be encouraged to emerge. This is a book that calls for participation, and the process will challenge you. It is arranged according to themes, and you can open it at any place to read.

We are a tribe of seekers; we think about creativity with patience and passion. I imagine that we sit in a circle near a fireplace or under my blooming peach tree as each of us contributes in unique ways to this exploration.

I experienced every encounter with the interviewees as a gift, and I feel deep gratitude toward them, touched by their authenticity and risk-taking. They shared their essence with me, and they are now part of my life; I feel love for them. They, in turn, appreciated being asked and listened to, honored in their personal search for this magnificent, and sometimes painfully unruly mystery called *Creativity*.

My own beliefs have been challenged by their opinions. Perhaps, I assumed, if I understood how creativity works—not only in those who were interviewed but also in you and in me and in the universe—I might be able to "tame" it, like the fox in Saint-Exupéry's book *The Little Prince* who asked the prince to tame him so that he would find wisdom. Or perhaps the opposite is also true: The creative force is an untamed and independent energy turned back onto itself and captured by the artist in moments of awakening and ecstasy or terror. I ask myself and you: Is creativity a force that needs to be involved and engaged in a way like that of love, which needs the link with physicality, with our senses, with real bodies and sweat and skin?

Tchaikovsky mused about the effect on him when being struck by this creative force: "It would be vain to put into words that immeasurable sense of bliss which comes over me directly when a new idea awakens in me and begins to assume a definite form. I forget everything and behave like a madman. Everything within me starts pulsing and quivering."

Yes, that quivering experience is the target of this book, including all the hesitations and resistances against such an orgasmic and engaging process which might end in glorious success—or in despair if the goal is not achieved and the artist's creation turns out to be flawed and disappointing.

Since I involved myself in this exploration, I see the works and objects of creativity everywhere. Nature is bursting with creativity, every tree or leaf, raven or rock, cloud or seashell is an expression of this creative force. As I listen to a small bird singing its warbled and complicated song, I wonder if it weaves this melody just to elicit pure joy and playfulness. Maybe its only purpose is to delight itself and us, as we stop in our tracks to listen.

And how is that for you, dear reader? Is creative endeavor a vital part of your life, or do you hide it like a secret love affair, shy to declare yourself an artist? This book wants to encourage you to accept and embrace your unique gift, your contribution to a continuously unfolding world. As artist and as therapist, I observe that we humans have a built-in longing for beauty and participation, but too often, we let daily tasks and duties squelch our expression of this yearning. In interviewing a wide variety of *Creatives*, I came to know their personal answers and solutions to such a split.

Creativity drives us humans to seek and shape the artistic visions that are locked inside our minds and souls. We are co-creators, and the bliss of being an active participant can be orgasmic. I am an elder, and have encountered the world and people for three-quarters of a century, first as a child and then as a chemist, a mother, psychotherapist, ceramic artist, writer, and seeker. So I was allowed some deep glimpses into human souls and into the mystery that surrounds us everywhere. The purpose of this book is to engage, to amuse, to be rattled and startled, and so to become intimate with the creative forces of this ordinary world and extraordinary Universe.

I engaged each of the interviewees with a series of about fifteen questions which became the titles of the chapters. In each, all the interviewees usually speak to the topic from their own point of view. The questions are listed at the end of the book if you would like to reflect on your own answers before you engage with the thoughts of others.

And so, dear reader, join our group. Walk along the pilgrim's path as we follow this ancient trail, exploring creativity and honoring the fact that we know very little about this great mystery. It is a worthwhile journey, the effort . . .

- to dig and to dance,
- to play and to plant,
- to sing and to sculpt,
- to paint and to putter,
- to prune and to plaster,
- to cook and compose,
- to write and to roam,
- to think and to sing

will bring you rich rewards.

The goal is revelation, the process is full of miracles, and there are dragons as well as angels along the trail; perhaps you'll even find a unicorn hiding in the thicket.

Each chapter deals with a different aspect of creativity, and begins with some thoughts of my own, followed by those of the talented people whom I interviewed.

I wrote this book for you, dear reader, as well as for myself, that we may listen to our muses and you too may become entangled in a hot-blooded love affair with a creative work of your own—that is the gift of creativity, and so it happened to me. Hold your life in loving hands, as you might a pebble found in a river or a shell on the beach. Quietly turn it around and look at it from every angle, hold it up to the sun or make it shine by licking the salt from its surface. In the same way, you may contemplate your own life and its expression, feeling awe and gratitude; you may recognize its beauty as well as its flaws, comprehending how unique this life of yours is, your gift, your special skills, your successes as well as your failings. Embrace and express them and all they stand for.

INTRODUCTION

We humans are not evolving but circling, and the stuff of our Souls keeps coming back for more attention and more living.
—Thomas Moore

Eating the Moon

In September 2014, I participated in a week-long Jungian workshop titled *Feeding the Moon*. When we gathered in the first circle and told our stories and why we were there, I realized that I had thought all along the theme was *Eating the Moon*. This mix-up brought me—besides some heartfelt laughter—a surprising realization: Yes, I am being fed and nurtured by the Moon Goddess and her Mystery. She is "edible" and makes herself available to be ingested.

As I grow older, creativity and insights are more easily accessible than in my younger years. It isn't any longer arduous work to dig for a seed-kernel of truth in a pile of leaves. After more than seventy-five years of life lived in great devotion to the creative Muses, they give back to me now in generous ways through inspiration and enlightened knowing. After a lifetime of *Feeding the Moon* and venerating her mystery, I am now "Eating the Moon," and the creative spirits of the night are intimately nurturing and nursing me. We are rubbing shoulder to shoulder, and they invite me into inner realms of vision. They reach out to me.

Yes, we have a mutual interest in each other. We are engaged in one love story, bonded inside each other.

I live in the high desert of the Southwest, and every evening for many years now, I step outside under the light of the stars and moon, watching the night sky spanning east to west with breathtaking clarity. Daily, I send my love and adoration to the Goddess and whisper prayers of gratitude.

I also have learned to camp out in the desert, and during the night, I put my head near the open flap of the tent so that at any time, I can raise my eyelids to observe the brilliance of the night sky, ingesting it into my being. The moon is a lover. She is part of my spiritual family. She is a quiet and deep source of creative inspiration as she strides in the golden sandals of dawn and dusk through the night and in my dreams. The Moon Goddess is one of my Muses. Her physical beauty is a witness to the magnificence of creation, her changing shape a lively reminder of the cycles of birth and death.

Creativity is always waiting for vision to be realized into physical form. It rattles the unborn work out of its slumber. At every breath, something yearns for gestation and birth. A tiny current of sound quivers in the air and expands into a song or symphony. A word or sentence in a poem stirs the imagination of the reader into a story. A quivering branch in the wind invites a dance. This exchange is mutual. We are the blank page, and we are also the moving hand that writes. We are the womb with a child and we are the child struggling to be born. Creative forces desire to be seduced into an inviting space. We need only to clear such a space and creativity will settle there, urging creation to burst forth. As William James said, *Action may not always bring happiness, but there is no happiness without action.*

I observe that my creative energy becomes sluggish and foul when I sit at the edge of the river of life and merely watch myself watching, distant to the river, separate from it, alone, without purpose. Then, just sitting and having time—though usually delightful—seems a waste of that time and a "sin" in the sense of uselessness. But when I am creative—as in this moment when I am writing—I stand with my feet in the current, watching what swims by and what happens under the surface. And I might even take notes and write about it. And in that way, I am engaged and

Introduction

become part of that twirling river. In this way, the artist is a witness to life's creative unfolding.

Active creativity is for me the most "effective" way to connect again and again with the vibrant force of life, igniting passion and joy. Active creativity is expressed through my hands, through writing or cooking or clay or alert stillness; it is my way to live life as art. The artist is the space-holder and the creator of action. The artist's happiness and satisfaction are rooted in action toward creation.

As artists, we should not take ourselves as too seriously, as we are just the channel through which the vision and ideas flow. Whatever project we realize is not so much our "gift to the world" but rather a product of the vibrant enjoyment of the act of creation. Creativity is self-gratifying and self-indulging; it satiates the creator's heart with delight and satisfaction. As I am writing this, I let my eyes wander to the window, to the New Mexico piñons shaking in the wind and the mountains in distance, the Stellar's jays at the feeder and my cat on her pillow. This moment and place are fertile grounds for the dance with the forces of creativity.

Most of my writing life consists of nothing more than unglamorous, disciplined labor. I sit at my desk and I work like a farmer.
—Elizabeth Gilbert, *Big Magic*

The Creatives: Their Bios

ANYA ACHTENBERG

Anya has taught widely, including at New York University, the School of Visual Arts in New York, Springfield College in Boston, Hamline University, the University of Minnesota's Split Rock Arts Program, the University of New Mexico's Honors Program, the Joiner Center for the Study of War and Social Consequences; and for organizations such as the International Women's Writing Guild, the Center for Contemporary Arts and Word Harvest in Santa Fe, the Leaven Center in Michigan, and Intermedia Arts' Writer to Writer Mentorship Program. She has developed and teaches a series of multi-genre workshops on Writing for Social Change (Re-Dream a Just World; Place and Exile/Borders and Crossings; and Yearning and Justice: Writing the Unlived Life). Achtenberg is Jewish; her father was born in the Ukraine. She favors the side of her mother, who was born in Russia and is of indigenous Siberian culture. Her mother's father was from North Africa. "That's where I got my wild, curly hair," she says. She was very young when she decided to become a writer.

I was always interested in human beings and how they function, so I decided to study psychology and comparative literature, and a lot of art history. I was homeless for much of my time in college. I was displaced, didn't have a place to stay, sat in coffee shops all night to study, could not go home. So even entering college at sixteen, it took me five years to finish. I graduated in January of 1970, when I was twenty-one. I had many notebooks and came out, doing some readings. Those were very difficult times, I was out on the street a lot. 1973 there was a nationwide depression, especially in New York, in specific neighborhoods. My life got increasingly difficult, and I was more and more involved with people whose lives were challenging; some were in and out of prison. But I trust myself: Give me that room full of kids who are lost, and I

Anya Achtenberg
Writer, Teacher

**Interviewed by phone at
her home in Minneapolis**

will be on the ground with them; I understand them. And that is art, that's living a life as art.

I was already politically radicalized by Vietnam and questions of race and civil rights. I was around those kind of people, and I kept writing. My creativity saved me. It is absolutely integral to the nature of human beings. The desire to create is a process of very deep union, a place to put the overwhelm of life, its light and shadow and shape. We live in a world that is overshadowed by so much suffering. For myself, suffering is part of my life and art. I ask about the unanswerable and unexplained mysteries. It's like someone gives you a most amazing gem; you have to do something with it, show it to others. Look at the ancient Greek tragedies, the plays; they are so very moving. I am overwhelmed by the world— some of it is so magnificent, other experiences so grievously sad. I explore all levels, from the grittiest of life to the most magical.

CATHY ATEN

Cathy Aten attended the Center for Creative Studies-College of Art and Design in Detroit, and received a BFA in textile design.

She was a well-established ceramic artist in Santa Fe when she was diagnosed with progressive multiple sclerosis. Her work is inspired by natural shapes found in the high desert of New Mexico: cactus skeletons, seeds, mountain ranges, the earth, and the lively shadows of cottonwood trees on adobe walls. The shape and texture of her clay creations have a magical quality; they are inviting to be touched and fondled.

Her illness diminishes her ability to work with clay and paint and to explore the wilderness as source of inspiration. She has been in the art world for more than thirty-two years. Dealing with the commerce of art and with galleries to make a living, her free spirit felt pressured to produce and repeat what was successful. She has focused her creativity now on the written word, keeping up a lively blog and connection to her followers.

I am not a team player, so I live and survive solo. I am comfortable and familiar with the insecurity of the artist's world, where my life's circumstances are not reliable. I have always been an action person, and I am at ease with the practical challenges of life.

People think that being an artist is really a glamorous thing; it's not. You see, there's the monster of resistance, expressed as procrastination. And there's something scary about it. It is the Void of creativity. Patience and non-action is not an easy thing; it means being naked, vulnerable, lost. Procrastination gives us time to catch up; it forces us to be inactive and experience silence.

My illness has turned my life into my palette; living with illness has become my art. My every day is shaped by creative action. Ordinary living is the same thing as making a sculpture or painting: I give shape to an object—which is my day—and see if it works, or

Cathy Aten
Clay Artist, Painter and Writer

**Interviewed at her home in
Santa Fe, New Mexico**

I might change it and do something different; living is basically the same process as creating art. Creativity is inseparable from my existence. All this is hard work for me. M.S. is an illness, and it sounds as if something is wrong, and I do not really believe that something is wrong with me. I am a survivor; some people think I am in denial because I seem so happy.

I can hardly walk, but I have all this space and beauty and time; that's a luxury. People think I am navel gazing, but I like this contemplative pace and don't make apologies for it. I live in the space shaped by my fate. I live my life how I choose to, and that is true freedom. The biggest thing I have done to celebrate my creativity is to cultivate a soft heart and to be undefended! The more I take down my own armor, the more God's voice sounds inside.

RUTH BAMFORD

Ruth Bamford has been a research scientist at Rutherford Appleton Laboratory (RAL) in Oxfordshire, U.K., since 1996. Her research areas are diverse and include space weather and fundamental plasma physics.

She is the principal investigator of the mini-magnetospheric project for spacecraft protection. The concept concerns "active" or electromagnetic plasma shielding of manned spacecraft for long stays in space and interplanetary missions, and also satellites in radiation belts. Bamford is a researcher on the potential use of an artificial controlled plasma barrier as a deflector shield for spacecraft.

When she first moved to RAL, she worked in the radio communications research unit on radio propagation and the Earth's ionosphere and space weather. From 1998-2001, Bamford devised radio experiments for the U.K. 1999 total solar eclipse, which used the brief night-time of the eclipse to make radio and ionospheric observations across Europe. She coordinated experiments for the scientist, radio amateur, and general public, for which she won a special early career researcher award at the SET for Britain held at the Houses of Parliament. Bamford is dyslexic and actively campaigns for greater awareness of the benefits of the dyslexic brain in science and engineering.

I live and work in a time and field and institution where women are represented in small numbers. The famous university of Oxford in the U.K. is still a male-dominated place. It took years until women were even allowed to study here. Born in London, I grew up in Yorkshire in the north of England, my mother Irish, my father English. I remember my own childhood being very happy actually, even if it does not sound like it. My mother came from a middle-class background; the family read a lot. She was bright, though in

Ruth Bamford
Physicist, Researcher, Professor

**Interviewed in
Cambridge, U.K.**

her generation, girls did not have the opportunity to carry an education beyond age fourteen. But she read profusely, like my grandmother. We did not have much money, but the family had an expanded mind, which she very much imparted to us children.

So I worked myself into a position where women are not honored and have to struggle for their place in science. Oh, God, yes, this power game interferes with my joy in work and creativity. My male colleagues try to squash everything and don't like my approach. I have constantly to fight for my place in this male world of science. I am only working here in this position because I encountered some open-minded colleagues. It is a lonesome position in the lab.

I am a rule breaker. If you are a scientist, that's what you do. It's your task to question the already existing. Never accept anything just because an authority says so.

MICHAEL BROOME

Michael Broome was born in Norfolk, England, and went to college in Leicestershire, graduating in 1966 as a photographer. He was a highly successful freelance magazine photographer in London for about ten years.

He participated in expeditions to Africa with Sir Ranulph Fiennes, photographing the Nile River from Egypt to Kenya. Then, following a calling, he settled in Wales, where he studied and worked as a painter and began to fall in love with clay. Moving to Ocamora, New Mexico, he opened his heart and vision toward the influence of Native American mythology and lore.

During the '60s in London, I met a lot of modern artists. Photography was a big thing at the time, a very open field, lots of new magazines and not many photographers. I liked the atmosphere; I loved the exploration of it all. And then we had this group coming over from America, called the Symposium of Destructive Arts. That was art at the time, trying to be anti-art. You see, art is about making objects, but that group despised the idea of a final object that would be exploited in the art market, sold and re-sold. The members wanted to make art that never got that far because it destroyed itself. Yoko Ono was a driving founder of this group.

I have always been interested in art and the people who make it. I slipped into that new culture, and I know all the arguments of abstract art against figurative art. It was a glowing time to be an artist and to meet kindred spirits. Great!

But then I moved to Wales, and the life there changed everything for me, because I got involved with visual art, with pure painting. And I realized that this was difficult and demanding. I had studied photography, and found out that painting was very different. I knew nothing about painting. It grabbed me, and so I devoted myself to studying painting.

Michael Broome
Painter, Ceramic Artist, Photographer

Interviewed in his studio at Ocate Retreat Center, New Mexico

And then I explored Japanese raku pottery, inspired by my friend Bernard. And I am still working with clay; it has become my love story. Now, living in Ocamora, I am enchanted by this land of New Mexico and the remote place where I live, and by all the experimentation with different materials and styles. I am never lonesome. Art feeds and nurtures me. I live a solitary life, but I am not lonesome.

Theodora Capaldo

Theo Capaldo is chief executive officer of the New England Anti-Vivisection Society, a not-for-profit founded in 1895 whose mission is "ending the use of animals in research, testing, and science and replacing them with modern alternatives that are ethically, humanely, and scientifically superior." She is also a licensed psychologist who has been in practice for over thirty-five years.

Capaldo has worked extensively with victims of psychological trauma, using her sensitivity to animals to enhance her psychology practice with an awareness of the consequences to children and adolescents of being forced to participate in inhumane animal use in education, an understanding of the development of morality and compassion, and a recognition of the psychological suffering and the toll that traumatic experiences take on humans and animals.

I am a Sagittarian, born in 1948. That's important; I am always looking up to the stars with my legs planted firmly on the ground. I love food and believe that cooking is a creative act. Food is not something to do simply to sustain ourselves. It is one more thing in life that I love. What else can I say? I am Italian. So imagine that those vegetables, herbs, fruits, and nuts hold within them fuel for our muscles and organs, but most importantly for our heart and soul. Eating is art.

Working on suffrage, on women's right to vote, working for children with anti-slavery activists—that is art. And the core—what they share and why it's near and dear to my heart—is the issue of justice, fairness, eliminating unnecessary cruelty and victimization. My passion for animal work is at once a drive toward beauty as much as it is a drive to fight evil.

Psychology doesn't just play a role in my work—it frames my entire ethical and professional activism. Remembering that psychology was originally defined as "the study of the soul," at its heart, it is

Theodora Capaldo
Psychologist, Activist, President of the Animal Rights Organization NEAVS

Interviewed at her home near Boston

a practice rooted in compassion. I don't look at issues from a species perspective. My overarching goal is to support the continual evolution of our species toward a more compassionate sensibility. True compassion has no boundaries. Every living being—whether it be a human child, an insect, a dog—is magnificently important and integral to the natural order. And so, to this day and to my final day, I am committed, every cell in me is committed, to this "work." I aspire to be one who helps to restore the balance and respect humans are meant to have with the natural world. I "work" so that the intricate and fierce and vulnerable life system can remain whole, as nature planned it to be. And you see, I see my rage, my sadness in the face of the atrocities, as simply one more proof of how much I love it all. Yes, I love it all!

Tim Gosnell

Tim Gosnell began his scientific career as an astronomy student, but, finding that he preferred working at the lab bench over staring into space, he changed disciplines to experimental solid-state physics. He received his Ph.D. in the subject from Cornell University in 1986. For the next fifteen years, he pursued a research career at Los Alamos National Laboratory, where he published numerous articles and books in a wide range of disciplines, including laser physics and engineering, biophysics, chemical physics, and materials science.

Feeling an itch for the entrepreneurial world, he then turned to research and development in digital image processing, image compression, and computational finance for several startup companies. He is now semi-retired and drifting into social science, partnering with a psychologist in a new venture to quantify and categorize people's attitudes and behaviors on fulfillment, health, and well-being, especially for members of the boomer generation.

When I was in high school, I became interested in Einstein's special theory of relativity. I had heard, like everyone, that the subject is extraordinarily difficult to grasp, and I wanted to prove to myself that I could master the mathematics and take personal ownership of the theory's radical statements about the nature of space and time. By that time, I had already committed to a physics career, as I believed that if I could comprehend something so challenging yet so contradictory of everyday "common sense," somewhere down that path, the truth of the world might lie.

If you ever feel inadequately humble, spend 10+ years of your life studying undergraduate and graduate-level physics at a major research university. That'll fix you right up. Follow then with a professional life full of relentless competition, scarce funding, unscrupulous colleagues, intrusive elected officials, oppressive man-

Tim Gosnell
Scientist Working in Physics and Mathematics

Interviewed at his home in Santa Fe

agement, politics, dollars, dishonesty, and diminished expectations, all the while believing that something like creative imagination still lives within you.

The true triumphs—I had one or two to be truly proud of—came emotionally tainted in ways I still don't really understand.

Now that I am growing older, and no longer caught up in the scientific "business," I've returned home to the motivations I felt as a teenager. On the bucket list are serious studies of topics in theoretical physics that I never had time for but which speak most clearly my longings to understand how the world really works. It's also about those old-fashioned, in-person conversations, time with friends and family in service of quieter needs. Call it a renewed respect for the sanctity of everyday life, as when fixing the sprinklers.

I look forward to the day when intelligent life is discovered on another planet. I hope humanity might then rethink a few things.

VIJALI HAMILTON

Vijali Hamilton is a visionary sculptor, poet, musician, performance artist, and author. She is the originator of the World Wheel Project: Global Peace Through the Arts. This global peace project combines sculptures in living rock to establish sacred sites with Wisdom Centers to address local problems and preserve indigenous cultures. Her work includes education, art, spirituality, and peace activism, and focuses attention on the awareness of environmental, spiritual, and social problems.

Hamilton spent ten years as a monastic member of the Vedanta convent. She received a master's degree in fine arts from Goddard University and is a fellow of the World Academy of Arts and Science. More than a thousand pieces of her art are in private and public collections. She lectures extensively and has offered retreats for many years. She contemplates the creative process of moving from the introspection of meditation and journal writing toward concrete art forms. Hamilton's work and life have been represented in numerous books. She studied Dzogchen under Tibetan Buddhist lamas and wisdom from native masters around the world. For forty years, she has been a teacher of spiritual practice and creativity (meditation, writing, sculpting, painting, drawing), as well as working in twenty countries with her World Wheel Project: Global Peace Through the Arts.

Hamilton has dedicated her life to working as a peacemaker. She collaborates with diversified communities and uses her skills as a sculptor, filmmaker, poet, musician, and author to further this mission. She started her World Wheel Project in 1986, circling the planet as she worked with the arts in her quest for world peace.

I started the World Wheel Journey in 1986, using environmental stone sculptures to build sacred space and to address the needs of communities and of the environment, the needs of children and

Vijali Hamilton
Sculptor, Filmmaker, Poet, Musician, and Author, Founder of World Wheel forPeace

Interviewed at her home and studio in Santa Fe

families, the need to understand neighbors who pray differently than ourselves, cultures different from our own, and the urge to call for a change of heart.

Tony Juniper

Tony Juniper lives in Cambridge, U.K., and is one of the top ten environmental activists of the last thirty years. He is a campaigner, author, and sustainability adviser to the Prince of Wales and various NGOs, and is working with corporations and other organizations to build sustainable societies at both local and global levels.

From a very young age, my inspiration came from nature. And it remains so; that's why I devote myself to nature's protection. What I am now is an environmental campaigner and writer, and I advise companies on environmental strategies. Spirituality does not mean a lot to me. I think I call myself a neo-pagan, more leaning toward Stonehenge than Westminster Abbey.

I work in slightly academic circles, and I lecture and write and share ideas. I came to this through quite a long journey that led to academic studies in zoology and a choice of whether the right way to go was to stay in academia and study the natural world or work through science and the disciplines in conservation, trying to hang on to the natural environment as much as we can, raising awareness through changing policies, teaching new approaches to companies. And I went down that latter road. I finished up working in environmental groups, working to conserve endangered habitats and threatened species, and then I went more into campaigning and the political side of it through working with Friends of the Earth for quite a few years. That led me into all sorts of experiences and questions in terms of global development. I ran Friends of the Earth in the U.K. for six years, and then I was the vice chair of Friends of the Earth International. I stepped out of that in 2008 to pursue a more flexible life, which I am in now, lecturing, advising, thinking, and contributing to teaching in different places. I am trying to reconcile these increasing pressures on the natural en-

Tony Juniper
Environmental Activist, Campaigner, Author, Sustainability Adviser

Interviewed at his home in Cambridge, U.K.

vironment with the increasing aspirations of people to have rising standards of living and this endless process of economic growth. What is the drive behind all of those things? How do we respond to all of those burning issues: climate change, resource depletion, the extinction of species?

How do we make that fit with the needs of nine billion people? That's all of my work today. The purpose of my life is to leave the natural world in the best possible state so that people can enjoy it in the future.

ESTHER MARION

Esther Marion has been studying, performing, living and absorbing the art of flamenco since she was a teen-ager. She studied in Spain with great dancers such as La Tati, Ciro, Merche Esmeralda, Joaquin Ruiz, Alejandro Granados, Carmen Cortez, and Farruquita. She has performed with nationally and internationally known flamenco artists while living in Santa Fe, New Mexico. In Seattle, she was the guest artist of Carmona Flamenca. She started the group Cafe Cantante, and, with the trio Andalibre, regularly performed as a dancer and singer. In spring 2009, she was a partner in the duo Arte Flamenco producing "Arte Flamenco Profundo" with guest artists from Spain.

After finishing high school in Switzerland, I did not go to college but instead traveled the world with my lover-friend Mark, trusting and risking, learning by doing. Such a path allows your life energy to build and move you forward. It challenges you to define what you really want and who you are and what your gifts are. That's the cauldron where you will be cooked. It's the place where you learn to trust in your guiding star; it's good to live like that when you are in your early years. My life and career have their own inner guidance. I crossed the Atlantic Ocean to come to the States, and the same month, my then-unknown husband crossed the other ocean and we met in Santa Fe thirty years ago. That was fate.

My sensually trained and finely tuned body is my vehicle and instrument for all I do creatively. I write continuously and redefine my own systems and vision. I speak four languages and also communicate through song, dance, and healing hands as massage therapist. There is a system of psychology that I study and explore. I am in my philosophy a Jungian at heart; I connect with my dreams, they are a true source of inspiration and guidance. I pay attention to my psyche and mind. The Muses and archetypes are

Esther Marion
Dancer, Mother, Teacher

Interviewed at her dance studio in Seattle

my source; they feed me, touch me, set me on fire. I live life as a daily creation of art.

I feel connected to a source inside that is free and spontaneous. The daily practice and training of creative skills is essential for me to live deeply, with wisdom, in family and society, in the world and in this cosmos.

Amanda McPhail

Amanda McPhail trained in graphics and illustration at Bath Academy of Art in the U.K. She worked mainly as a freelance illustrator for publishers in London and for magazines and books in Cambridge, where numerous pieces of her work were commissioned by Cambridge University Press.

McPhail also taught graphics and illustration in the Foundation Art Course for eighteen years, first at the "Tech" and then, after it was transferred to Cambridge, at the Regional College. On leaving teaching, she set up her own studio, where she is producing illustrations on bone china by using on-glaze paper enamel.

I believe creativity is not just a visual art thing; it is also in the person who raises children and cooks their meals and lives their life with satisfaction. They cope every day with what they got assigned by life.

My favorite days are those when I put on my red hat and go into my studio and do my work undisrupted. A creative day is wonderful. I am doing what I love doing, and there are so many different ways of expression.

I need to have a studio space which is solely mine. I have to clear out everything that's not related to me and my work; that's very important, this one space, my studio, where I can leave out everything there that I need.

I think that we are not producing just out of ourselves. We always integrate inspiration and new ideas from the people around us; we are not totally unique in what we produce.

I think there are differences between the modes of art. I always thought that painters are more serious about their art than creatives of other modalities. They would probably define creativity much more eloquently. We have never been good in artistic verbiage. I don't care much for it. I want to look at art and get a feel for it. I

Amanda McPhail
Sculptor, Media and Ceramic Artist

Interviewed with Wesley West at their studios in Cambridge, U.K.

don't want it all explained in art-speak. Art-speak annoys the hell out of me, because you can pass off bad work with clever words.

So Wesley [West, her husband] and I take all those ideas from others or from nature and combine them in a very personal way, or make them out of different material, and that for me is creativity in action.

PEGGY O'KELLY

Peggy O'Kelly left a stable job as "big eight" CPA in 1994 to follow her true passion: harvesting olives and practicing the ancient art of olive oil production. She moved to the Napa Valley of California, and started the St. Helena Olive Oil Company, producing first-class olive oil and other pantry and beauty products.

I grew up in Oakland, California, in a very chaotic household. Mom was a trained schoolteacher; Dad was a doctor. Art and creativity were not respected. In their eyes, that was not the way to make it in the world.

In high school, I fell in love with philosophy and writing, wanted to be a writer, and did well. I grew up with a math mind and I thought I had zero creativity. I was into sports.

In college, I went into nursing, pre-med. Dad—who was a surgeon—said, "If you want to be a doctor, you have to give your entire life to it."

That was not for me. So I went back into accounting and finance and finished with a double major. I built my own business after my divorce, when I had to provide for two daughters. I am successful in what I do and dedicated to lead an enterprise in a way that does not harm but honors the earth.

Building my business began back in the early '90s with two small girls in tow and "Under the Tuscan Sun" in hand. I worked in finance and loved it, but it was not conducive to being the mother that I wanted to be. So I left my career in San Francisco. I left financial security and traded it for a life of risk, adventure, and creativity. I learned a lot along the way. This change of occupation changed me. I opened several outlet stores, but today I restrict my business expansion for the sake of my personal peace and freedom. I do not have to practice the bigger-is-better thing. That is my new way of living a creative professional life. Being successful usually

Peggy O'Kelly
Visionary Businesswoman, Producer of Olive Oil and Bath Products

Interviewed by phone at her home in Napa Valley, California

means having multiple stores, creating a national brand. Now, I shape that path differently: I build only one store in the way that it brings basic income—and also feeds my Soul.

And I reach out beyond my life. I have the vision and plan to support women worldwide in their craft and skill and ability to create a livelihood for themselves and their families and their villages. I faced many challenges along the way, but I have always stayed true to my core values of living an authentic life with deep connection to spirit, to others, and to our beloved planet. I break bread with those I love and drizzle on a little Napa Valley Olio Nuovo! Carpe Diem.

CHRISSIE ORR

Chrissie Orr was born in Scotland, received an MFA from Edinburgh College of Art, and then proceeded to develop her skills as an artist in unconventional places and ways. She was a circus performer throughout Europe and a muralist in Corsica, and has created community-based projects in America, Australia, Europe, Iran, Mexico, and Turkey. She was co-director of the Aran Community Arts Project on Scotland's Isle of Aran, one of the first rural arts projects funded by the Scottish Arts Council.

Orr has been a community artist for East Lothian, Scotland, a guest artist at the University of Michigan, an artist-in-residence in South Georgia (for the Millennium Project developing innovative projects gathering stories from diverse communities), and an artist-in-residence at Grand Central Art Center in Santa Ana, California (designing portable, urban edible gardens). She is the founder of the nationally acclaimed Teen Project in Santa Fe. Her vision and skills have been recognized by the U.S. Congress and the National Endowment for the Arts. She has been nominated for numerous awards for her work with youth, and lectures internationally on her work and process.

I grew up in Scotland, was born in a small town called Motherwell near Glasgow, still a mining town, and lived there until I was five or six. We kids lived with my grandfather because my father was studying.

My purpose in life is to live for the arts; it's just something I have to do! I think I was always a creative person, beginning at a young age. I cannot imagine not being actively involved in the arts and in community.

I live it! Every moment, I am watching, seeing, being awake in the environment. Would I do something different today? No!

Chrissie Orr
Painter, Muralist, Community Activator Through Art

Interviewed at the Warehouse 21 performance center in Santa Fe

Everything that comes into my life—all the hardships and disappointments, the mistakes I made—add up to a really vibrant, adventurous life. I made wrong decisions and will continue to make wrong decisions; that's part of a creative life. There were a lot of hard times, but it brought me to the place I am now.

I worked and studied in community with the purpose of building relationships through the creative process. At the School for the Blind, the children came and touched, explored my face; they touched to get to know the body and the person. It was an incredible experience for me. It allowed intimacy. Working with art in community opened me up to a greater level of humanity.

ELIAS RIVERA

Elias Rivera was born in 1937 in New York City, In 1982, he moved to Santa Fe. In his paintings, he explores the colorful costumes and street life of the native populations of Santa Fe, Guatemala, Mexico, and Peru. He lives outside Santa Fe with his wife, artist Susan Contreras.

Classically trained and using large canvases, he portrays people in their pursuit of daily life.

In 2004, Rivera received the Governor's Award for Excellence in the Arts. In 2005, he was named Distinguished Artist of the Year.

Rivera is a painter whose work both creates timeless images and displays virtuosity of technique. During his long career, he has painted the human drama as it unfolds in settings as varied as civil rights demonstrations, subways, rodeos, and the marketplaces of Central and South America. His classical training and "old master" technique evoke a true narrative quality rarely seen in contemporary realist painting. Regardless of the particulars of culture, place and time that appear in each painting, Rivera consistently captures the essence and soul of humanity.

I grew up in New York in the Bronx, and as a young man, I needed first to educate myself. In my home, my family had no sense for culture; my mother mostly read the Reader's Digest. But I took art lessons, and my teacher, Frank Mason, was a great pedagogue. He had a sense of the ideal. I read art books, I visited museums, I reached for stars.

I studied the old masters. There's Velasquez, and especially Rembrandt; his genius hit me between the eyes and in the heart. He was a guiding force for me all throughout my life, and he is still one of the greatest artists who lived. Ever.

Life in New York inspired me deeply. But in the 1980s, the city that had nurtured me all those years began to destroy me as an

Elias Rivera
Painter

**Interviewed at
his studio in Santa Fe**

artist. I entered the world of art in New York at the wrong period, what was "in" then had nothing to do with my style of expression. I was running against too many brick walls. When I came to Santa Fe, I approached the town and looked down on it from the hill, and I fell in love immediately, and I am still in the quiver of that love. This is home and a place that nurtures my art.

Aaron Stern

A composer, teacher, and internationally recognized consultant on learning, he conducts consultancies and seminars throughout the United States and Europe.

While serving as dean of the American Conservatory of Music in Chicago during the early 1980s, Stern met his mentor and friend, Leonard Bernstein, and the two embarked on an intense ten-year collaboration.

Stern is a Fellow of the Mind & Life Institute, which was co-founded by the Dalai Lama. He conceived the Academy for the Love of Learning with Bernstein, and serves as its president. As educational leader of the academy, Stern designed and directs its core curriculum and foundational program, Leading by Being.

The question of biography is an interesting one. I could enter it in the frame of education or where I grew up, but since the topic is creativity, I will enter into it as a creative biography. When I was a kid, around six or seven years, I remember vividly that I would sit at the piano and create thunder and lightning storms with my music. I would create whole symphonies in different moods. Understanding more about how music is composed, I would say today that all the components were present at that young age. Those are my earliest creative memories.

Through musical expression, I was trying to make sense of the world. Where I grew up, there were some very challenging stories in our family—very painful and explosive, deeply unsafe and confusing—and I was not clear what this was all about.

So finding a narrative in the middle of an unsafe family situation was a creative act. It created wholeness and a sense of rightness in the midst of chaos, in which music was a powerful healer for me. Music helped me to survive that challenge.

And this is what happened to me: It was in the Ming tombs during a trip to China that I said to myself "I know what I am going

Aaron Stern
Composer, Musician, Teacher, Founder and Director of the Academy for the Love of Learning

Interviewed at the Academy outside Santa Fe

to do." I had this flash of knowing what I would dedicate the rest of my life to. I knew that I was to create this place, the Academy for the Love of Learning. It was a mystical experience, a great opening. And I got completely lost.

And today, after years of work and struggle, this academy exists in Santa Fe and attracts people from all over the world.

UWE WALTER-NAKAJIMA

Uwe Walter-Nakajima was born in Germany and dedicated his career to theater arts. But in 1979 when he heard the sound of the Japanese bamboo shakuhachi flute, he was so mesmerized that he moved to Japan to devote himself instead to studies of this instrument.

Fully trained in the dance and chant of Noh drama, he is now a performer and ceremonialist and a shakuhachi recording artist, while living as a rice farmer and teacher with his family in a mountain village near Kyoto,.

Walter-Nakajima lectures about the techniques of shakuhachi and "Ma" (roughly defined as "space") in Japan, where he often appears on television. He has taught at the main temple of the Komuso Society in Tokyo and makes his living playing Honkyoku shakuhachi music. He belongs to the "Kiri no Kai" Komuso group in Higashi Hoshino. Since the 1980s, he has been an active musician and performer in Japanese streets, temples, and media.

Walter-Nakajima's creative spirit knows no limits. He organized a pilgrimage to Auschwitz for eleven Japanese Komuso monks to contribute to the process of healing the wounds of the past in his country of birth.

I studied and live in Japan. I think my purpose is to connect these two cultures and collect all the new trends and bring them back to Germany, especially for young people. They are hungry, seeking for answers, particularly after the Fukushima nuclear accident. There is a mistrust now. That's new in Japan. The country was functioning because people trusted each other. It's a society of consensus, and that is lost now. After the Fukushima accident, people feel hurt and cheated, almost paralyzed.

The young people are moving now. Many of them are leaving Tokyo and coming to the villages, like the one where I live. The

Uwe Walter-Nakajima
Dancer and Mime

Interviewed during a visit from Japan at the Railyard Performance Center in Santa Fe

leaders are lying, and the young folks know that; they look through the web.

I always hope to change the environment through art. That's why I devote my life to the arts. I have a message about truth and magic and spirit, a universal message If you don't have a message, you should not be on the stage.

Sara Warber

Sara Warber graduated summa cum laude in 1973 with a BFA in drama from Illinois Wesleyan University in Bloomington, and in 1993 with an M.D. degree from the College of Human Medicine at Michigan State University. She was elected to the Alpha Omega Alpha Medical Honor Society and received the Janet M. Glasgow Memorial Achievement Award for women who graduate from medical school with academic distinction. She joined the University of Michigan Department of Family Medicine, doing research in Native American healing and studying complementary and alternative medicine.

In 2006, she established the Integrative Family Medicine Clinic at the University of Michigan, and in 2008 was promoted to clinical associate professor. She was offered a Fulbright Scholarship to study "nature-deficit disorder" at the European Centre for Environment & Human Health at the University of Exeter Medical School in Truro, U.K. She has published fifty peer-reviewed publications, twenty-one book chapters, and five books. Warber was promoted to professor emeritus of family medicine at the University of Michigan in 2008.

I am an artist—to please my Soul! I am a physician—to help my patients.

I am a researcher—doing the work in the world that makes apparent the connection between human health and all that is; that's fundamental to my life philosophy.

I had decided to go to medical school just before I met my Native American teacher: Keeaaydino Quny Peschpel. From her, I learned about herbs and spiritual medicine, parallel to my traditional med training. She influenced what kind of holistic doctor I would become.

I charge my creative batteries in nature. That's where Spirit is, where reality is, where I check into refined states and find balance,

Sara Warber
Physician/Researcher, Cofounder of the American Holistic Medical Association

Interviewed by phone at the University of Michigan

where I let go of the trivial and disturbing. Nature charges me as human being and a physician. I go into a prayerful state in nature when I am really struggling with creative work, which often means writing. I am describing here somebody who needs to be alone a lot; that's true with me. The way I construct my day is to be home in the morning for my work, and in the afternoon teach and see patients. I feel generally exhausted after that. I have to go home and curl up in my place here, on the couch, to recharge. I will be mindless for a while, and next day, I am ready again.

In a really creative moment, there's a sense of flow. That's when I feel united with greater universal forces. I am absorbed, expanded beyond myself. And that can happen also in normal activity, and it makes me feel on purpose and fulfilled.

CAROLE WATANABE

Carole Watanabe established the first nationally recognized Gallery for the Fiber Arts in San Francisco, and founded the Apprentice Alliance (a non-profit organization dedicated to placing apprentices with masters in all fields of creative endeavor). She is dedicated to a lifelong commitment to create supportive communities that nourish the wild-art-spirit in all of us.

Her tapestries, sculptural handmade paper works and paintings hang in private collections, hotels, banks, hospitals, and corporate offices across the country. Since completing a bachelor of fine arts degree at the California College of the Arts in Oakland, she has studied indigenous weaving at Lake Atitlan, Guatemala, traditional Japanese papermaking in Aichi-ken, Japan, and, in the last fourteen years, painting with masters in the magical countryside of Southern France. Currently, she is living and teaching the concept of "life as an art form" during the winters at Art Heaven, her art school in Sebastopol, California, and summers in the French fauvist village of Collioure where she paints and sells her work in her own gallery L'Art Vivant.

My favorite saying is, "You live a brilliant life by creating your environment." I need to create the lifestyle and the environment that inspire me. And I need to keep it fresh and changing so that I feel continuously inspired, and that philosophy comes through automatically in my work.

When I'm feeling down or lonely, I paint what's down and lonely. My work is all over the place. That's what they tell you in art school not to do. You are supposed to have a style and be predictable. And in galleries, when you change your style, they go nuts.

I trained a lot of people, and they ended up buying land around us out there in the wilderness of California, and now a community

Carole Watanabe
Painter, Textile Designer, and Teacher

Interviewed at her home/studio in Sorèze, southern France

of weavers has been established; my first husband still lives in that community.

It was survival out there. After six years in the wilderness, I moved to San Francisco and had already established markets there and connection to sellers for my weavings. I was weaving those beautiful pillows and shawls, large, for couches, and they were being sold at design houses. They introduced me to different design centers; one was called the Ice House, at that time owned by Henry Adams. He was building a brand new huge design center, and Henry's wife, Claire Ellen, was a weaver, and she knew me and my work. I told her that I wanted to open the first tapestry gallery because there was not such a thing at that time anywhere in the U.S. that offered tapestry for big corporations. So I started that project.

YAEL WEISS

A captivating presence on the concert scene, award-winning pianist Yael Weiss has been hailed by many of today's greatest musicians and critics for her visionary interpretations of surpassing depth, immediacy, and communicative power.

Weiss has performed across the United States, Europe, Japan, Korea and South America at such venues as Carnegie Hall, Lincoln Center, the Kennedy Center, Benaroya Hall, Moscow's Bolshoi Hall, and London's Wigmore Hall. Her New York recital debut, presented by the Metropolitan Museum, was acclaimed by the *New York Times* as "remarkably powerful and intense."

Winner of the Naumburg International Piano Competition and the Kosciuszko Foundation Chopin Piano Competition, Weiss has recorded solo and chamber works by over a dozen composers. She presents master classes worldwide, and has served on the faculties of Indiana University and the University of California at Santa Barbara. Her mentors have included Leon Fleisher and Richard Goode. Weiss is the creator of "32 Bright Clouds: Beethoven Conversations Around the World," a global commissioning project aiming to inspire harmony and unity through musical performances of Beethoven's thirty-two piano sonatas and related new works.

I was born in Israel and started playing concerts when I was seven or eight years old. Coming from a family of musicians, that was a natural thing to do. I played solo recitals and orchestral pieces.

I moved to the U.S. when I was seventeen years old. I knew since I was little that America was my destination. I don't think anybody in my family has been as serious as I was. I was highly encouraged by my family. Music has been for me always such a profound way of speaking truth. Through music, I can seek understanding and

Yael Weiss
Musician, Concert Pianist

Interviewed by phone at her home in New York

self-realization. For me, it's the only way to grow and to understand this world.

When I perform, I long to express truth about human existence. Through my music, I inspire people to seek truth, too. I want them to feel how they get transformed when they listen. They wonder, they are excited, they perceive the brilliance of the moment. I want to contribute to people's life and happiness in that way.

I am looking for the magic in every performance, so I observe that it is very special and also just ordinary. And it happens only once: music is fluid; it comes, and the next moment it is gone. For me, everything is Art.

JERRY WENNSTROM

Artist and author Jerry Wennstrom was born in New York on January 13, 1950. He attended Rockland Community College and the State University of New York at New Paltz. After producing a large body of work, he set out at age twenty-nine to "discover the rock-bottom truth of my life." For years, he had questioned the limits of his creative life as a studio painter. He was a successful artist in New York when he decided in 1979 to destroy all his art, give away everything he owned, and begin a path of unconditional trust, allowing life to provide all that was needed. He lived this way in New York for fifteen years. In 1998, he moved to Whidbey Island in Washington State, where he met and married Marilyn Strong and produced a large new body of art. His island home is now filled with his unique interactive sculptures and paintings. He has participated in over fifty radio, TV, and magazine interviews and art features.

I think art in the truest sense is always a radical departure from the known. You have to die with your own ideas of art and be ready to change. You have to live it like a religion and then step off the cliff; that's the birth of art. Most of what I see in art is before that final leap.

Yogananda says: To set out on any holy purpose and to die along the path we walk is to succeed.

I seek balance in my creative life. For example, if I write too much, I get into the garden and plant vegetables. Sometimes, supposedly mundane activity is more important than our so-called art.

You have to develop your craft, of course. You have to use your best skills to build your creation, following the nature of that beast that is your specific bent in your art. I have worked my butt off to develop my craft.

When we talk creativity, we talk what is beyond that, what's the next level of "Ta-daaa!" You work up to the place where it becomes

Jerry Wennstrom
Sculptor, Painter, Inventor of Movable Art, Bold and Colorful Life-Size Interactive Sculptures

**Interviewed at his studio on
Whidbey Island, Washington**

a prayer. If you hold to the integrity of what you want, something larger kicks in.

Creativity is our birthright; it's inherent in us.

It's not a lazy game. Surrender is the end product of a whole lot of hard work.

WESLEY WEST

Wesley West was born in London in 1949. His father died when he was eight years old. He joined the Royal Navy at age thirteen and left it at age twenty-two. He entered art school at twenty-six, which was the official beginning of his creative life. He delights in it, and hasn't looked back since. Wesley's life up to his present age of sixty-four "has just been completely fun. Enjoyable!"

His initial education began with his father, a talented artist, who taught to draw at an early age. He also inherited his father's amazing memory

He changed courses for a foundation B.A. honors and then went on to a three-year degree at Bath Academy of Art, studying three-dimensional design. At Bath, he met Amanda, later to become his wife, who played a huge part in his future creative life.

After leaving college, he became head of ceramics at Cambridge School of Art, a post he held for eighteen years. During this time, he was also making teapots in a small studio in Cambridge, fine art pieces, some of which took two years. From there, he went on to work in advertising, making weird and wonderful pieces for TV as well as still shots, including *Cabbage,* a short film nominated for a British Academy of Film and Television Arts award.

Exploding with creativity, he still works as an artist in TV, other media, and marketing.

I went to Bath Academy of Art and studied ceramics, pottery, and three-dimensional design—not because I fell in love with clay but because I fell in love with the people who taught me clay. And I still see them now, Blake Mackinnon and Ed Harvey, I wanted to be like them. So that's why I chose ceramics.

I have always drawn, beginning in the early years, as soon as I could pick up a pencil, because my father was a magnificent

Wesley West
Sculptor, Media and Ceramic Artist

Interviewed with Amanda McPhail at their studios in Cambridge, U.K.

drawer. He never would tell you just stories; he would tell you the story of an orchestra while he was drawing the orchestra. Even at only four years old, I could do caricatures and draw stories. I have always drawn, my whole life.

When my father died, I carried on trying to be my father. He was very, very imaginative, bordering on the insane. He was a nut case, but he was wonderful to be with. He is the source where all my creative spirit came from. Drawing was my playground; it got me out of troubles. My drawings helped me save my life. I could always translate a dramatic event into a drawing, and that helped me to stay balanced, even in the Navy. I feel so lucky to live the life I have.

Chapter One. What is Creativity?

The most beautiful thing we can experience is the mysterious.
It is the source of all art and science.
—Albert Einstein

A Web of Beauty

I am fascinated by real things, real people's stories, naked and earth-grown stories that have their roots dangling out in the open, dirt crusting the ends. That's why I write non-fiction, and that's why I am a psychotherapist and deeply interested in the shaping and twisting forces that motivate our actions as human beings. Answers to questions flower and bloom in secret and sacred places where it might need the innocence of a child or the stubborn rustiness of an inspired, aging mind to mid-wife them toward the light. Such a magical place is for me most easily encountered in nature.

Nature has always been a source of inspiration and creativity for me; it is playful and bursting with innovation—either practical and purposeful, like the robust and simple shapes of seeds, or whimsical and playful, like clouds or snowflakes or caterpillars with tiny horns on their heads, seemingly existing just for the sake of beauty and delight.

This morning when I walked outside to get the paper, I found the rear window of my car covered with a most astonishing blue-white, paisley-patterned lace curtain. The patterns mimicked the shapes found in the veins of leaves or riverbeds with swirling eddies and sand paintings arranged by the wind. Here, just in front of me, I discovered the most intricate beauty, woven during the cold of the night, a beauty that made me burst into tears of joy.

This was art shaped by nature. Some force had crocheted beauty by turning water into ice. It played with shapes for the sake of splendor, extraordinary and sacred, but also normal and simple, just by the side of the road. It was not precious but ordinary. Divine creativity was simply playing around and enjoying itself.

This icy beauty demonstrated the miracle of creativity. I devote my life to it. I explore and cherish it. Creativity grabs any opportunity to express life force in refined or raw shapes. The magical force that wove these patterns on the glass of my car decided to show up just here today, on this frosty morning in December. There is no logical explanation for such a gift of beauty. It is not driven by any purpose but only by its delight to create and mimic the playfulness of the Universe.

Those objects of creativity want our attention; they long for our recognition and love. They fill us with soul food and inspire us to be creators ourselves. The Sufis say: "God wants to be known through his creation."

This morning, I was the audience. I provided the eyes to see and the attention to behold the Divine at work in creation. On our globe, creativity rarely lives in an empty space or in a vacuum. It comes to life in interaction. We encounter it. There is no music without a listener; there is no beauty without a viewer to delight in it. There is no dance without the wind that curls around the dancer's hips. Creativity is action on behalf of the creator and the receiver. The ice crystals I saw vanished in minutes after the sun hit them and they returned to water. But I have taken their image into my heart and memory. My soul has been nurtured and ignited. As a receiver, I am part of the process of creation. My delight infuses the created object.

Creativity may show up one day like an angel knocking at your door. It stands outside and offers you an inspiration, a gift. It loves to play, and wants you to get involved. You can hear the knocking and might get up from your seat; you might drop the "to do" list of your ordinary life and respond.

If you are too occupied with "important" things, or you don't even listen and disregard the knocking, the angel will leave and go somewhere else to deliver the gift—and you have missed an opportunity. To use Joseph Campbell's expression, you will have neglected "The Calling."

This ice crystal curtain was *l'art pour l'art*, beauty for its own sake, lavishly created for a short moment of life. The first rays of the sun had begun already to melt it at the edges. I observed in front of me the utterly pure and unblemished expression of creativity, just for delight, "useless" and timeless, emerging and dying seemingly in one breath.

Yes, creativity elicits joy, fun, play, and lightness of being. All the energy needed to bring a new shape or form or sound or movement into existence is already there, pulsating and vibrating, floating in space; we only need to step into its flow as we try to unleash its secrets. Creative acts seem to hover at the edges of the "ordinary," reserved for the genius and the artists and the bystander. But *who* crocheted the icy lace onto the car window? Was there any purpose to it, or a need waiting to be fulfilled, besides the satisfaction of our craving for beauty?

Do we take creativity too seriously? Or not seriously enough? Maybe it's like breathing, in and out, naturally, or like our heartbeat, ceaselessly driven by its own inner purpose? Creativity just *is*. It can be activated and used, or neglected and denied. Does it need an end product and sustainability to make sense? Does it need a witness, like my observation of the crystal lace as I walked by the car? Or can it exist without being noticed, just for the delight of offering itself for consumption? Does it need the midwifery of an artist or scientist to translate the raw energy into a refined object?

Right now, as I formulate these thoughts and questions, I sit in front of my fireplace and gaze with soft eyes into the red and orange flames that dance along the edges of the piñon wood. And at the same time—so rare in New Mexico—I hear a strong rain drumming on the slanting red metal roof of my home. Our long-haired Maine coon cat is curled up and snores in my lap. The only equally satisfying action—besides sitting here and thinking—would be to do purely nothing. Creativity cannot be produced, but it can be invited into such a space of yielding to this present moment. We can lure it, seduce it, flirt with it. We offer an invitation. Invitation comes from the Latin word *invitare,* to fill with life.

I believe that creativity is born out of our own substance of life, like a spider's web is created out of the substance of the spider. Right now, I create these thoughts out of the substance of my experience; they are not constructed from stuff, they emerge from an inner source that flows through all of creation. My thoughts already exist. I am just the container who caught them as they filled the room where I sat with my cat in front of the fire.

So creativity needs cooperation between the creator and the object that is being created, between the artist and his or her vision. There seems to be always a threesome in interaction: the creator, the medium, and the object that emerges. Creativity needs cooperation between those three, even if the artist works alone. And what if the artist expresses the universal energy of life, like the one that created the intricate ice lace on my rear window?

I am aware that I am walking a fine line here as I offer these very personal reflections and examples to you. I offer them humbly, believing that creativity lets us open doors to its mystery from various points of view. A more-sophisticated approach might hinder this secret's being revealed. But the ordinary—like the ice crystals on the window—might generously, and with ease, reveal its creative source. I experience the exploration of creativity like being in love: I want to know everything about the beloved and can listen to the beloved's stories with tireless attention. I want to know about creativity's origins and manifestations in people's lives, in all its guises.

I Want to Write About Creativity

I want to write about Creativity

About the fire that scorches the heart
About mistakes that turn into art.
About the medicine that heals the scar
About the crack in the jar and
About the delight of creating
About the pleasure of mating
About audacious flight toward light
beyond the boundaries of wrong and right.
I want to write about creative Art
And how it tears us apart.
I want to write about creativity
with its clay feet on the ground,
and its squabbles between square and round.
Its messy outbursts, and smelly piddlings
Its failures and mediocre fiddlings
Its piercing doubts and lousy moods
Its sharp-edged rocks in worn out boots.
About its lust for fame.
And disgust for the same-old-same.

I want to write about creativity,
How it gives shape to the dreams of a child
or to the cravings of the wild
Self during dreadful doubt
When hungry ghosts rumble and shout.
I want to pose my questions to *you*
and to the angels as well as the gru-
some forces of the Dark.
Where shadows and brilliance meet
We artists stomp with enormous feet
Across the glowing ember

Remember. . . ?

Fire in Water

During early childhood, my parents used to rent a room in a fisherman's house with a thatched roof near the North Sea, where we spent our summer vacations. The beach was endless and flat, so when the tides went out, they left a long stretch of white sand, and when the waters came back in, the waves rushed speedily toward the dunes and the little village behind the dike, called St. Peter Ording. Sometimes my sister and I were so involved in playing and building castles and running along the silvery rim of the waves that we had to hurry in front of the incoming tide and it was scary to see the sea suddenly chasing us, as if it wanted to swallow us all with our shovels and towels and woolen sweaters. This sea was sweet and playful at times, monstrous and rough at others. It mumbled and rumbled like a being with moody character, mysterious and powerful.

So it was summer again, and my sister and I packed our small bundles for the yearly vacation at the North Sea. We loaded the scruffy blue boat and rakes and balls and hats with strings to be tied under the chin because a mighty wind was always blowing along the water. And then we left Hamburg for the long drive to St. Peter Ording. We girls fell asleep on the back seats of the car, and when we stopped, it was pitch black outside. My father turned around and said, "We have arrived! Let's just step out and listen to the waves before we go to the fisherman's house for the night."

We all stood quietly in the dunes, and from far out there in the dark, we heard the rustling sound of water breaking along the beach, and we felt such a longing to be back with our beloved sea and the salty wind and water that we took each other by the hand and ran, ran toward the splashing sound and the wide space in the dark, and we delighted in the familiar sensation of fine sand between our toes. We ran and stumbled and arrived breathless at the water line and tore off our clothes and put them in a pile to find again in the dark, and then we all hopped and galloped and slithered and slipped stark naked into the water, screeching and singing and getting utterly lost in joy and ecstasy.

Oh but then, a mystery appeared: Wherever we moved was gold, and there were golden sparkles in the dark, and they fizzled like bubbles raining from the sky down and back up, rolling through the spaces between my fingers and along the rim of the waves and underneath my belly and between my thighs, and golden light was all around us as we floated in a starry sky, black around the moving gold and behind it, and the black was penetrated by golden sparkles and jumping golden balls, something I had never seen before. A miracle had happened and wrapped our little family in gold and invited us to a playful chase between the night and the stars that were on the ground beneath us and above in the sky, and the golden water jumped upward as we threw ourselves into it with glee and wonder.

My father later explained that this was called Meeresleuchten, *Fire in the Sea*, caused by small fluorescent plankton in the water. It needed a very precise temperature of the water and air, and movement of the water rubbing against our bodies to trigger the light. It was quite rare, he said, and only children born on a Sunday, like my sister Helga and I—and their parents—could see it, too.

We found our pile of clothes and put them on our wet, salty bodies, and we held hands as we walked back to the car and away from this mystery, turning around many times. It was a moment in my life, I was aware, that I would never forget. I placed it securely inside a chamber in my heart, and that is the place from which I am telling you this story now.

> *Creativity is the residue of time wasted.*
> —Albert Einstein

What is Creativity?: The Interviews

ESTHER MARION

Creativity is lived life, idea, and action. It's a source of energy. It's a passion.

I move and dance in my studio, or I ride my bike through the luscious green valley, and then I stop and sit down and write my ideas or questions. I always have my notebook nearby to capture ideas and visions. The sensuality of nature stirs images in me and opens new potentials for my dance.

Many art forms have their roots in an ethnic tradition, and I am so enriched by studying those traditions and their wisdom. I have my university inside me; that's where I learn. I study the books of life. Flamenco has been a chapel and library for me for more than thirty years now.

And there's the other big topic of creativity: birth. When I expected my daughter, Sophia, I turned the whole house into a temple for this most creative act of human experience: gestation and birth. That was such a big change in my perception of life that I almost forgot who I was before giving birth. Being a mother changed me. After giving birth, I felt another richness to my being, a new outlook on life. C.G. Jung said: At the moment the child is born, the mother is also born.

Each of the two births of my children initiated in me a different form of dance. First it was not flamenco, but Kathak. Dancing in a real temple, on the cold tiles, with my baby-son inside my belly made me conscious of my body as a source of creativity. And when I was pregnant with my daughter, it was African dance and its undulating movements that inspired me to celebrate my fruitful body. Almost as if the masculine child inside demanded manly, harsh movements, and the girl more-feminine ones. After Sophia's birth, I yearned for flamenco, and that's when I founded the Arte Flamenco group, inviting guests from other states or Spain to come to Seattle and perform with us.

And for some time now, there's a new dance theater piece emerging. I call it "Cosmos to Earth." It is still in gestation, and I am not complete yet, because it takes a lot of dreaming and exploration to create a dance theater. This new dance performance is an "underground" piece; it grows slowly and demands its own slow timing.

What is Creativity?

Creativity emerges freely when given a place to live. It initiates the birth of art and cooperates with our own longing for creation.

MICHAEL BROOME

Art is alchemy. It's first an idea and then a craft, and then there's this other mysterious thing that we don't know what it is, but without it, the art does not work.

Creativity is the willingness to do what is on your mind. Whatever the inspiration, the artist *will do it*, not only think about it. Thinking about it, that's the philosopher; an artist does the doing of it. I am passionate about that. Artists *make things*. And when they don't, I am very suspicious. Many artists today who have become famous have a *system* produce art. Is this really their art, or is it just cleverness?

What motivates art? I think it is frustration. We are not satisfied with what is, and that drives us. The Buddhists call it Divine Discontent. We want to make a change, leave a mark, create something new. We want to shape something that is an agitation. And when you engage in the doing of it, the calm settles in, the frustration goes. But remember what gets you going: If you were satisfied, you would not do anything. I admit it's a little obsessive for me; making art is obsessive. What are we obsessed with? I think it's the urge to not be dying. Art will definitely help me not to die. It's not the ending of life we want to avoid but the ending of this moment in time. This moment is much closer to death; it's not over there, it happens right here.

Yes, and it's also boredom, boredom. We can't stand boredom; we have to fill the moment and be challenged and vibrantly alive.

Yes, we could fill that time with many other things, like baking a pie or driving around, but art is the much better way to avoid boredom. If we have to live with this neurotic creature that we are, let's do *art*! Because it's a great way of having a true relationship with that obsessive energy. And then you get a lot of contentment and joy out of your creativity.

TONY JUNIPER

Creativity is the ability to synthesize in different ways, taking different bits of truth and putting them together in ways others have not done before. It also has something to do with confidence to step outside of what is the "right" answer and find connections between different things. At the heart of creativity is the ability to look at something and connect it in new ways.

Creativity in science and the arts is not very different. Both require an open mind and a readiness to do new things and create a new point of view, and so to see things the way other people might see them. That's another insight I had over the years, to observe that two people might have a totally different way of seeing, perceiving completely different images of what's going on.

That is actually quite empowering, realizing I can be an active player in shaping points of view. I step constantly into new points of view. That's creative thinking for me. Five years ago, when I left Friends of the Earth, I thought I knew everything. I had been in this game of environmental activism for twenty-five years. But in the last five years, I probably learned more than in the first twenty, realizing how things actually are, finding truth, compared with a simplistic common view.

I see the predicament in which we are today less as problems with technology, policies, or information than as a crisis of *perception*. The prevailing culture's view is that technology can solve every issue: Nature is obsolete if we just invent something to replace it. And that's the space where we have now arrived.

We are looking here at a fundamental misunderstanding! A misunderstanding of how this whole system works. And that is a crisis of perception! And that is, in my opinion, the main problem. So shifting this crisis of perception becomes one of the main jobs at hand. How to do that, I think, is through storytelling and creating a different perspective. You need to connect with people in ways they can understand. And that's quite a creative process: You are putting together many pieces; you are putting science together with plain English.

Carole Watanabe

To me, creativity is a spiritual practice. There's nothing mysterious about it; you just need to show up again and again and use your courage. There is discipline behind it, yes, but for me, it's more like an addiction. I could not be without it. If I don't paint for a week or two and make something beautiful, I feel like I am just wasting life. I need to make beautiful things; that's essential for me. It's a real longing of my soul. If I don't care about this urge, it goes nuts on me, it screams.

Rumi said:

Let the beauty we love
Be what we do.
There are hundreds of ways
To kneel and kiss the ground.

Creativity is the courage to trust yourself completely. Every artist has those moments when you stand in front of an empty canvas and think, "Oh God, how will I start?" and you always hear the negative voice in your head telling you, "You really don't know what you are doing. Who do you think you are?" Blah blah blah . . . and you have to confront that with your courage and send the demons back into the closet. "I do know what I am doing, and I trust however this is unfolding. Even if I don't know how to begin, I will know how to end."

A friend asked me to show at an opening in her gallery, so I began to paint intensely, while dealing with my low mood and frustration and the question if I just should take a normal job and not struggle with art any more. The paintings were dark and powerful, wild and demonic. That was all I could paint, because that was what happened to me inside at that time.

And then we prepared for this show, and I showed her my work and apologized. "That's not my usual stuff, that's not what you expected, but that's what is stirring inside me right now. And if you don't want to show my work, I completely understand."

She looked at it and said, "Oh my God, this is some of the most powerful work you have ever done. I really want it." So we hung the show and there was an amazing response.

Creativity is life energy for me; it is food for my soul.

Cathy Aten

Creativity means bringing a little piece of God into this world, so that it is a bit more beautiful. I am surprised by my words, because God was not in my vocabulary for much of my early years.

I am curious about this whole process, about life. I have always been curious. Curiosity is the root of creativity. It is something magical for me, to use my hands and bring something into form, taking the dirt and shaping it; it's very visceral for me.

I took it for granted for many years that I was a creative person, after having devoted myself to art for so many years.

Creativity is inseparable from life, and now I am confronted with my diagnosis of multiple sclerosis. My body challenges my life and art profoundly. All this is a hard thing for me. You called M.S. an illness, and it sounds as if something is wrong, but I do not really believe that something is wrong with me. The biggest thing I have done to cultivate my creativity is to cultivate a soft heart, to be undefended! Because I feel that our culture is so defended, we are all so armored that creativity cannot get through. The more I take down my own armor, the more God's voice sounds inside me. We are in this together. It's my own voice and it's God's. Creativity is an expression of the Divine.

Everybody has some sort of genius. My gift in this lifetime is to be a voice and a way-shower. The right side of my body does not work at all. My illness has segued into my life as my work of art, no distinction. M.S. has become my artistic path.

Because my whole life has turned into my palette, my whole life has become my art. Every single day is art; living with M.S. is the same as making a sculpture or painting. I create something and see if it works, or I change it and do something different with my life—same process: creating a piece of art through the way I live.

Aaron Stern

There are many books that try to define creativity. In short, I would say, creativity is making something out of nothing. For me, it means taking all the material of all time and fashioning it into something that did not exist before. Some percent of inspiration and some percent of craftsmanship—and then there are Muses, other forces to inspire us.

The place where creativity can flower and bloom is very important. I think that such a Muse is Leonard Bernstein. His spirit is active here in our Academy for the Love of Learning because he was so much a part of its conception. Creativity lives and breathes in this place.

Once, we prepared for a performance with the Vienna Symphony, and we were in Spain, intending to meet Salvador Dali, and he took us to a place called Figueras, where he lived and worked—an incredible place, magical. The place itself breathed mystery and creativity.

That's when I made the life-changing decision to create this academy, and for the rest of my life, I would use what I know about music and implement it and create environments for that. I devoted my life to the building of such a space where the real experience of Leonard Bernstein's music can happen in a sustainable way. What I know is that creativity can be part of the physical place where it lives and inspires.

Some people think of me with anger in relationship to this building. "How dare you spend all of this time and all of these resources on making this Academy and calling it a space that can hold silence?" And I don't care for this critique, because from my perspective, in this noisy time, we need places of quiet. We need to quiet our minds. Music and silence are brother and sister.

Last week, I was just sitting here with eighteen people on Thursday, the first day of a new training, telling them that the way I facilitate learning is that I stand and listen to all the different voices and instruments in it: "Oh, there's the piccolo, and there's that voice connecting with that one, and there's the fundamental, a low C. They are all one system." As a composer, I don't have to make anything right or wrong; I just balance systems. A conductor is a conduit, connecting and balancing between all the voices in an orchestra. Creativity lives in those places of gestation. The Muses are alive here; they are forces that connect creative endeavors.

ANYA ACHTENBERG

Creativity? It's a yearning to bring something to life that helps you understand the world. As you write, you recreate a part of the world so that you can really focus on it. It's a place to follow the extraordinary, a constant invitation of the spirit of the planet and its people. It's a process by which we confirm that all the species are constantly inspiring us. It's a process by which we sort through the overwhelm that this world is relentlessly offering. We let the music of life flow through us and connect us with the planet, whether here, in New York, or in a small place somewhere else.

Creativity is a powerful, profound human urge, a constant yearning and desire. And I obviously appreciate its products tremendously. But the products are not the first motivation for it. The *doing* is.

Creativity is absolutely integral to the nature of human beings. The desire to create is a longing for very deep union, a place to deal with the intensity of life, its light and shadow, and to shape reality.

My purpose in life is treasuring and noticing the world, even when I feel terrible. I observe and express. You know, I am a political activist. As an artist, I am with all I observe; I treasure it to be awake. Why do people do the things they do? The artist explores that with the help of their art, from the grittiest of life to the most magical.

Elias Rivera

Creativity is the need and capacity to express yourself through a specific medium. It chooses you as well as you choose it. You have to give your visions a specific form: writing or singing or dancing or anything that allows you to be expressive. Usually it is a God-given, specific talent you have, and you train your skills to use that medium. Discipline is a very important part of this process. If you don't have discipline, you are all over the place. There are so many so-called talented people who don't get anywhere, because they miss discipline. Again, that devotional part of yourself allows you to take it to a special place. In the end, to be an artist is a gift to yourself. What a gorgeous gift to have, to be able to create something beautiful. I feel so honored to be part of creation.

I am very, very careful not to be haughty about that—or it goes out of the window very quickly. I know where I want to go; it's eternal growth and beauty. I honor that with gratitude.

I paint the people of Guatemala, but now, I can't easily travel to that culture anymore. I am fragile now. It takes strength to travel, especially to that world.

I am so grateful that my art has directed me to such a beautiful culture. It's healing, and I give that back to the world in my paintings.

Yael Weiss

What is creativity? That's a big question.

Sometimes we think that creativity creates something *new*. I actually don't see it like that; I see it as bringing forth something that is already there. It reveals itself through human senses. That is hard to understand without the senses, but is it already there, has existed before we can see or hear or touch it. The work carries something like a certain general truth or understanding, so it can be perceived by others. I am always learning. My feeling is that this is really what creativity is: understanding the already existing through a new point of view or vision, a new access to an already-existing truth.

We don't really create something *new*, ever; it might be new on the surface because we are combining certain elements in new ways, but all those elements are already there. Just a new way of putting those elements together so that we are as precise as possible to convey that truth to others.

I play music. The composition is already existing, but I give it a uniquely personal interpretation; that's my creativity.

UWE WALTER-NAKAJIMA

Everything that leads to creating the space for art is part of the creative process, and it changes with each new performance.

Noh theater is a part of a four-hundred-year-old tradition in Japan. Tradition means devoted repetition. Through the eyes of my Western colleagues, this might not be creative, because you don't create something new. I think it is in that sense creative, that you are part of a tradition, of absolute timing and rigorous discipline, lived and practiced for hundreds of years.

The creativity occurs in the interplay between the season, the audience, the place; it's always different. Creativity in Noh theater for me means to create a space and to use it in a perfect way.

It is important to be open to the audience and sensitive to time and place. That requires the ability not to be in the center, but to concentrate on the whole space. The audience becomes part of the story.

The mask, the chorus of eight men, and the musicians are all part of Noh theater. They give me the backbone; then I can let go. Even if that form is hundreds of years old, I am creating something new in that moment, and it needs a lot of training to master that.

But I quit Noh theater, and have not become a member of a group, because I would have to commit myself to the old pieces, could not create new ones of my own. Now I create my own pieces and forms. But I work still in the essence of Noh with its extremely refined tools and expressions. The question is here: Can one respect an old artistic tradition and still be creative? I found out that I feel too restricted, but there are many different opinions about this.

TIM GOSNELL

Creativity—at the end of the day—is a mistake with a positive outcome.

The brain is sublimely organized in trying to recognize patterns and imagine possibilities. There is an evolutionary reason why our imaginations are as viral as they are. Example: You are on the plains in Africa, and something is rustling in the grass. You immediately compare: Is it just the wind, or is it a lion who intents to eat me? The cost of getting that wrong is pretty high.

It's okay to be creative—imagine the danger if you are not!

I suppose that the creative ending of such a story very often leads to false predictions, false positives. It's about imagining possibilities. Creativity is imagination.

Artists need to make a direct connection to people's experiences with their senses. The scientific world can be very different from that. What you are studying has all kind of amplifiers in between the world of science and the human being. For example, the microscope and telescope are creative amplifiers. These monstrous machines, like at CERN—they are amplifiers, and they are multibillion-dollar kinds of machines. No matter what, scientific exploration needs an interface somewhere, often very sophisticated ones. It's less the case in art. Scientists' creativity is often bound to those machines. Artists' is free.

JERRY WENNSTROM

Creativity is about finding the sacred in the moment, finding the God of that moment. Creativity is our birthright, it's inherent in us—but generally so suppressed. Even in school, they do not teach you to risk and do creative things. Creativity is inherent in children. We lose it, and then we have to claim it again as we grow up.

You have to develop your craft, of course. It needs will, an inherent intelligence and skills. You have to do your best to make your creation following the nature of that beast that is your specific bend.

It's not a lazy game. Surrender is the end-product of a whole lot of work. Those beings I create, they find me. I begin a new piece, and they find me and inspire me. But I have worked my butt off to develop my craft.

When we talk creativity, we talk what is beyond that, what's the next level of, Tada! You work up to the place where it becomes a prayer. You hold to the integrity of what you want—and then something larger kicks in.

Creativity happens outside the common box. But even that statement—couldn't that become the next box to sit in? Boxes, I could not stay in them. I risk everything to be authentic and get out of boxes, over and over again. When I start seeing that box, I blow it up. I risk it all for honesty and my truth. The tendency would be to stay in that nice place of complacency, but I am always risking my own self—have to get out of the box, be authentic. That's living creatively in every moment.

VIJALI HAMILTON

Creativity has expressed itself in many layers throughout my life. First, in college, I was a painter, and then I switched over to sculpture and environmental art. So I went to Italy and worked in the marble quarry of Carrara. I got my stones in the quarry and had my studio there, Henry Moore was next to me and Isamu Noguchi on the other side. We all shared this courtyard and shared ideas and discoveries. And if you got your stones from that quarry, you could use their tools. That's how I started into sculpture. Oh, those were brilliant times, overflowing with creativity!

Spiritually, in the middle '70s, I had a breakthrough of consciousness: I saw light in everything, I literally saw this boiling light and how everything was connected; boundaries were arbitrary. We were made all of the same substance. That awakening continues to be the base of my work.

I reduced my studio work at that time. I needed to be outdoors. I needed open space, and began to do my environmental work. I worked like that for ten years before I started my global work. That step included all the arts, also ceremonial performance.

I had a base in Utah, on this five-acre place in the most beautiful wilderness in the Canyonlands area. After I had finished traveling the first *Wheel* around the world, I built a straw bale hogan and used all natural materials. I felt I needed to be grounded on earth because creativity comes from the ground.

My journey with the *World Wheel* has been over twenty-five years now. I started in 1986. Originally, I didn't have any base in the U.S. and considered every country my home and my family. But now I have a base here in Santa Fe and that is a different situation.

WESLEY WEST AND AMANDA MCPHAIL

Wes: How do I define creativity? Creativity is a way of life. I think it's just doing what you want to do—and the freedom to live the way you want to live, dressing and eating the way you want. What physical works you actually create come from the way you lead your life. Being authentic! You have these forces inside you that need to get out or they show in anger, temper, love, frustration. Whenever you, as an artist, do something or create something, it's like taking all your clothes off. It is a difficult thing to describe, but I think it's three-dimensional personality; you basically paint or write yourself. Creativity is the turning inside-out of a person. It can feel frustrating when the creation does not happen the way it is inside your mind. But when it works, it's the most amazing buzz. It makes you glad that you are alive. For me, creativity is my home.

Amanda: We are lucky that creativity is part of us. I believe it is not just a visual art thing; creativity is also in the person who raises children, cooks their meals and lives their life with creative satisfaction. They cope every day with what they got assigned by life. I remember one of my first visual impressions was a lady downstairs when we lived in London. This lady had two children and an unusual way to cut the bread, and buttered it upside down before she cut it; it was amazing. I had never seen something like that. It worked perfectly for her. It used to fascinate me how there were always perfect pieces of bread. I watched and giggled, and she smiled. To live life daily with the freedom of creative expression is great joy! And this is just one example of this freedom. It's an approach to life!

SARA WARBER

In really creative moments, there's a sense of flow. That's when I feel united with greater universal forces. I am absorbed, expanded beyond myself. That can happen in normal activity, and it makes me feel purposeful and fulfilled and in sync with myself. Creativity shows up at any time when I experience myself to be completely responsive to the moment, like in good encounters with my patients. And in medicine, that can touch the boundaries of life or death. Or when I read another scientist's work and it sparks a new idea that relates to my own experiences. I write it down and remember it. That's an Aha! moment. Very exciting.

The source is inside me. When I am unhurried and engaged with the process of this encounter, it flows freely.

Before I studied medicine, I was an artist. I felt a strong pull toward the theater and graphic arts. I give an example here: I love M.C. Escher and his art. He forces you to see the world in a new way—non-normal and normal in relationship. That's how I see the world too. I perceive the familiar and mysterious at the same time. I weave them together. Creativity is born out of that weaving. It's a shock when we see the world in new and different ways;

it rattles our brain. We experience ourselves as strangers. A great resource for that new view is my Native American teacher. She sparked creativity in me. I learned from her about herbs and spiritual medicine, parallel to my traditional medical training. It influenced what kind of doctor I would become. I feel deep gratitude toward her.

Ruth Bamford

Creativity is not leaning on memory. It has to give birth to something that is unique and new and original. And there is an element to creativity that *feels* right when it is authentic. It fits in with the whole of the universe. And you can hear it in words that you can understand, even if it's the work of a genius: It's simple and very clear.

Peggy O'Kelly

It's hard for me to accept that I am creative, because I think about art and not business when being asked about creativity. I am used to thinking that creativity means painting and drawing and playing music. But creativity is sparked when you take your time and allow a vision to emerge and then you go with it, not through a lot of thoughts but let it come alive by listening to your intuition.

People look at me as an accounting and finance person. I am good at branding and product development, and it comes all from this inner place of creativity. My conflict has been that I am *not* really an accountant and finance person. I have to fight with myself to keep my books organized. I am good at it, and I believe that financial statements can be very creative, too. In my first job, I was very successful and worked extremely hard. So I got promoted into Public Accounting, but that's not who I really am.

Creativity means bringing something to life that is just sitting inside your mind. Nobody else can perceive it but you yourself. For example, the inception of my company. People thought I was crazy when I designed it. Bringing it to life changed my career path. Now I create natural products and enjoy my work very much.

I had to go through certain structured steps to build this business, and maybe that does not feel like creativity because of the logic and order in it. I produce olive oil, soaps, and body oils, and when I give them color and shape, make them pleasing, that does not feel like creativity. I do it naturally and delight in the process. But yesterday, when the soap was ready and I held it in my hand, I was so excited. It was beautiful. I assembled all our products for inspection in my office, and then I opened the box and thought, "Wow!" we have a complete brand here. That's very exciting. So creativity sneaks into my daily work.

I am creative. I do the labeling and branding and create pleasing merchandise. I used to think that art is apart from daily life, not producing an "ordinary product" that can be used. It is so common to see art and creativity as separate from our day-to-day activity.

But my path is very similar to an artist's. They always think it's not good enough yet, like me with my products. I never think I am there yet.

I believe that part of creativity is trusting. It's trusting that what you have created is worthy. And it means that you love what you have created, and you have a bond with it.

CHRISSIE ORR

I work mainly in community. Creativity is given birth through communal action. Artists working in community are like *animateurs*; we animate the culture and the old stories, and that triggers new stories to be born. That's the mystery to live with, the question of how to shape the new story of a culture. Look at the mural on the school in Santa Fe. We created the plan and the piece together. There were all those young people and they told their stories, and then they came up with images to represent those stories, and the community said, "Oh, yes, yes, that is our story!" and then we painted it, all of us together. It's not that I bring a plan; it emerges out of the interaction and the storytelling. We had no idea when we came together where this would lead. I work best in community. It's a wellspring of creativity.

Creativity comes out of collaboration, and that collaboration is very structured and needs a strong foundation. The craft used in the creative process is a foundation. Listening to each other is a foundation. Otherwise, it would be scary and chaotic. Inside the structure, we can be creative and free. Look at a canvas: It has clear boundaries and shape, but inside that shape, you can do anything.

If I work for myself alone, creativity is an ecstatic moment. I am looking for ecstasy, and when I put those two colors together in a certain form, and suddenly everything comes together, that's, Aaaahh! Orgasm!

Theodora Capaldo

It's creativity that transforms the ordinary. It's one of the paths to the realization that there is something bigger than our normal reality. You can call it Soul or Spirit or Creation.

The other point of view that I want to shine light on is that the product of creativity is not always an object, a house, or a song or a piece of sculpture. In relation to the animal activism I do, it's the transformation of somebody's point of view. I believe that is another form of creativity. Social activism is in the same vein: "Let me show you this piece and that piece—and now can you see it differently?"

My creativity is active with new problems and new solutions to them. I think my work with patients in the psychology realm has really helped to hone that capacity. That means not to just offer the "right answers" but ask the right questions. Working with patients helped me to find the approach that involves them and their best capacities. It is strategic, creative work to do that.

Creativity is the courage of seeing what's there and what's not there. Making something! You have to see both, the existing and the non-existing.

I appreciate artists who can evoke an emotion through a concrete thing. Like they can paint an eggshell, and then it has all this emotional content to it. They see what is there, the form, and then they create what is larger than just the thing in reality. They infuse what they paint or write with the bigger meaning. It's not just the sentence they write, it's the stark implication of life in it. It's a metaphysical place. You see a sentence—let's say with fifteen words in it—but when you read it, it's enormous; it might contain the whole truth of everything. It's the entry into what is not so easily accessible, beyond the fifteen words. As it passes your ears and mind, it leads from the physical presence into a spiritual, esoteric one. It transports you someplace else, like in music. It moves me to a bigger place. It guides into a more spiritual and metaphysical world, even just those fifteen words on paper or a violin concerto.

CHAPTER TWO. THE CREATIVE PROCESS

Where the spirit does not work with the hand, there is no art.
—Leonardo da Vinci

*How do you keep the risk-taking alive as you
learn the basic skills and craft?
Risk is a breeding ground for the unexpected and
new; it's the Muse of courageous invention.*
—Aaron Stern

Embrace education; it's a source of creative thought and action.
—Amanda McPhail

I think that a creative object emerges and develops when it is "ripe" to manifest. That's when the artist feels called to be the *birther* of it; that's when we are urged into action and get engaged. We play with options and, like hunters following a track, we are alert! Our hearts beating, we expect at any time to be struck by the Muses.

For me, creativity is always linked to physicality, to the senses, and to the human embodiment of spirit, idea, and perception. Just touching the tools of the trade is almost erotic, especially when working with clay: moist earth and transformative fire. This soft and silky wedge of soil is flexible. It allows the artist to change shapes and correct mistakes. Clay is so forgiving. It transforms its consistency when it hardens in the ferocious heat of fire, where the soft earth becomes stone again and glazes melt into glass. Archetypal alchemy occurs throughout all the stages of creation with earth and heat.

Or imagine a dance and how the body shapes the wind around the hips of the dancer, or a song's invisible vibration seeping into the chambers of the heart, emerging from the human throat. Or envision a painting that transports you in seconds to the sunflower-filled fields of southern France. *Tournesol* is the name of this glorious plant, because it turns with the movement of the sun. Or imagine the creative use of food. We encounter familiar or shockingly strange tastes as we open our mouths and ingest the art of a good chef or grandmother.

An artist delights in the encounter with the instruments and tools of the trade, and often the tool is her or his own body: the hands digging into clay, the ears full of music, and the dancing feet overpowering her heartbeat. The artist dares to get engaged with the sweaty embrace of creative action. Through invigorating and patient practice, and with assistance of her body and the equipment of her trade, the artist invests her courage and skills into the process of shaping a new reality.

The flow of creativity is fostered in situations where a strong trigger for the imagination is matched by a solid skill level. When I engage in such an encounter and face the challenge, I experience joy and satisfaction: "Yes, I can do it!" That conviction sparks my courage and supports the feeling that I can manage my life and live up to its demands and callings. A sense of urgency and passion—and often play—invigorates such a creative endeavor. Skills and tools are companions in an artist's life; they nudge our longing for action. Handling them well does not exclude failure and frustration, but they provide a solid handrail, as we climb—or fall. Failure is such an intrinsic challenge for any creative person that many aspiring artists hide their ambition and talent or drop their attempts in artistry—until they discover that it's so often our failure that drives us to find new approaches. It urges us to dare and get lost as we stumble into unknown creative territory.

On the other hand, when I fail—which means when I don't respond skillfully to the demands of a situation—the effect stymies me and strangles my creative spirit. As an example: When I am confronted by an electronic challenge and am hampered by my lagging skills, that leads to frustration triggered by the feeling that I am clumsy and will be left behind by modern life, where kids the age of twelve, like my granddaughter, are more apt at dealing with computers than I am. This is a challenge where I feel limited and uninspired. Creativity expands the mind and heart, but obvious limitations make me shrink. I could acquire the skills and tools to make the electronic world a friend, but I am lacking the motivation. I am at ease with physical tools, with hammer and nails, but I am not living well with the logic and hidden mechanics of the electronic age. I feel like a bird in a cage or a mouse in a spinning wheel.

I wonder often if the creative life that involves the senses and the body is fading out in our electronic age, where the pseudo-experience in our sheltered living rooms or offices replaces the wet, messy, sweaty real encounter with the objects of our imagination. Creativity gives birth to a physical piece of work that I can hear, see, taste, dance, and touch. Electronic devices seem disembodied to me, unrelated to human senses and being-ness.

So why are acquired skills for creative activities so important? Skills grow through usage, devotion and training. Skills grow when we do what we love. We want to repeat and do well what we love. We return to it; every morning, we can't wait to put our hands to our object of art and meet its challenge. That does not mean that highest levels of skills bring best results; we need also a willingness to fail and to stagger. We need an adventuresome spirit to give shape to the unfamiliar and not-yet-born—and so to step into the unknown wilderness of imagination—and find the Unicorn or dragon in the underwood. Creativity can flow even when a person doesn't have a high skill level yet. That is how we artists grow in our work: Our early work evolves into the maturity and mastership of later years.

Creation asks for skills. Skills are a part in the triangle of creator, object, and the physical process of creation. We learn how to swim when we step into the universal river of manifestation. The acquisition of skills allows us to make real what is hidden. That is joyful and satisfying and utterly magical.

I remember when I raised my three children in Switzerland. Every winter, we took off into the Alps and skied on a mountain called Schilthorn. Sometimes I just observed and wondered with amusement why we went upward in a gondola just to put on our skis and slide down again, to go up again and slide down again; this repetition seemed foolish. So why did we put money, time, effort into that activity? We wanted to build and test our skills. We were eager to risk something and face the dangers along the way, the spirit of competition, the speed of the wind in our hair, the cold air on our hot cheeks, and the steady increase in skills. And all of that just for the experience of the thrill? Yes! Nobody was needed to admire or care. That's *l'art pour l'art*. The activity in itself was worth the effort. It provided great joy and exhilaration, again and again. There is a childlike innocence in such an endeavor. I believe that we humans love to learn and enlarge our way of being and doing. It brings sweet satisfaction and opens the vista into future success.

Doing something well—or just a bit better than the day before—is exhilarating and motivating. This is what happened to me: I had written my whole memoir with the support of a coach and several trainings in creative non-fiction. And when my coach said, "I think this manuscript is ready to be sent out to agents," I began to hesitate, questioning if I had produced the best I could? So I got suddenly gripped with the desire to become a "real writer," a professional. I believe in education and in the transmission of knowledge and skills. I love to learn. So I enrolled in graduate school to earn a master's degree in creative writing from Goddard College, daring to invest a major part of my retirement savings.

Those two years brought me some of the best times in my whole life. I was on fire. I was engaged. I learned and felt the pleasure of practicing a whole variety of skills and tools. As I approached my seventieth birthday, I was back on campus and into the student situation. How delicious that was at my age! It was deeply satisfying to till the mature soil of a long life and plant seeds and water the grounds in the field of the arts. Creativity blossoms and grows in those fields.

Yes, creativity needs the achievement of skills and the practical application of tools. Writing my memoir meant that I was able to turn a vision into a book, into an object of art that I could hold in my hands. I knotted the strands of my life experiences into the weaving of a whole tapestry. I learned how to apply words as tools and to listen to the intricacy of language. Skills are servants that support a desired outcome. Acquired skills are a humble and devoted manifestation of our love for creation.

*The feeling of frustration—the act of being stumped—
is an essential part of the creative process.*
—Jonah Lehrer, *Imagine*

Perfection

The Japanese have a deep and intrinsic love for beauty. The masters of Japanese arts devote many years to reaching perfection in their field. The following was told to me by a master player of Japanese shadow paper puppets, an ancient theater art in which puppets are moved with help of sticks fixed to their arms, legs, and head.

Five artists are needed to bring the larger-than-human puppets to life, the shadow theater performer explained, with each puppeteer holding and directing one of the sticks. The players are dressed in black, and disappear into the black backdrop so that the audience registers only the puppets' movements, enchanted by the creatures' breathtaking elegance and grace.

The puppeteer explained the lengthy training required by this ancient art: ten years needed, for instance, before the artist humbly begins to gain enough skill to call himself a master of the movement of the legs. Then he steps up to move the puppet's arms—another ten years—followed by the last stage—ten years more devoted to moving the head in ways that exude magic and brings to life the mystery of the stories that are being performed.

So after thirty years of rigorous training, the master is appropriately trained to awaken these puppets to life and so to tell Japan's ancient tales in the most graceful ways—touching the hearts of the people who watch and listen with great reverence and deep joy.

Why such urge for flawlessness?

It seems that we humans have a built-in longing for perfection; we naturally strive to be increasingly skillful. Our limitations are painful blocks; they stunt the flow and strangle our enthusiasm. Perfection can manifest as a deeply satisfying sense of meaning sparked by Divine inspiration. But on the other hand, this hunger for perfection tortures the artist as "not being good enough," and drives him or her with a restless urge for better results.

How do we register perfection? Is it a question of taste or of education? Can spontaneous creativity still spring to life if a culture imprints such strict rules, like the traditional Japanese? Or is perfection a deep longing that awakens delight and bliss when we get an inkling of it in a fleeting moment? Is the urge for perfection an expression for our longing to encounter the Divine as a creative manifestation?

No, art does not have to be perfect; creativity can sprout in a flowerpot as well as in the work of a highly refined painter. Or the silly charm of child's play may be so contagious that it triggers our own creative playfulness. I believe that the driving force for creation is enthusiasm and curiosity. The Greek word enthusiasm means being-possessed-by-the-Gods. Perfection might point to that state of being possessed by the Divine.

In 1990, when I lived in Tokyo, I visited the Japanese National Museum with its varied collection of treasures born from and created in this exquisite culture.

In one room, I walked slowly through the many rows of ceramic wares behind protective glass. Being a ceramic artist myself, I felt a sensual delight as I observed their shapes and surfaces. Plates and pots and bowls were glazed in the most splendid, slightly subdued colors, slick or with textured surfaces.

And then I came to a sudden halt in front of a bowl not much bigger than what my two cupped hands could hold. My breath stopped for a moment, and I broke into tears of recognition, touched by the encounter with *Perfection*. In front of me was a quiet product of human hands and imagination, a simple object that had reached its completion in excellence.

The recognition of its beauty came from inside my body. There was a feeling of utter happiness, an orgasmic rush of energy. I was rattled by an intrinsic knowing, like the golden mean, not learned but planted into the cellular wisdom of my physical humanness. The creator of this bowl had stepped into the space of the Sacred, and was able to bring back to us the gift of this encounter with a final product that cannot be improved. He offered to us the experience of perfection.

I believe that we encounter our own Divinity in those seemingly ordinary moments.

Writing always changes the writer.
The person who completes the writing
of the book will be different than
The person who began the book.
—Unknown

Give your own story to the earth as an offering, full of meaning, full of possibilities, and full of the song of the soul.
. . . Just find the seed of your own story; open it with love and place it in the heart of the world, where it will keep alive the fire that burns there,
that is your offering.
—Llewellyn Vaughan-Lee

The Redemptive Power of Writing

In 1991, I settled in for an all-winter retreat on the sacred island of Iona in the Hebrides, off Scotland. The main gift of a retreat is *time in abundance,* an open structure that allows a place for contemplation. I was undistracted and free-flowing in my imagination. I didn't have to hunt for ideas and insights because they came voluntarily, knocking at my door. The loneliness of those days left me naked in a heartbreaking and mind-scrambling way. But this emptiness in solitude was pregnant with possibilities.

So I began to remember and write my story of childhood in Nazi Germany.

Not because it was a special story, but it was—for me—the most familiar tale and full of questions that caused bewilderment about being human, about war and loss and survival. The act of writing led me through that bewilderment toward clarity and compassion. I used words to shape my inner memory into outer language; I sorted the threads of the weaving which we call life, and knitted them into a tapestry made of words that had special meaning in my childhood, like *grandmother, mother, garden, tree, bomb shelter, air raids, fire alarm, hunger, love, family, fire, death, fear.*

And as the story unfolded, the words changed into grown-up words, like *survival, shame, guilt, horror, grief, love, community, forgiveness.*

As I allowed these words to percolate and shape themselves into sentences, the story came to life. It had a voice. It became a calling that wanted to be heard. The story carried a vibrant life-force in and of itself. I crossed the threshold where the history and I became partners and walked shoulder to shoulder. That's my experience of creativity: My own longing for truth and expression is mysteriously supported by the Muses, and the action of writing kindles fire beneath the cauldron of alchemical transformation. Thus, creative writing turns into a redemptive power.

I discovered that creativity carries profound healing power; it transforms and cracks open our habitual and frozen mechanisms of thought or belief. What was a nagging, torturing, nightmarish thought or memory inside my brain turned into something that could be perceived as an object of my senses through the process of shaping it into words. It became a *vis-a-vis*, a partner with whom I can negotiate, and that was the beginning of letting go.

Remember the fairy tale of *Rumpelstiltskin*? The princess had to find out the name of the dwarf who wanted to force her into marriage. She was smart and found out the name of her ugly oppressor, and as soon as she could speak his name, he lost his power over her and she was free of his spell. This story reveals the power of language, the power of naming and speaking truth. The artist and writer is a transformer and alchemist. Speaking the truth unlocks the spell of lies and distortions. Speaking the truth reduces the power of the ghosts that feed on past curses and lies. That process also happens in psychotherapy, where a witness is present to hear and receive the story and hold it with grace and compassion. And that also happens when we write memoir, where the process of turning the inner world into outer language invites a redemptive healing of past wounds.

Writing memoir activates and energizes remembering of the past, but it also opens doors to the present and future. As we gather and weave our story, we collect all the separate pieces of the quilt of our life in the attempt to arrange them into one big picture. As we write, we understand and integrate the past with the wisdom of today. We learn to embrace the losses and shortcomings of our youth with the acceptance of a more-mature age and attitude. And so we celebrate our life of today, inspired by the child we once were in the past, the child that still lives inside us. We discover who we are through the process of writing, and that will help us embrace our own humanity as well as that of other members of the human race. By knowing and accepting our own story, we feel compassion for others. It's a humbling and fulfilling path, to live the "examined life" of a writer.

As I stumbled around in my past with the help of the process of writing, I began to bring order into the chaos of memory. The shaping and forming of language on paper enabled me to *name* the experience. Language is magical; it catches a thought like a bird in flight and places it into the web of a whole story, the story of our life. Language is a bridge between you and me, and between me and me—between the outer and the inner. As I express my life, I can understand it better, and that inspires me to understand you better. As I look into my history's hidden corners and remove the spider webs covering truth and lies, structure and meaning emerge. Wounds and pain turn into paving stones along the path of life that I share with other human beings. As I name my experiences, I uncover secrets and ghosts, and thus, they lose their suffocating power.

The writing of my book about growing up in Nazi Germany turned for me into a question of existence, a *must*. I wrestled the truth from the angel, like Jacob at the foot of the ladder to heaven's door, clutching the angel's heels and yelling "I will not let you go unless you bless me!"

So I discovered how my humble and small endeavor initiated me into a bigger understanding of life itself. I made a commitment to the healing art of writing. And today, I keep showing up at my desk.

When I write and live in the flow, the sentences arrange themselves as in a dance, forming paragraphs and filling pages. The process of writing my memoir took more then ten years. What emerged was nothing extraordinary, just one child's life, moving like a river shaping its own bed and the surrounding landscape.

Creativity is love in action, grief in action, anger in action, awe in action. And there's relief from pain and anger through those actions. So the unwritten book inside me grew like a pregnancy, where there's a moment when the child is ripe and has to be born. No avoidance is possible anymore!

I called the book *Dancing On One Foot*, because I realized how much I loved this life, even if it was flawed and awkward at stretches; I saw that it was a dance, and it deserved to be celebrated.

Now, I am celebrating my eightieth birthday, still dancing. I am entangled in a hot love affair with writing. And the book, *Dancing On One Foot*, conceived on a small island in the Hebrides, has grown up and walked out into the world.

The Creative Process: The Interviews

ESTHER MARION

For me creativity is in all of what I live, including biking, hiking, yoga, cooking, gardening. Flamenco is a deep creative exploration like a journey into death.

I write a lot. I rehearse my dreams. And then the flow might just stop, be stagnant, but that's not boredom, it's like a vacuum; I slow down and wait, allow it to be there, this nothingness. I allow time for this internal process of emptiness, I am patient, and it does its own work inside. And then it wants to come out; it needs community. It turns around naturally. Like a seed coming out of the ground, or like a bear in the cave, waking up and coming out after hibernation.

Mother Earth inspires me; she is the ultimate artist and Muse. Nature, this mother we are living on, is so intelligent. Children are tuned into that and respond instinctively, and so am I. We go to the woods or hike or run around; nature is always there, full of creativity. I watch the light and the shadows, fully immersed in the Earth's magic. This is ultimate art, this is where creativity starts, with those observations.

The place where I live is essential for my creativity. I remember being in New York. I was overwhelmed. The energy there put me into grief. It tripped me out. I was in psychic pain. I couldn't handle such a big city, as fascinating as it is. The pollution and the noise were so intense.

I lived for some years in the Southwest, in New Mexico, and there on that land, I feel the opposite. I am familiar with it, I calm down and go deep. That's how I find my way into creativity.

My creative flow opens when I really devote myself to the art. Dancing is like putting out a prayer into the world; the prayer is the starting point. I live my art and my life in a state of prayer. And then there is performance, stepping out and dancing on stage, or on the land, or in the forest. I always receive inspiration when writing, reading, or experimenting with movement.

I am working on a new dance piece, and sometimes I smoke a little bit of marijuana; it comes from the earth and wants to be used in a sacred manner. It enhances the archetypal images that want to be expressed. I choose the music carefully and pick melodies that trigger deep, dark visions, leading the listener into their own process. It might take years for the piece to be ready for performance. But I cherish the process of gestation.

There's a system of psychology that I study. I am in my philosophy a Jungian by heart. I connect with my dreams; they are a true source of inspiration. I pay attention to my psyche and mind. I want to be efficient and go forward. The Muses or the archetypes are my inspiration; they feed me, touch me, set me on fire.

Michael Broome

I am interested in the alchemy that charges me, like putting things together, placing red next to blue. Or I take scrap clay and do something new with it, let it come to life. That's how these clay *katsinas* are being made. It gives me great pleasure to make something and find out what it is. You can't help but mess with these pieces. I think that's true art, moving without destination and without any purpose or expectations, but I am doing something at the same time. It's doing itself and letting me know its intention; we are a team.

I think it's a great feat of a human being to do something without purpose. And what comes out can be very playful. That's what I want: I try to create good play and enjoy it. If I am not playing, it's not fun. If that blockage happens, I give myself a break, take a book and read.

But I always come back to art and charge my batteries through the doing of it. There's a product at the end. It's not so difficult to follow this natural pull because I am really a person who wants to be creative. Even if I am not giving it any thought, I find myself doing something creative naturally.

It's always the same: I am *playing*. I am getting into pottery without knowing or planning what I am doing, but finally I get to it. I roll the clay out or pinch it; I just start and let it move me. I do the simplest thing until I have an idea. It's the idea that emerges and then drives me. If I don't have this idea, I just unconsciously play with the clay and wait.

That's how I make these *katsinas*. They are not really my inventions. They originate from the Native American culture. I am the one who elected to make them, but they have their own life and idea. And they really interact with me and talk to me, and I see, "Oh, that's what comes out, that's what's being born here." It's not born from my culture, but those *katsinas* don't seem to mind. They want to play, too.

I have shown them to people who understand them, and they think I am catching something about their origin that the old traditional ones don't carry and that is related to our modern times. You see, modern *katsinas* seem to move more toward action figures. Like Barbie or Spiderman, those action figures have dropped the mythological part of their character and just look like people. They tried to go past the mask and make real figures, which I think is a mistake. I dropped that and moved toward the mythology of those figures. That's where the magic comes in.

TONY JUNIPER

In my work, I have learned to come in *through the back door*. That's an important strategy. Friends of the Earth has over the span of eighteen years tried to get some political attention for the environmental issues of our time. It's an art. In political work, you have to reach people where it touches their personal lives. You have to be quite thoughtful how you approach those issues. Through years of experience doing this kind of work, I learned that you don't get very far until the problem interferes with the personal interests of the people. If you discuss the birds and the bees and the impact of chemicals in the agricultural industry, you might encounter deaf ears. But if you come from a different point of view and say, "Actually, your drinking water is contaminated with nitrates from the fertilizers, and this is a health issue for you and your family," then people get alarmed and approach politicians and insist on getting some answers back.

From that kind of experience in my work with Friends of the Earth, I learned to see things from a different point of view. And you find a new way to approach it; I call it *through the back door*. You find a more literal than rational approach. I suppose that is creative, and inspires new ways of thinking. It's about strategy and how you conceive plans for change.

The purpose of my life is to leave the natural world in the best possible state so that people can enjoy it in the future. From a very young age, my inspiration came from nature. And it remains so now; that's why I devote myself to nature's protection

How do we make that fit with the needs of eight billion people? That's the center of my work and engagement today.

Let's look as an example at the genetically modified golden rice. There is a tendency just to see this as a scientific, ecological issue. But it has to do with power relations and all the choices we have in agriculture. It has to do with vested interests. Unearthing all of that is for me a really important part of the conversation. These wider questions need to be embraced and spoken; they are still hidden from view.

We live in a world that is driven by finance and business. But we need to be able to make a case for nature in a way that can be understood. People see on the one hand economic growth as a choice, with nature on the opposing side, so it's either the one or the other. We devastate nature, and that sacrifice is just seen as the price we pay. But the truth is that the bees, the birds, the trees, the wetlands, the swamps, all these things are actually adding value to our economy. They bring concrete money into the banks. If we are saying economic growth is the primary objective, we are definitely losing.

This is a problem of perception and interpretation of facts.

That's where the work is needed. In my process, I merge the ideas and the factual reality, including the loss and gain. I have my feet on each side of the divide.

Carole Watanabe

My favorite saying is, "You live a brilliant life by creating your environment." For my creative process, I need to create the lifestyle and the environment that inspire me. And I need to keep it fresh and changing, so that I feel continuously stimulated. That philosophy comes automatically through in my work.

My houses have become my art form. When I look back, that has always been so; I have created environments since I was a little kid. I was always the one building the fort. I remember that I had a tepee when I was little; I created the fabric and then I invited others and held court inside.

I paint in France. I stand in the middle of the field of sunflowers and paint the beauty of it. It heals me. It seems like a very simplistic point of view, but my art got me through a lot of trauma. I often wonder how people who don't paint get through their trauma? I assume they are writing or dancing or making music.

I always think that I want to go out by myself and paint, but the reality is that it always evolves into a community. I am happiest painting with other people. I have always needed the engagement with community. Artists tend to isolate themselves too much. I have the idea that I need this kind of peace and quiet to concentrate, but I also crave creative feedback. We need to know from time to time that we are on the right track. We require willing and supportive friends and other artists around.

CATHY ATEN

My creativity has segued into my life as my work of art, no distinction! Multiple sclerosis has become my Path. I do believe there is a depth that you can never reach unless you have been shattered.

Creating art has a lot to do with the tension between knowing and not knowing. Three years into the diagnosis of M.S., I realized that I had no idea what to tackle next in my art, in my work. I stopped creating. Nothing was coming through. What I did was flat and without substance. So I stopped and hiked around a lot, and prayed, "What shall I do?" And I received the message: *If you love the land so much, why don't you use the earth for your art?*

I gathered the actual earth, the dirt, the red dirt of the high desert of New Mexico. I got inspired by branches, shadows, the place itself, nature. And that's where I go for my inspiration now. That's where I feel nurtured.

I am a wanderer and watcher, I feel drawn to places, I listen well. I am from Michigan, but that was never my place. I had never gone west of the Mississippi. And then I came here to New Mexico—and I never went back; it was home, it nurtured me. This does not happen if you are not in your place; for me, place is vital for an artist! I came here, it felt like home, and so I stayed.

I was a visual artist, painted and created objects out of clay, was quite successful. Now, as symptom of M.S., my right hand is basically without power and is lame. I had to change my creative expression, and began to write just using my left hand and the keyboard. I keep up my blog on the website and share my insights and struggles in ordinary daily life, and I share openly about my struggle with the monsters in my inner world.

Creativity is inseparable from life. All this is a hard thing for me. You called M.S. an illness, and it sounds as if something is wrong, and I do not really believe that something is wrong with me.

I think that if God would have come and said, "I am gonna give you a really hard job to handle that will transform you, but it's going to be hard work!" I don't think I would have wanted a smaller lesson than this one.

AARON STERN

My process? I am sitting at the piano, playing. I am "doodling," and all of a sudden, an inspiration hits me. Who knows where that comes from? It's a mystery, impossible to know. I try everything I can to turn off my mind. I am just there, freely improvising, just wondering, and all of a sudden, it sparks, and I like what I just heard. And I play with that a bit more, find out where this is heading, rather than trying to make it be something according to my will.

That's my creative process. Usually there is a story, like right now as I am talking here to you, it is like a creative act as I weave this in between the Leonard Bernstein story. It's a creative act right now as I am reflecting on it. I am connecting it with that felt sense of familiarity and recognition. That's a process, and I am conscious about it. Something touches me, and I pursue it. And where the original stuff comes from is a mystery. It is already existing somewhere, and we are waking it up when we give it attention.

Whatever materials you choose, whatever methods you use, as long as you stay connected to that felt sense of knowing, you let it inform you. The familiarity is the touchstone. The essay I wrote is about that; it is written as a dialogue between me as a composer and a music listener and teacher.

ANYA ACHTENBERG

All of my processes are fueled by a certain level of possession. When I create, I am possessed.

It was always important to me to write stories and poetry. All of my processes are fueled by a certain level of possession. When I create, I am possessed; it's gift from a mysterious place. I work very hard on a lot of things but especially on my art, my writing. When I am doing it, when I am in the middle of it, it's not hard.

When I was younger, like teenage years, I had to fight a huge amount of fear. I felt stifled, as if someone put their hands over my mouth. I was in terror. So I invented for myself what they call today "free writing"—writing in a solid block, not watching punctuation and so on. And then I looked through it and found out what I was given, and it was often really worthwhile. So then I would shape and review it and cut and move it, listening to its voice with great devotion.

I wrote stories from time to time, but I am essentially a poet. I began with the I, I, I voice, and then I wrote in a persona. I would get possessed. I remember writing a poem about a person in a wheelchair, in that person's voice, being and living this person's experience. I got possessed by this person's story and world, a person I had created—she took on life.

Very specifically, in terms of writing, we are instructed and illuminated into making something. I am a receptor. I feel lacking if I am not active. I see the world unfolding and I don't have a place in it. I am often amazed what surfaces just in the act of writing. I echo experiences that many other people have had. I tell the stories that want to be expressed and come to life. That opens me to understanding this world. My own writing triggers my own transformation; that's the gift given to artists.

Elias Rivera

When I paint, I leave this all behind and I go where the Soul expresses itself.

I have a specific orientation. I could have easily been an abstract painter and dealt with different issues for my art. I took a certain path. I was a peasant and I am so interested in people and their faces. I look at people all the time. In the subway as a child, going to school, I was always watching people, watching people. And sketching. My soul was always interested in human beings. And their soul expresses itself in those faces. The eyes are the most expressive part of the body. So I had to be a figurative painter. I had to.

The people I paint are the people of Guatemala. They are tough and work hard, they are of the earth, there is something deeply ancestral about them. They have Mayan blood. They have survived all kind of hardships. That's why for these past years, I devoted myself to painting them.

When I am involved in my art, I go back and back and deeper and deeper. I try to take the object of my painting to a very deep place. I observe the face, the movement of the body. I paint mainly women. There's so much beauty. I go to Guatemala and take pictures and paint from them. They don't mind the picture-taking; they are so much in the here and now in their life. They feel that I am honoring them. I have such respect for them. I have such a connection to the Mayan culture and their people, and to women. Ninety percent of my paintings are women. I have such a deep connection to them. It makes me really comfortable to enter their world.

YAEL WEISS

Silence is what defines sound.

Music is for me such an actual way of speaking truth. Through music, I can seek understanding and self-realization. It's for me the only way fully to grow and to understand this world around us.

It's funny because I am working with sound, but I am actually preferring silence. Silence is what defines sound. What I mean is that the quality and meaning of sound can be only evaluated according to silence, as supposed to a different kind of sound. For me, silence is the source of sound. Silence is the foundation of everything. And then, on top of that, one can create, as if one is studying a new sense of gravity.

From time to time, I take the opportunity to actually do nothing; essentially doing nothing is really important. It is a major part of my creative process. Trying to give myself complete rest, mentally and physically, is how I recharge. As I do nothing, my hunger for the creative process is gradually growing. Then I actually feel deprived of my work and music. After several days, I feel such great excitement and can't wait to start a new project. That works better for me than being busy with listening to recordings and so on.

Its funny: I am motivated from the inside, but deadlines, constantly, are very, very helpful, because they are defining elements. There is time to prepare a program and a structure that helps. Performances and the discipline of deadlines help in the process.

If I don't have those, I could get stuck in the mud. It was Artur Schnabel who said, If you rehearse a specific piece for more than three days, you need to stop and choose a different one. It's important to keep balance—for a pianist, not difficult because we have an incredible amount of choice, not only in quantity but also the range of styles.

It's essential to me that I practice things that are very different: new music, French music, Ravel, or Bach—he is the greatest, incredible.

I have some tricks: I practice variety; that's important to keep me going. For me, the most important thing is the purity of the music and to connect the audience with the music I play. The most important experience for the listeners is to realize the creative impetus of the composer. That's what I want to trigger and provide.

As an example, I love passionately Schubert's last piano sonata, in B-flat major. When I begin to perform it, I imagine that the basic beat in the music is like a heartbeat. It was there before I discovered it. It always existed, and somehow the performer just joins that beat as it emerges into awareness. The source of it is timeless existence that is already there. So it helps to imagine that, quietly, before I begin to play.

Uwe Walter-Nakajima

What inspires my creative process?
Nature inspires me.
The mountains!

The wind! They inspire me and fill me with vision.

The rhythms of the river; I observe how it changes its surface and its reflections when I toss a stone into it.

And then I listen to the birds. I can answer those birds with my shakuhachi flute.

The goal is to open and awaken the creative flow. To do that, I breathe consciously as I play the flute, or I go swimming and dive in the sea. I take the shakuhachi with me everywhere. I sit in bamboo groves and let the inspiration come to me, and then I write it down. I have developed a special way to do that. I always have a pen and paper with me. I write down the inspirations that penetrate me, coming from the ground, the rock, the trees.

When I have questions, or doubts are confusing me, I dance in front of the shrine. Yes, I have doubts. For instance, after ten years in Japan, I wonder why I am here and not in Germany, where there is success and fame. My friends always ask me that. They made a career out of their path. But I am living here in this small village in rural Japan.

What am I doing here?

I think it's my personal problem, this doubt, so I go to the shrine and dance; we talk with each other, the Gods and me. I connect with Benzaiten, goddess of music. She was a dragon and landed on this island and settled. She is the goddess of everything that flows: water, words, speech, music. Creativity. Always, Benzaiten answers my questions, and then I am calm again and see clearly.

I love to work with partners, in groups. I am performing now with six monks. I brought them over from Japan to Germany. We trigger and enrich each other in our creative imagination. So we mingle with my jazz friends, dancers and sax players. We come together every year now as the Wandering Monks; they call it "blowing the sutra."

Once a year, we are coming together and gather in a temple in Japan where I know the monks. One day, we sat together and planned, and I suggested that we go to Auschwitz and play there.

That's a seven-day trip on the Siberian train. I felt a calling to go there, to play my flute for those who were tormented in that camp. So the monks agreed, and we went there and offered our music in that place of darkness.

We have also performed in Polish churches and in Germany. That was another story, with eleven Japanese monks, in 2003. And in 2010, I went with ten monks to Berlin, and we performed in the *Heilig-Kreuz-Kirche*, the memorial church for World War II. We did Buddhist chanting, and then—very carefully—jazz music mingled with the chanting of the monks. I choreographed the music and included dancing. Observing how the monks were offering their rites in a German church gave those celebrations new energy and meaning. Old became new. One could feel the deep connection between the audience and the monks. It was palpable and powerful, and very healing.

I always hope to change the environment through art. That's why I am an artist. I have a message, a universal message. If you don't have a message you should not be on the stage.

That's what I am working on now. New ideas emerge out of the flow and lead to new ways of expression. Creativity is always in flow.

Tim Gosnell

. . . it's almost an out–of–body experience. I hesitate to say that, but it's a kind of altered state.

My creative process? I don't have much idea about that, but I know the circumstances under which it happens. Most illuminating things happen to me in the middle of the night or early morning, when I am staring into the dark space. It's quiet, no people around. There is a lot of creative inner activity, space as a pushback, almost a psychological space. I found that for me, this is an intensely imaginative situation. I don't have my hands on the computer, don't mess with paper, no equipment around. That tends to help me to reach out further than I normally would; it's almost an out-of-body experience. I hesitate to say that, but it's a kind of altered state. Once awake and going about my normal everyday routine, this altered state experience evaporates.

It actually takes some energy and courage for me to turn that nighttime material into everyday reality. It takes some ability to connect those two worlds, but that's where the most *Eureka!* kind of experiences happen. That's where art and science meet inside me.

Many things in the science world require creativity, like writing a report or proposal. You have to do that in the light of day, with people around you. It's a gutsy process and a different kind of space. As a scientist, you have to activate that creativity in all kinds of different settings, like solving a problem in the lab. It demands innovation. Most of the creative processes in science are not an altered state experience and do not produce these Eureka experiences but lead to simple problem-solving.

It always seems that the ideas for scientific experiments are easier to birth than the footwork, the instruments, the action part in the institution. That demands more discipline, more routine work, more patience, and has less celebratory luster about it.

Jerry Wennstrom

I don't discern between creativity and just living my ordinary life. There's no difference; you are not always being creative, just alert to what the next moment might bring. It's the creative moment or response to what *is* that saves the day. How could you separate creativity from daily life? We need creativity daily. It's the only way to solve a problem and to act in new ways. I get my creative sparks when I work in my garden or clean the bike or light my studio, seemingly ordinary actions.

I do not follow routines or rituals, but I listen to rhythms. I allow much time when I work on a piece. When at the end, I sense its completion, that's when I work through the night. I listen to its own intrinsic timing. I know—and it knows—when it's done. I follow its lead.

That's what I have given my life to: Everything counts. The next and last moment in this creation isn't about art but completion;

you get the piece done and get it out of your life. It's an impossible paradox. Not everybody creating something is creating art. I think art in the truest sense is always a radical departure from the known. You have to die to your own idea of art.

There's always a place where you have to die from the known. You have to live it like a religion and then step off the cliff; that's the beginning of discovery. Most of what I see in art is before that final leap, because it's hard to let go of what we construct and believe. Art is always a journey toward the unknown, the new, the not-yet-defined.

Yogananda said: *To set out on any holy purpose and to die along the path we walk is to succeed*. When I work, I don't allow myself to get scattered. I get overwhelmed too easily. When I work, I do what I do, at the expense of everything else. I am exclusive; I focus. The hardest thing to do after destroying my art and giving up my studio was doing *nothing*. It's good to know how to do that, because we all have to finally do that at the end.

I don't worry. If we live who we are, if we live our dream and calling, we will attract what we need. There's no reason to worry, just trust. Your life is what it is because of the *choices* you make. If you really wanted to, you could do whatever you want to. All of it is God, even when you can't do things anymore. Be open to the time to stop action and just be. Find the courage to arrange your life so that you don't *have* to deal with so many details. How many can you let go of? Live simply.

That's part of the creative process, to sort out and be clear of your involvements, but the daily and ordinary stuff is accepted as part of it and not something that intrudes.

VIJALI HAMILTON

When I started the *World Wheel*, I didn't know where the locations for my work would be. I had to let the place find me. So one day, I spun a globe, put my finger at the place where I was living, and followed the line around the globe. The countries jumped out toward me—they just clicked—and I knew those were the countries of my dreams, and we were on a parallel. I have been tempted to get off this line, like in Mongolia where I made this soul-mate connection with a woman. She wanted me to do my piece there, but I knew I had to go on to Siberia.

When I find a place to work, I first ask the earth and the stone. I stay overnight on the ground; I listen well. I need to get permission from the owner and from the place itself. I use sage and dance and let the earth be a conduit, let the people of the country speak.

How I find places—it happens right by itself. I stay alert, I walk around, and they speak to me. I have a dialogue with the place and the people. I ask them my three questions. As soon as possible I have them translated into their language. No matter where I go and what I am going to do, I ask:

- What is your essence?
- What keeps you from living it?
- What needs to happen to heal the split?

I keep those as my focus.

In Siberia, I talked to the women on the bus; they invited me home, and I stayed with them. They introduced me to the Tibetan monks in the monastery. They wanted me to carve a Buddha, but I had to say no,; it was not my calling. I did not want to fulfill their expectation of a traditional sculpture.

The power of the place, I think, is everything. It's really elemental, because the creative spirit and energy come from the earth and sky. I am missing that here in Santa Fe. Yes, I am so grateful that I have this place here in the senior complex; I could not afford normal Santa Fe rent. But Thursday, I am going up to Abiquiu to look for some land. I don't have the finances to build something, but if I could just go out and spend some nights under the open sky and meditate. . . . I feel that's very important to me and my process, that there's nothing that can take the place of that. I need to fill myself with that earth and sky energy and bring it back to the city. I crave that shot of nature.

I keep my life available at every moment. That's why I think simplicity is very important, so I am available and can let go and move with the calling. I am always watching out; life is a dynamic process that invades that free space, so I keep it simple. Life around us is always seducing us to be busy and become complicated. And so it's a challenging task to keep your life available and simple. When you do that, you are ready and open to move on the creative and spiritual path. I never resist a calling, just keep my life uncomplicated so I can follow it.

We all have those choices as we live with art. I assume that it's my art that keeps me busy, so I accept the intrusion of ordinary life and make it part of my creative endeavors. The emails I have to answer become part of my art projects, and I accept them without complaint, but I stay alert. That's part of the creative process, to sort out and be clear of your involvements. But the daily, ordinary stuff is accepted as part of it and not something that intrudes. It's my business and part of the major work. I do not separate my daily life from my artistic endeavors.

Much of the creative work is based on the space where it can happen. Yes, you need to be able to focus on your artwork. You decide and set boundaries. You clear the space, and that's the balance to be created every day. For me, that's meditation. I also sit, it brings joy to me, but the real meditation is every moment; it's those little tasks, or the deskwork or the computer—it's all meditation. That's our life. It's the biggest challenge, that technology—yes, that too—wants to be loved.

Amanda McPhail and Wesley West

Wes: My creative process always starts out with cleaning. How the place presents itself is important for me. I could never go straight to my workshop and begin working. I'd always have to Hoover-up or sort things out. That's part of my ritual. Some of my friends work in a complete mess. I can't do it. I need to first get my act together. And last, I clear my bench, and then—pfuittt—here I go, full steam.

Amanda: Me too. I always have to do the washing up first. I remember listening to the BBC station where an artist was interviewed, and she said she is doing anything first, to avoid that moment when you have to actually get down to what you meant to do, which was for her to sit down and write. She said she had a needle book, and she would even rearrange that needle book to avoid the start of her writing. So now, when I am fiddling around before I dive into the actual work, I always think of her needle book and that I am doing it too.

Wes: Before I dive in, I always leave my studio and go over to the house and open the fridge and roam around in it, and think, "Can I not just get on with it?" and then I argue inside, "But I am not quite ready right now," but when you get finally into it, you don't want to stop or have anybody interrupt you. The preliminary fiddling is like foreplay; one cannot just drop into it and begin.

Amanda: I need to have one space which is solely mine. I have to clear out everything that's not related to me and my work. That's very important, this one space, my studio, where I can leave everything out there that I need.

Wes: Yes, I do that too, all for myself, all my stuff. Like my office, where I have all those funny things hanging everywhere, things I have made. So when I lean back and look around, it's inspiring and it's all geared toward my imagination. If I would be sitting in another room where others left their things, it would not work so well, it would be distracting my mind.

There's something strange about creativity: You can't just kindle it, you have to court it—yes, that's it.

Sara Warber

I charge my creative batteries in nature. That's where Spirit is, where reality is, where I check into refined states and find balance, let go of the trivial and disturbing. It charges me as a human being and as a physician. I go into a prayerful state in nature when I am really struggling with creative work—that often means writing; that's where the struggle is. I am describing here somebody who needs to be alone a lot; that's true with me. The way that I construct my day is to be at home in the morning for my work. In the afternoon, I see patients and feel generally exhausted after that. I have to go home and curl up in my place here, on the couch, to recharge. I will be mindless for a while, and next day, I am ready again.

In really creative moments, there's a sense of flow. That's when I feel united with greater universal forces. I am absorbed, expanded beyond myself. And that can happen also in normal activity, and it makes me feel on purpose and fulfilled, in sync with myself. Time and space play a role in creativity; it needs to be unpressured. When I am fully engaged, hours can go by without me realizing it. And I am very, very happy in such a state. Time is such a luxury to have, undisturbed.

Ruth Bamford

I need an atmosphere of cooperation to be creative and to transmit what I think.

To be creatively active, I just need a lack of distractions, no disruption. That's not easy, because I have two small children. It can take a while to get into the zone. I call it focus. I don't go into a science paper and allow myself to get really excited if I have only half an hour before I pick up the kids. If I get into A and B and then C, and only half is done, that's very frustrating. But these are practical issues, and I need to manage them. I put music on; that helps me to focus. Music—sufficiently good to be not annoying but not so good that it takes the attention towards itself. I can't put Bach on, but Mozart is perfect. Can't listen to something too passionate or soulful. Elton John works well for me.

Using all my senses activates my brain and all the elements of the creative moment. Sensuality is an important part of my creative work. That's why I can work in science, especially physics. It's not about the details but about being truly conscious in what I see and want to invent. I am fully awake when I work. Right now, I hear the sound of the water in the fountain behind me, the pleasantness of the temperature; I notice the walls of the building nearby. I am a part of the whole surrounding, not separate. I think this approach is specifically feminine, and looking at my process, I can't separate the facts that I am female and also dyslexic. Most of my colleagues in science and research are men, and I find that they don't think like me at all. Most of them don't understand my process, even Bob, who is very imaginative. I am embracing in my process the metaphysical meaning of the event and my specific way of thinking.

I encounter snobbishness from male colleagues in board meetings. Often I listen for long periods and watch the intellectual arm wrestling about "Who is the alpha male?" The men don't care about me in this group where they are fighting about hierarchy. I know that I am not going to be an alpha male under any circumstance. The only way I could intrude into this game would have caused a lot of disruption, by having a woman behave like a male. But they are completely unconscious about this dynamic. I need an atmosphere of cooperation to be creative and to transmit what I think. I rarely get that as a woman in a man's world.

PEGGY O'KELLY

I integrate nature so much into my life that it turns into art.

My methodology is that I approach an idea by first gathering a lot of information around it—until it all comes together, and that's the most nerve-wracking part because I wonder how I best can make sense out of my experience and all that material and then build the next step. Like when I stretched into business with Morocco, I felt carried along, things unfolded seemingly effortlessly, as always for me.

For example, when I opened my first store and I had the first tasting room for my olive oil company, it was a unique idea in America, and I didn't know if it could succeed. I had no money and had to furnish a whole building for office and production. Then I had an idea and put it straight into action. I went to a salvage yard. (That was not like today, when use of salvage and creative decoration is "in.") A friend of mine brought his big truck and we loaded it full of furniture and things needed. I picked out the pieces almost randomly, and it all looked beautiful when arranged; it had class and style. People loved it and wanted to know who my interior designer was—and I laughed because I had designed it all myself! That happens to me: Life just works out.

In my daily process, I enter my office where I have all my products exhibited, and then I light a candle and read out of a prayer book. I have a lotus candle which I love to light. Lotus is such a wonderful symbol for beauty that grows out of the mud. I have pictures all around me on the desk; there's a wolf, and there's Ganesh.

That's how I approach the process of living my life and building business, and I have finally gotten comfortable with it and enjoy it. This is how things unfold for me, and there's ease in it now. An idea appears, and then when I give birth to it and turn it into action, it flows. But in the beginning, it's like a puzzle: You don't see the whole picture yet. I just observe and bring order into it, asking, "Are these all the right pieces and how do they fit together?"

I integrate nature so much into my life that it turns into art. In my house, the way it's decorated, the way I eat, the things I read, how I relate to my daughters, the way I work—I am always thinking of natural ways to produce and to show my products.

I always look how to do it better. I adjust to the constant changes, like selling from websites besides the stores; that's creative change. As owner of a business, I have to rethink the situation, including the life of my daughters, one of whom just started college. When they plan to have family and children, I want to have time and be available to them.

CHRISSIE ORR

It rips me open to hear people's stories as I work with them. I think this being ripped open is necessary when you work as an artist with community.

I am not creating much just for me. And when I do, I do drawings. It's a wonderful process, just the pencil on the paper—delightful, healing. It puts me in a meditative state.

The inspiration is always there, and I never know when it's going to hit me. Sometimes it disappears and then it rushes back in. It's in the movement of the leaf of grass, in a sound from the wind, in the light and shadow moving along adobe walls, in an encounter with someone, a story they tell me, the words they speak. It comes from somewhere else and is right here in front of me. Maybe this little drop of water or a mark on the floor, and it hits me. I say "Look at that!" and catch it in that second.

As an artist, you have to have your antenna honed all the time—keeping your vision totally open constantly, having your perception alert. It rips me open to hear people's stories as I work with them. And I think this being ripped open is necessary when you work with community. This collaboration opens me up to know things I would not have come up with all by myself, or by being in communities where I would normally not be. It's a challenge. And that challenge is what I am looking for to be able to create. It's like a blank canvas or wall in front of me.

I'm pressured by the question "What do you put up there? How do you start?" You can just wildly put some color on it to start, just to get rid of the white, and then you see what emerges. That's how I work in community: They put their mark on the white canvas, and however those marks inspire, we glean out a way for the process. We help the story to be born.

THEODORA CAPALDO

Somebody asked me years ago, Why do you do this animal work? And I said, Because the moment when people understand the depth of the issue, when they *get it*, is like nothing else! Watching that is the creative aspect of my endeavor. That's the product you are searching for. It's not about "you have to think like I do"—it's much deeper, a deep understanding emerging.

Here's a recent example. A film of an amazing whale whose fin was trapped by a fisher's net, and the fisher was in a tiny boat, and the whale had to dive up and again up to breathe, and they realized on the boat that she was in trouble, that she was held down by this net in which she was caught. It would have killed her.

So they freed her from the net, and you can watch how she is celebrating and full of joy, having her freedom back, and the viewers see it and they are transformed in that moment. That's social activism. It's bigger than mankind. It's what everything is made of, and we have constantly to figure out how we are in relationship to that in ways that do not destroy it. What Cormac McCarthy says in *The Road* about the wolf: "It is that which mankind cannot afford to lose."

That relationship is what I see as the core of my animal work, the creative transformation of this relationship to the Other, the creature world. This is a kind of social activism that helps people to see and understand in new ways.

How do I use my specific creativity in my animal activist work? That's a really provocative question for me.

First, what I bring to that is: I am always thinking outside the box to get from Point A to Point B. My abilities: I am a very strategic person, and I am a very creative person. What I brought to my position as the director of NEAVES is the ability to take a very new perspective on an old problem. As with any artist, I have my color palette, and mix and mingle and adjust.

It's the same thing with my advocacy program. I can see a bigger picture—like right now, we have a whole campaign on common ground, an environmental and feminist approach, including the animal connection, and the goal is to expand consciousness on how people see things. I started focusing strategically on very specific points, which may seem simple, but the implications of them are huge. For example, we focused on chimpanzees as our closest genetic relative. We are creative around the question of which road to take to avoid animal testing, and to see the variations that offer themselves. So we ask, what road are we likely to get the best effect from? Which means, how does it help people to get the biggest view on the problem of respect for animal life and avoid suffering?

For example, the environmental group: They work on a safe chemical act, and we are helping them. Yes, we all want safe chemicals, but if you do animal testing for that, you are creating tons of toxic, dead, animal waste products, elicited by the testing procedure, so you have to mandate the alternative—the toxicity testing can happen now in petri dishes in the laboratory and not in living animals.

CHAPTER THREE. ENCOUNTERS

In fact, even fleeting feelings of delight can lead to dramatic increases in creativity.
—Jonah Lehrer, *Imagine*

Aztec, A Love Story

One day, I fell irrevocably in love with clay. My love story began in summer of 1985. I had traveled through New Mexico and stopped at Aztec Ruins. And at this remote place in the high desert of the American Southwest, I walked into a small museum that was part of the Anasazi archeological site, and needed a moment to adjust my eyes from the piercing desert sun to the dim light of this cave-like space.

Single shards and whole, restored bowls and pots stood on shelves behind glass, the famous black and white Anasazi pottery "characteristic to the Mimbres culture," said the tourist guide. As I approached the clay works, I had this gut feeling that I knew these patterns with the power of an ancient memory in the very cells of my body. They were familiar, and I recognized them like old friends.

These patterns seemed to represent abstract designs of our modern times. They told the story of the Universe and contained the wisdom and vision of the elders from centuries gone by. The mystery of ancient gods and the stories of the people were depicted here, describing the movements of planets and of our Mother the Earth. Painted on these wares was ancient wisdom: a sensual chart of the great skies, transmitted and shaped through living beings. The lines defined the universal systems of creation and destruction, the web of the skies and its planets and stars.

At that instant, I fell in love with clay and with the art of making hand-built pots decorated with intricate patterns, black on white. Spirit contained in form.

* * *

Three days later in Santa Fe, I walked through an exhibition of the works of graduating students at the Institute of American Indian Arts. With great surprise and excitement, I learned that those old patterns and the skills to make hand-built ceramics are still being taught at the school.

I turned around and found my way to the IAIA's admission office, asking, "What do I need to do to study here?"

"Take these forms and apply," said the secretary. And so I did.

Following a deep inner instinct and yielding to the creative current of fate, I wanted with all my heart to learn about this craft. I was dipping into something deep and familiar. I am not Native American but was accepted into the program, and I never doubted my path. At the time, I had just graduated with a counseling degree and was committed to a job in Boston. So I went back to the East Coast and fulfilled my agreement. But a year later, in 1986, I returned to Santa Fe and began my journey into this mysterious and challenging desert land and my love relationship with Santa Fe and clay.

Since then, this sensuous material has become a life companion for me. I had planned to stay in Santa Fe for a year, and that's more than thirty years ago. I am still here. I studied at the IAIA for two and a half years, building pots in the traditional way, studying the Native American mythologies, and also educating myself in contemporary styles: creating clay masks, ceramic sculptures, and large reliefs and mosaics. They have become an intricate part of my life and my creative endeavors. The passionate affair with clay has turned into a devoted marriage that fills me with deep joy and inspires playful escapades as well as serious work.

Clay is extremely sensual. It is soft, squishy, muddy, humid and rich in its fragrance, the smell of Mother Earth's body. It yields to your shaping, demanding or enticing hands like an aroused lover. Yes, there are rules to be obeyed when working with clay, rules about consistency, water content, firing temperature, and glaze quality, but other than that, you can play, get dirty, involved, muddy, and utterly happy. You will stroke, knead, bend, smash, rebuild, and invent without limit or regret. There's rarely a "failure" in work with clay because you can always change, add, cut, break open, or close. Clay is forgiving, gentle, and intimate.

Clay is the skin of the living body of our planet. Through a process lasting thousands of years, wind and weather grind stone into silky sand, wash it, soften it, and turn it into clay. The artist scrapes it out from the body of the Mother Earth and adds water. She kneads it and forms it with her hands, and then surrenders it to red-glowing fire that hardens it, turning it back into stone again.

In 1989 and 1990 during a yearlong sabbatical, I traveled to Australia, Japan, and Scotland. In each country, I found a clay artist who opened his or her studio to me. I would settle into a space and work beside them. I created masks related to the culture and mythology of these countries, and I found lasting friendships with the artists. Clay is a magical element and has been so for thousands of years. It has brought much joy into my life. It triggers the creative child inside and does not squeeze the artist into those debilitating doubts about skills and ability—"Can I really do that?" or "I am not an artist." It builds a bridge between the ordinary and simply crafted objects of daily usage and all the grades toward highly refined objects of art. I am still in love with it, and will be so until my own human body will decay and turn back into earth.

Facing the Mystery

At about age fifty, I planned my first LSD experience. I was a novice to this kind of drug, inexperienced and anxious. So I created with great care and reverence a sacred container for the journey, choosing my most beloved Mozart *Requiem* as musical background.

As the journey unfolded, my spirit expanded deeper and deeper into unlimited space. I shifted body shape and identity, and as I floated for some time inside the powerful music as in a great ocean, the sound spread into every cell of my being. Then a stunning transformation happened: I became the composer himself. I was inside Mozart's body and mind and observed the movement of the music, which had a cloud-like consistency, flowing like heavy fog from the right side to the left. I found myself sitting on a fence separating two worlds:

On the right side stretched the unformed, pulsating and undefined mass of sound, and on the left was a wide landscape, a real and physical world. In this material universe, there were yellow wheat fields, undulating grass in green meadows, hills and rivers, and swallows sailing in the air catching mosquitoes. But to my right was the source of the music, an inexhaustible and unlimited field of soft fog. It streamed across the fence, and as it arrived to my left, it turned into sound. And I was Mozart, and I was shaping these vibrations into the movements of the *Requiem*, into the sounds of violins, bassoons, celli, and the whole orchestra, including most beautiful human voices. I, as Mozart, created that music through pure use of my imagination. I heard those divine tunes inside the unshaped musical fog and transformed them into the *Requiem*.

I found myself positioned at the divide between form and nonform, between the spiritual universe and the physical world. By shaping music out of sound, I made it real and accessible. In this form, it could enter the human ear and consciousness. Sound-fog became physical; it had a sound-body, it was able to encounter and "walk the world."

When I later contemplated this experience, I realized that I had been allowed a glimpse into the mighty creative process that turns unshaped vibration into music and universal force into earthly reality. We know so little about the source of creativity. As humans, we are urged to be involved in the process of creation. We are persuaded to participate and actualize the power of creativity. The world is constantly being created. Everything falls away and is reborn again. The joy of creating, of building and shaping and embodying our fantasies is built into the cells of our minds and bodies. Sourced by this cosmic energy, we become co-creators and rejoice like children in a sandbox or flying a kite or dancing and skipping or dabbing paint on a piece of paper.

The creative process is intrinsically energizing and inspiring—*inspirit-ing*. May it ignite the genius of Mozart or the innocent fantasy of a child. Creativity fills our human batteries with life joy, with playfulness and deep gratification. This involvement can be dangerous and overwhelming; it can be destructive in its urge for expression. This ability might be neglected in some, and blossoming in others. But it needs us human beings to be co-creators in this mysterious universe.

> *There is a crack in everything*
> *that's how the light shines in.*
> —Leonard Cohen

> *There are encounters that will change your*
> *perception of the world—and of yourself.*
> —Unknown

Encounter with Mark Rothko

In 1971, Mark Rothko's work was exhibited in the *Zuerich Kunsthaus*, a world-renowned art museum and gallery in Switzerland. I remember the afternoon I encountered his work. I bounced up a long sandstone stairway coming from Lake Zurich; the lively and nervous water glittered in the sun. I was excited to have some child-free hours to see the art. My skin tingled, and I had a physical sensation of anticipation.

When I stepped into the space where the huge abstract paintings were displayed, I stood still, rooted like a tree on a cliff. The cliff was in front of me; I peered into a shockingly new and also deeply familiar mythological landscape where the inner had become the outer, the life of Soul and psyche had taken on shape and color. As if being awake inside a dream, I was in my personal space as well as in the dream of Rothko's universe. I could not fathom what had touched me so deeply and shaken me to the core.

Stepping forward, I leaped off the cliff into his world. Rothko painted messages from "the other side." He lived over there; he knew the entrances and exits, how to cross the borders and translate the experience onto canvas and into artistic language that could be deciphered and read by his viewers, without the use of words. The landscape he revealed stretched far. He ripped open a psychic space and made it available for me. More than forty years later, it still roams inside.

As I observed his "soulscapes," I experienced those spaces in their contrast to each other, color leaning against color like separate worlds, borders between colors as if they defended their "otherness" by acknowledging their differences and coming to life in this encounter.

Rothko killed himself in New York by cutting into his arms; he let his life bleed out of him. Before he destroyed his body, he painted a last picture in shades of black and gray, depicting the soft border between the one and the other world, the living and the dead. In its utter simplicity, it left the viewer naked and vulnerable. This document of death revealed the experience of transition across the dark river towards the realm of shadow—a masterpiece. It moved me to tears as it lured and whispered from across the dark river, hungrily grasping toward the living. And this murmur was tempting; death appeared as seducer, as vast nothingness that would eliminate all struggles by dissolving life itself. The painting hypnotized and embraced like a dark lover, strangling the beloved with his beauty.

Reliving this encounter today as I write this memory stirs tears of awe and gratitude. I don't know the suffering that broke this artist. I know that it evokes powerful visions into inner territories, harboring the intrinsic mystery of life. I believe that such a talent might always come as a burden as well as a blessing. Here again I see art as the key to open the chambers to our heart and soul. As in the myth of King Bluebird, when we enter that key into the lock and open the forbidden door, we might find slain bodies and blood and horror, or angels disguised as monsters.

For beauty is nothing but the beginning of terror which we are barely able to endure, and it amazes us so because it serenely disdains to destroy us. Every angel is terrible.
—Rainer Maria Rilke

Where the spirit does not work with the hand, there is no art.
—Leonardo da Vinci

The Great Mother Thanacupe

I didn't know it then, but the moment I took her book in my hands, our story began—a story of deep friendship and discovery, a story of bonding in the realm of creativity and Magic.

As I walked slowly through the National Gallery of Australia in Canberra, I was stunned by the burst of creativity on display. Sunlight poured in from crooked angles pointing toward specific pieces of art. On a lower level, the "Aboriginal Memorial" depicted a gathering of spirit totem poles decorated with intricate patterns of dots and stripes, the unique Aboriginal style of storytelling. The colorful poles stood in irregular patterns, like people in a marketplace, mirroring a lively scene that had frozen suddenly because a meteor might have stopped the movement of time. The poles quivered against the serene backdrop of gray, wood-marked concrete.

And then I visited the gallery's gift store and felt drawn to a book on the shelf depicting an Aborigine woman with wild curly black hair, sitting at a beach, marking mysterious circles in the sand: *Thanacupe the Potter* explained red letters above her.

I fingered through the pages and found shapes and forms incised and painted on ceramic bowls, bottles, plates, and murals that took my breath away. The shapes were intimately known as if already existing inside my own vision of clay works. They seemed to fit effortlessly into the physicality of my body. A familiarity and power radiated from them that filled me with the joy of coming home, of arriving on familiar ground, a ground that I had been missing and didn't even know it until then.

I bought the book and read it the same day, learning that Thanacupe is the first Aboriginal Australian woman potter, and has developed a signature style that is unique and unmistakable. Her markings on the hand-built pots are stories told in symbols like those we see in the petroglyphs of the Native American people. They are archetypal images that come from dream-zones in subconscious levels of awareness. I had learned from the Native American artists of the Southwest how to build and decorate hand-built pots. Hers were similar but very personal, building on a different culture and expression of self.

After finishing the book, I was gripped by the desire to meet her, a desire that was intense like a ravenous hunger. I had found a sister I didn't know existed. So I called the publisher, who connected me with the book's author, Jennifer Isaacs.

"I just discovered your book, Ms. Isaacs, and I feel a deep longing to meet Thanacupe. I am a potter and ceramic artist, and her art stirs me in ways I cannot even explain."

"Yes, she is very powerful in her art, and she is also a woman with a big and generous heart," said Isaacs.

"Do you think," I asked, "Thanacupe would allow me to meet her and work beside her, assist her in her work in the studio, like an apprentice?"

There was a moment of silence on the phone, and then Isaacs responded: "Let me tell you, what I think. Thanacupe has a major show scheduled, and she needs to create new work. But it is rainy season in Australia, very hot and extremely humid. That makes us all sluggish and slow. If you just work with her in her studio and create your own pieces, you are busy in her space, and she has a reason to come out and join you. She will not be alone, she will be inspired by somebody showing up regularly—and that will support her to do her own work."

My heart was beating; the suggestion went beyond my expectations.

"Shall I write her and ask her permission to knock at her door?" I suggested.

"You can write her and she will probably not answer. She usually doesn't like to correspond. So you just announce in a letter when you might be there and assume she received your letter. She doesn't own a phone."

There was thoughtful silence again, and then Isaacs said: "Thanacupe lives in Trinity Beach, north of Cairns, in a small wooden house with an open studio and big kilns in her garden. She loves chocolate cake. So before you go there, buy some and then go and knock at her door."

Claude and I had planned to drive in our decrepit little car through the red, hot, and immense desert of Australia to climb Uluru, the great sacred rock. Now we changed our plans.

We would go north to Cairns and humbly invade Thanacupe's life. It was around Christmas, which is summer in Australia, and five minutes after any shower, the sweat would make one's clothes stick to the skin. There was no air conditioning in the car, and we just left the windows open so the speed of the air rushing by would make it seem a bit cooler.

We packed our suitcases and drove north from Sydney. The best traveling was in the cool of the night when crickets chirp and the roads are quiet.

Some of the most remarkable creatures on the continent are the birds and insects. One night, as we drove through a dark forest, I had to step out of the car to relieve my bladder. As I hunkered down beside the road, a kookaburra, or Laughing Bird, in the tree above me burst out into wild laughter; another joined in, and soon there was roaring laughter all around me as I fumbled in the dark to pull my panties back up. Soon, my own startled laughter joined the chorus of these totally eerie birds who seem like a reincarnation of souls from a Scottish pub.

I remember our walking in the evening through the suburbs of Sidney with a small tape recorder taking down the sounds of crickets and birds, especially ravens. The ravens in Australia utter a unique call, screeching out the deeply sad sound of a hungry, suffering baby. Crickets sound screechy too, and intense like lawn mowers; one sometimes has to cover one's ears.

The day before New Year's Eve 1989, we arrived in Trinity Beach, a small town just past Cairns. Sweating and amused, we had greeted the young year with champagne at midnight, calling our friends in the U.S. for whom the calendar had not changed yet since we were a day ahead of them. I felt it inside: This was a good year to come. The next morning, I would visit Thanacupe. I was very nervous—and happy.

At about ten o'clock, I stood in front of her door, chocolate cake in hand. The wooden house was small and simple. Held by surrounding tropical palm trees and bougainvillea bushes, it rested like a sleeping cat. Moss softened the path to her door. There was a huge kiln in the back yard. I knocked and heard steps, the door opened, and we two women looked at each other and then we laughed and laughed, bursting with joy, and embraced each other like lovers. Thanacupe was round and big and mighty like a Goddess. She stood as if her feet had grown roots into the earth, and her deep black-and-gray, wild frizzy hair seemed to reach to the stars at night. Her skin shone with intense darkness, and her cheeks were soft and round. She had those Aborigine hands that I adored, with long fingers and slim wrists.

That was the beginning of our story: We touched each other's life for a month in January 1990, and forever. Every morning, I walked along the mossy path and stepped quietly into her studio to work on my own pieces. I made masks related to Aborigine lore and learned to integrate their patterns into my own style. I used the cultural imprints of these gentle and deeply spiritual people, and felt great reverence and admiration for their myths and their love for the earth and her creatures.

Later in the morning, Thanacupe would walk in and settle into a comfortable chair. She sculpted her round pots in her lap, between her thighs; the palms of her dark hands were light. We shared this space and enjoyed each other's presence. After some time, she would softly fall into the remembering of a story, usually the one she had been working on in clay. She called her pots her "story books." She told the tale how *Quichan* the red kangaroo would build those distant hills with his mighty feet so his children could live there. Or the story of the corroboree, where *Ayala*, the white-necked messenger bird, and all the other animal people danced into the late night, and Ayala grew very envious because *Arough*, the emu, was so obviously the better dancer. And *Chara*, the fire man, had to be fed every evening so the fires would not die during the night and leave the people in the cold.

Thanacupe cherished her tribal stories and saw it as her calling to gather and tell them, carved into her pots and bowls and mosaics. She taught children her wisdom and invited them out to the beach, where they drew symbols and patterns in the white sand and shared the stories of Aborigine Dreamtime.

We worked and created pieces in clay, and I listened to her ancient and new stories: the painful events of her early childhood and the suppression of Aboriginal people under the white man's rules and regulations.

One day, her friend Henry Welzman, a jeweler and designer, came by and was excited by our creations. "I have a great idea," he said. "As I see you working and producing, I think we could arrange a show for all three of us together. I am opening my new gallery in Trinity Beach at the end of January, and we could combine your work and mine."

And that is what happened. Flyers and invitations went out. Thanacupe and I worked into the night. She was energized, and the enthusiasm of that month invigorated our creativity and joy. On Friday, a day before the show opened, we still were firing our works and carrying them with big hot-gloves out of the warm kiln to place in the gallery.

The next day, January 27, Thanacupe's friends came from Cairns and Kuranda and Trinity Beach. Fifty bottles of champagne filled the fridge, and—later—us. Henry wanted it elegant, so we drank champagne against the thirst and for the pleasure, and everybody enjoyed friendship and art and life itself.

Before we parted, Thanacupe and I exchanged our work, I chose two beautiful pieces of hers, and she picked two of my masks. Three days later, Claude and I packed and left Australia. Those quiet days with her in the studio are a highlight of my life. I think that the Muses guided us to meet. At my home here in Santa Fe, her artwork has a special place, and I revere and love it. Maybe the big egg is a depiction of *Thwawaal,* the black-and-white eagle, or *Peethereethe* and the *Willy wag tail* he loves when people adore him, and he swings it just for the fun of it.

Thanacupe was born in Weipa, on the western coast of the Cape York Peninsula in Far North Queensland. Her charming personality enabled her to make friendships easily. She loved her ancestral land and customs. She was graceful—and, yes, she had a big and generous heart.

Thanacupe died in 2011. She was one of the greatest and most innovative clay artists in Australia, and was proclaimed a National Treasure. Clay is not a part of the bush people's culture. They use leaves and tree bark for cooking and food serving because they walk about a lot. She used her creations to tell stories, to keep alive the ancient wisdom of her people. Her whole heart was dedicated to serving and preserving. She loved children and thought them her art.

I believe it was our creative work and our mutual devotion to clay and its sensual character that bonded us. When artists are energized and on fire about a specific art form, it lets the heart open, allows trust to bloom and inspiration to ignite creativity on a deep and soulful level. We were in love with each other and with the clay. The magic of this encounter has settled in my heart, and there it flowers and blooms like a seed.

Encounters: The Interviews

ESTHER MARION

At about age eighteen, I saw the Japanese butoh dance for the first time, performed by a group of about sixteen dancers. It was mind-blowing and transformative for me. When we came out of the performance in Zurich's international theater festival, I was in a trance.

And that happened to me in a similar way when encountering the music and dance of flamenco. I was walking in Zurich's Niederdorf and came to a music store where I heard a flamenco singer. It hit me in my core. This woman's voice and song ignited my love story with flamenco. During a tour in Switzerland, this singer came to Zurich and I heard her sing. That was my initiation.

Very soon, I found the dancer Nina Corty, and with her I began to dance and to learn. Then I lived in Madrid and had many transforming encounters with flamenco performance in those beautiful old theaters. That's unforgettable for the rest of my life. Those memories are a never-ending inspiration for me.

MICHAEL BROOME

Who really influenced me was that teacher who got me out of night school and into art college, where I studied photography. He did these enormous photographs, ten feet long and six feet high. He went to this old chapel in the village, and I would come along and assist him. He had built a great enlarger and used unusual means; it was fascinating for me! He inspired me enormously.

You find out who you are by getting involved with art. You need conversations with others and with yourself through your art. That conversation is feeding you, and you are always newly discovering yourself. The more problems you are producing in your art, the deeper you are digging. And in that digging, you will discover who you are.

After photography, I met Ted, and that encounter got me into pottery. He made stoneware pots. He was a student of Michael Cardio and worked in the traditional way and associated with Bernard Leach. They were all potters in the modern movement in London. Bernard had been to Japan and studied with some of the masters there and came back with all those ancient Japanese ways of making pottery, including raku.

He set me on fire, as did my partner, Karen Harris. So I decided to help her build the kiln and get her going on this specific style of pottery. That all happened in England, in Wales, when I stepped into the realm of painting and pottery. Karen lives now in Paris. And it's funny to think that she is now a photographer—and quite well-known too. She does pinhole photography. Interesting how our paths meander. Creativity plays with us. It loves to derange our steady lives and opens new gates of expression.

Tony Juniper

A person who made a deep impression on me is Vandana Shiva, the Indian environmental activist. She is one of the giants in the world of sustainability. Just being in the same room with her and listening to her changes you. She is amazing! Her ability to synthesize and have the confidence to change things is transforming. She has the ability to marshal and argue based on evidence—

which is the complete opposite of how most people are thinking. She is totally inspirational.

She talks about the way the economy works and about the big corporations in the world. She is one of those people who is able to paint a highly convincing and inspiring picture of a possible future. Yes, she inspired me deeply, Vandana Shiva.

And Satish Kumar, the editor of a magazine called *Emergence*—he is another one who can rise above the details. He does that with stories; he uses stories to look at a challenge and what to do about it. He is a man who walked from New Delhi to Moscow, and than to Paris and to London, and then he took the ship to America. After he landed in America, he walked to New York and then to Washington. The reason he did that was that his friend, a demonstrator against nuclear weapons, was imprisoned. Satish Kumar and his friends were sitting in a cafe discussing, "How come an old man stands up against these issues and we are doing nothing?" So they decided, "We will walk to Moscow and then we walk to London and to New York."

They didn't take any money with them, just walking around the world without any security. It's outrageous. And that set off a wave of support, people standing in the villages and cities, greeting the pilgrims. They had receptions prepared and the media came, and all of this had a huge impact. Their ability to decide to do something had extraordinary effect, on the world and on me personally.

Satish has this story as the root of his own philosophy that is expressed in his recent book *Soil? Soul? Society*.

Another man of influence on me is the Prince of Wales, the husband of the queen. I work closely with him. I wrote the book *Harmony* with him and learned much in the process of doing that. I practiced putting those philosophical and historical views in context and understanding the place where we are now, and the way we have lived the last five hundred years. That opened my eyes really widely. I thank the Prince of Wales for that. He is one of the great thinkers of our time.

Carole Watanabe

After doing tapestries for a while and after some of my big pieces were stolen out of the design center in San Francisco, my insurance was canceled, and I got really depressed because I had a wonderful business going. I could no longer sell there because the insurance would not cover me.

That's when I took my first trip to Japan, and there I discovered papermaking. In a tiny village up in the Japanese Alps, I asked a man, "Could I come back and apprentice with you?" That was really a life changer, because they were making shoji screens, very traditional Japanese paper, gorgeous paper! I was taken and enchanted.

On the weekends, when the studios were closed, I had full range of them. I was dyeing and cooking the paper pulp and putting it in squirt bottles. They had these huge screens. I started making these large pieces, and I would collage them.

When I got back to my studio in San Francisco, I said to my weavers, "We are making paper now!" I would take all those woven pieces and cut them up and put them into the paper pulp and made "sandwiches." I made them big and three-dimensional, like sculptural pieces that were placed into big plastic boxes. Those became a hit, and I started selling to corporations and galleries.

I no longer had a place for my tapestries, but I was anyway kind of burned out on it. It had come to the end of its excitement. I had twelve employees and did not really have time for new ideas. And I was getting really frustrated toward the end because I was so busy. So I changed art form and did paper-making for about ten years. It was very successful, and loved creating the pieces.

And then we moved from San Francisco up to Sebastopol. We got twenty acres, my husband and I, and that's where we built our house. But then I got Lyme disease. It was a time of struggle, an encounter with limits. When I came out of that disease, I realized that I wanted to paint. So I went to France and encountered Juan Morteaux; he had a great influence on me. His style was to simply paint what he saw, no compromise, just the naked truth. So I overcame my dilemma with art school and the teachers who were not useful for me. So I began "painting what I saw" and deeply involved myself in that process. That was twenty-five years ago and I still love painting passionately. I could paint for ten lifetimes and never explore all the options. There are so many directions to go. I am still discovering and surprised—I still love it!

Cathy Aten

There are very few artists who really touch me deeply. I can go through a museum and pick out one or two pieces that hold the substance of life. I believe that for myself, when I am in a very high state during the creative process, something of substance wants to come through. I become a channel for that.

I don't see it often in other artists' work. But here's a positive example: the artist Anselm Kiefer. He is inspirational to me; he integrates the opposition of dark and light, I look for that. Shadow is an important element for me. He offers me powerful inspiration. A great artist has room for not-knowing! Creating art has a lot to do with holding the tension between knowing and not-knowing.

Aaron Stern

Yes, I do remember life-changing encounters! Interestingly, it stirs up emotions even right now as I think back to those meetings.

When I was eleven or twelve years old, my relationship to music was profound. I could hear something and in that moment, I would begin to cry. I was so deeply touched. Music took me over. I remember how it overwhelmed me. It brought me to a place of wonder, asking, "What is this power that almost breaks my heart?"

And then I encountered Bernstein's music, and Leonard had these young people's concerts on TV. When he became the director of the New York Philharmonic—he told me the story later, when we had become friends—that he came to the decision to take on the N.Y. Philharmonic only if they gave him a TV program, and so to reach millions of people. That was in the '50s, just at the beginning of TV.

So I watched that program and was absolutely transfixed, stunned, taken. He explained how music works, and I was educated by him about music before I ever met him. There was something about him and his music that I actually recognized; it was familiar. I can remember that I was twelve years old when *West Side Story* came out and was made into a movie. I went thirteen weeks in a row on a bus from my house to get to the theater where that movie was shown, every Saturday, and it took me an hour to just get to that theater. I would take friends with me from school, and I went there again and again. I never forgot the experience of that music. I felt like I knew it and felt like I could have written it. I learned that piece inside and out. Later, I became a camp counselor and mounted a production of it. But simultaneously, there was another piece called *Kaddish*, his third symphony, and I played it repeatedly on my old record player in our house, and my father burst into my room and yelled, "Turn that screaming soprano down! What kind of crap is that you are listening to?"

My mother loved music, but my father could not accept the fact that I was a musician; it drove him crazy. I was so different from what he always wanted as his son. He would make fun of me viciously because of my passion for music and how moved I was by it, my crying with emotion. He ridiculed me.

He later met Leonard Bernstein, who had a story similar to mine, a similar father who was interviewed about his son, Leonard. He was asked, "Mr. Bernstein, we understand that you did not encourage your son as a child to become a musician?" And he answered, "How was I supposed to know he was going to grow up to be a Leonard Bernstein?" So he came around when he realized who his son was. My father and I had a big reconciliation just before he died; it was beautiful. That does not erase the earlier difficulties, but it certainly healed the relationship.

You asked if there was a moment of transformation: I think it was Bernstein's *Symphony #3 Kaddish* more than anything else that changed my life. It's a prayer that is sung at the death of a loved one. Bernstein took that symphony and used that *Kaddish* prayer, and he hired a gorgeous soprano who sang that part. And then there's also his wife, Felicia, who was the narrator. It's about the death of God in the twentieth century—it is an amazing story and an amazing symphony! It totally changed my life. It made me see what is possible in music on levels that I had never imagined. It broke me open, and I was about twelve years old.

I had never thought I would ever meet Leonard Bernstein, not in a million years. Isn't that funny? And when I met him, I was twenty years old and I was on my honeymoon. It was in 1971 at the world premiere of his mass at the Kennedy Center in Washington. It was a theater work for musicians and dancers and actors and multiple orchestras, a stunning piece. The piece had been commissioned by Jackie Kennedy for the opening of the center. So my wife and I—through a mysterious set of circumstances—found ourselves at this event, and when it was over, my wife said to me, "You've got to meet him!" And I said, "I could not possibly meet this famous man, and why?" And she looked at me and said, "He has to meet *you*!"

I looked at her, and it felt true; she had an intuition about it. So we found our way to him, and as we approached, he was standing with a cigarette in his hand and a scotch, and he turned around and looked at me and asked, "And *who* are you?" He was like the mad hatter from Alice in Wonderland. And I said, "Oh Mr. Bernstein, we are on our honeymoon, and we just wanted to come back here and congratulate you," and he said, "Nonsense, it's I who should be congratulating you. Mazel tov! And he took our hands and then—just like that, I swear this is what happened—he leans over to me and asks, "Do I know you?" It was like an echo of the experience I had with his powerful music. I was somewhat outside my mind, and I said "No!" and he asked, "Are you sure?" By then, he had his hands on my shoulders and was just looking at me, and then he embraced me and said, "Well, I don't know who you are, but I know that I love you."

It was a deep recognition and initiation.

Anya Achtenberg

I remember the encounter with a piece of art that ripped me open. I was in Paris and saw a self-portrait by Van Gogh; it was greenish. I stopped in my tracks and stayed rooted into the ground. Everything that I thought I understood about art was transcended. The energy in that portrait was alive and vibrant; it was of *him*. I could not stop looking into his eyes. He looked back at me. It helped me to experience the magic of art: This energy does not die when the artist does. I could not leave. I felt that, in spirit, we were connected. It was very real and happened in that moment of encounter, beyond time and place.

Elias Rivera

As a young artist, I studied art books, I visited museums, I reached for stars. I was young, and I needed first to educate myself. I was full of passion and longing. In my home, my family had no sense for culture; my mother mostly read the *Reader's Digest*. But I took art lessons, and my teacher was a great pedagogue. He had a sense of the ideal: Frank Mason. And there's Velasquez, and then Rembrandt—he hit me between the eyes. He was a guiding force for me throughout my life. He is still one of the greatest artists who ever lived.

As you start painting, you seek in different directions, which allow other forces to impress you. The list of artists who influenced my painting became broader and wider as I extended as an artist myself. New York City is the mecca of great museums, and I was a regular visitor. Oh, and the music! I was able to go to Carnegie Hall and to great concerts.

And later, there was my father-in-law: He had all these phenomenal connections to European intelligentsia, like Kurt Weill and Bert Brecht. He was an incredible human being who enriched my thinking and imagination.

YAEL WEISS

I got initiated into a creative life very early, four or five years old, in Israel. I grew up in a house full of music, and was actually taking piano lessons at that time.

One day, I remember, a violinist came to play a sonata with my mother, and there was one phrase, in the Beethoven *Spring Sonata*, just a few measures. I heard it and I felt it was amazing that somebody could create music of such incredible power. I was stunned. And it left an amazing impression on me, even today. I could not put words to it.

Later on, the actual decision to become a musician was inspired by this original encounter and my reaction to it. That moment and that music set me on my life's path as a musician.

UWE WALTER-NAKAJIMA

I worked with mental health patients in the Institute Reichenau near Konstanz in Germany. One morning, after a long night of demanding work, someone put on a tape with Japanese shakuhachi flute music. I got all turned inside out and knew instantly that this was what I was looking for: a sound without a player, just existing as sound. It played itself effortlessly, and the sound had a smell of mud, like a lotus flower.

This sound gets off the ground and becomes a flower that is holding beauty—sound in its pure form. I was mesmerized. It changed my life. Within three weeks, I left Germany for Japan. That was in the year 1980.

I had no money at all, which is great; it leaves you hungry and open for all that offers itself to you. You are dependent on strangers; you cannot read the signs, don't understand the words; people are smiling at you, or laughing, and you cannot get into arguments or political discussions.

I tried to find the man who would teach me to play the shakuhachi—of course, in Japan the flute is played by men only—I was told he was in Kyoto. I did not know his name, but everybody told me to go to Kyoto; he was there. I was a pilgrim on his path.

So I finally found the teacher in Tokyo, a monk who had trained young soldiers in the war. He had seen a lot of horrible things. That was the reason he started to meditate with the shakuhachi flute; he needed to heal. He thought I was not serious, a westerner who just came to study one year and then he thinks he understands. The Japanese training is ten years, five hours each day. That's how it settles down in your spine. It becomes part of your body.

I went back to Kyoto, got a free apartment there, and through a divine coincidence, I met this Noh theater teacher. I found out later that he has the same birthday as me, September 18.

He gave me a ticket to visit the theater. Noh theater is very expensive. And it happened that I had the same experience as when I heard the shakuhachi for the first time: It played itself, and the actor with his mask was moving without ego existence. This whole Noh theater seemed to me like the church I went to when I was a kid. I remember that the experience in the church stretched beyond the walls of the building. There was a drummer, but he was not really playing; *It* was playing, and this *It* was deeply connected with *breath*. It was not his breath or my breath or our breath but the drums' and their rhythm through breathing. Those who witnessed—the audience—were part of it and we merged in one big breath. It's hard to describe this experience of union.

I heard the flute that day and knew that this was what I had been looking for all along. I asked the teacher to accept me as a student. It was very expensive, but I would work at a school to teach French. He saw that I was very serious, and he accepted me.

I told him that I did not need any special treatment as a foreigner. I spoke a little Japanese, and he spoke a little English.

My stay required a visa, so I went to his *dojo* and I asked him for help. He was quiet, and he brewed a tea for me; there was only silence. I was so uptight. I felt that something very important was going on. Tea in Japan has meaning and power, and I wondered and was nervous. After the tea, we talked, and I told him about my vision for the future and that I would like to commit myself to music, and then he gave me a paper for immigration and put a stamp on it. And I began to study. I think he wanted me to be his right hand.

He was the best teacher in Noh theater.

Studying Noh had to do with studying Zen. Kinto, the way of God, is similar to the German *Edda,* the ancient teaching of the Druids. I found that within the container of form there is complete freedom. If the art is in your spine, you can let go and let it do itself. You don't have to think of being creative. You just allow it to happen and support it by practicing five hours every day. Devotedly. You get up at 4:30 in the morning and practice. I know people who are so dedicated to Noh theater that they sell their car to have the money that pays for the training. A Noh performance can be $26,000. A friend of mine has a factory in Osaka. He is so intoxicated with Noh that he paid that price for one performance. There is much mystery in these traditional arts.

Tim Gosnell

I search for the building blocks of the universe. It's an ongoing story. And that seeking built up to the decision to go into physics. That moment was the fundamental and initial step into my future in science.

I was really interested in what's called special relativity, one of Einstein's discoveries. In 1905, he published that paper. There's something mythological around that. This topic is very counterintuitive, and that feeds the fascination. Things move fast, speed-of-light fast. They are unknown and mysterious and don't make sense at all for my understanding of reality, based on my everyday experience. I was elated when I read it; it turned me upside down.

I thought, these are the "secret teachings," and I needed to find out about that secret. So I decided to study physics. It was not a job; it was an identity. Later on in graduate school, I went on to quantum mechanics, which is even more crazy and outside of my everyday sense of reality. It's not just an activity but is a way of viewing the world.

And then in graduate school, the most thrilling moment of my life was the demonstration of a particular type of laser that I had built. It had not been done before. I turned it on and . . . it was working; for the first time, it was functioning! I was ecstatic. This was one of the rare occasions in the life of a scientist when something like that happens.

It was unique; it was thrilling. I had been in school for seven or eight years to arrive at that point.

Science is often about more mundane things than the big questions, and I might not be the person to dig into those fundamental ones. Most science work is an awful lot of hard plodding. Ecstatic experiences are not part of everyday work. One of the things I discovered when I got to graduate school was that there are two basic types of physicists: Einstein and Stephen Hawking—they are theorists—and the experimentalists—they work hard to prove their theories. Or the other way around: The experimentalists find something that the theorists will then prove.

I am an experimentalist. I measure, create, and build the thing that captured my imagination. I have an abstract image in my head of how reality works. I design something that might never have been built before, and might find out an abstraction. I master an understanding of the physical world that will make it real. When I demonstrate it to others, I get a real kick out of that.

Jerry Wennstrom

My father had great influence on me. I unconsciously lived my father's life. He wanted to be an artist, hiding in the attic where he painted secretly. But I did the real thing; I lived his dreams.

I loved art class in school, but not the other classes. I was good at art already as a child. Art education—that was the one thing I could do, the only skill that was acknowledged. The universe was not supporting any desire to be a doctor, lawyer, Indian chief. I did not have a choice. I got this gift of art.

Art became my intense passion; that was not healthy. I was addicted, and produced a large body of work. I could not do anything wrong. In New York in the '60s, when art was all the rage.

Underneath, I started getting an inkling: Who am I beside this addiction to art? Being a painter had become my persona. I wanted to encounter nothingness, the empty space, the divine. I always had a spiritual longing, could talk about it, talked myself onto a higher ground, but then I had to live it, occupy the territory that I had created. I usually was able to.

Passion is not always healthy. We can be very passionate about our neuroses. There is a great quote by Simone de Bouvoir: "I can't imagine a more profitable life than to be completely free and to defeat boredom and find inspiration in the emptiness. . . ." What does emptiness mean for me? Emptiness means I am available, without interruption, to do anything at anytime. I am an open space.

So I gave my belongings away and destroyed my art to come to terms with *nothingness*. I wanted to live it and so to encounter it. You have to find meaning in emptiness. For me, that's the great encounter—the nothingness. It's like learning to dance. At first it's clumsy, and you don't know what you are doing. It's even meaningless; what are these steps for? Later, the music comes on; you get in tune and into harmony with what you are doing. And it's a beautiful experience: You are one with the music and your body.

In my life right now, the music is on, the music is playing, and I am living it as my second nature. I am flowing with it.

If you are so completely available to what is in this reality, you learn a lot, you learn to fix things, be practical. There is a usefulness that comes with this simple way of living. You learn to make things.

You mow your lawn and you plant the garden and grow veggies. You hold an appreciation of things if you don't feel entitled. I don't need lavish living to feel fine. I can do with almost nothing.

But earlier, when I gave everything up and fell into nothingness, it was really difficult; I didn't know the territory at all. I didn't know if it would work; I didn't know if I would die. But at the end, it has become celebratory; it has become my life. Nothingness, no possessions, no home, no income—utter devotion to living in the now would became my deepest inspiration.

VIJALI HAMILTON

I remember moments of awakening that changed everything for me. My mother and father divorced and I was placed in childcare or lived with my grandparents; this did not work for me. My grandfather was a fundamentalist who was very harsh and beat me every day. I had scars on my legs. He used switches, cut from the tree, to beat me, and I would bleed. I felt like I was just a problem for him, was just dumped there in his household. I was not social; I was very shy. I just put my head in the couch and cried, but when I was given crayons and paper, it helped me to come out of grief. And when I painted, everything was okay and I was happy again. I found a magic power in colors and drawings.

When I was seven, I remember, I lived with my grandparents, and our next-door neighbor was very sad and stressed. She was thinking of suicide, as I was told later. She was just divorced and ready to let go of her life. So, with great enthusiasm, I drew a picture for her. I drew what I really loved, a tree and the sun shining through the tree. I gave it to her and she took it in her two hands and looked at it, and I saw how her whole expression changed immediately. I could see how it uplifted her, and my grandmother was saying that it changed her and at that moment, she decided to live.

I remember that I went into my room after my grandmother told me that about our neighbor, and I decided at that moment that I wanted to be an artist. That's what I would be doing in this world: I would help people through my art! I wanted to bring joy to other people's life through my art.

And the same year, I went to a museum where they showed the art of children. There was some native girl's artwork that really spoke to me, and it confirmed to me that this was what my life would be about. It touched me deeply, and it filled me with hope to see that a child, like I was, could create such work. So art would become my path and lead me all around the world to different cultures and peoples and religions and ways of life. I began to use art to create peace and well being.

Amanda McPhail and Wesley West

Amanda: What changed my artistic life was Cartier-Bresson's photography exhibition; I was blown away by it. And the one artist whom I admire most, brilliant and moving, is Picasso. I love his immediacy and his incredible freedom of line.

Wes: What changed my life? It has to be the moving art of Tinguely, his sculptures—massive movements, massive change and surprises. It's alive, fills me with excitement, just wonderful! It was the only exhibition I have ever been to where there were signs saying "Touch!" "Break!" "Snap!" "Push!" There were kids pushing the football-launching machine, and a wonderful bicycle that you could sit on and it was attached to a pencil and did a drawing. I just loved it! It was noisy; it screeched and it rumbled! It made me giggle and jump up and down. It inspired me. That's what I wanted to create!

Sara Warber

I had a dream, in which I was in a powerful way ordered to "Sacrifice!" and I answered: "I am willing to sacrifice for the people." And that was my initiation into medicine. But I am an artist too, and I care for the arts. So I often wonder how can we create community in this country that honors the arts so that the artist can live and has food on their table. This is a fundamental question that has bothered me for a long time in my life. And one of the things that drove me to be a doctor is that need for the basic values.

I would have been very happy not to be a physician. I would have been very happy to not have been any other thing than just an artist. When I was younger, I would have loved to just stay with theater. All its aspects enchanted me—not the acting but the creative activities around that: the environment, costumes, lights, and that. I think now I would choose more two- and three-dimensional fabric art. But theater arts is what I studied in college.

Yes, I am a doctor now. You cannot look from the back end of your life and say, I would have been this or that other. When I engaged with healing and medicine, I felt I was truly stepping on my path. When I registered for that first class in med school, I knew that it was right. Today, I am expressive and artistic as physician; that's the way I am integrating and living my creativity now. In the latter half of my life, there's always the draw for a more-personal engagement of my creativity. When I don't practice art, I miss the joy of color, absolutely. I miss the artistic and playful aspects of the arts. Yes, I see that there's something like sacrifice in my service as a doctor.

RUTH BAMFORD

As I grew up in rural England, I was inspired by my own intelligent and creative mother. She was very eager to stimulate our inner world.

One of my earliest memories during that time was the Apollo mission. When we talked to other people, I realized that what she did for us children was a lot different than what other parents did. She rented a TV for the Apollo mission, a black-and-white one from radio rentals, and she got us up in the middle of the night to watch Apollo landing. I was sleepy the next day when going to the nursery, and she told us, "This is more important than nursery school," so I knew something big was going on. She said she wanted us to tell our grandchildren that we had watched that landing together.

What I vividly remember is standing on a chair looking out the kitchen window and trying to imagine that there were men walking on the moon that night! I remember squinting, trying to see them. I wonder if this Apollo landing shaped my choice to become a physicist.

My mother had the capacity to see the importance of that moment, and I am sure there are many areas where she implanted in us this point of view. Even my cousins, older than me, did not have this kind of inspiration and enthusiasm about this event. And other people around me, I could not believe it—"You have not seen *that*?" I would ask. My mother was eager to provide what was needed so that our imagination got stimulated.

It was about the same time—I was about three years old—a woman made a big board for us children, and we painted it black so that we had this massive blackboard for us to draw on as we wished in our house. I remember that I drew Saturn V all over the blackboard, and my mother was astounded how I got the proportions actually right. And I tried to get the astronauts into it too and managed just to draw two small stick figures in the tip of the rocket, and she thought it was astonishing for a little girl to be quite so accurate with that. I think it is important to keep these childhood fantasies alive in the young. Look what I took up later in my life: My work in physics is mainly focused on outer space. Thanks, Mother.

Peggy O'Kelly

In younger years, I experienced a sudden shift when I gave birth to my daughter and became a mother. That was a profound stage of change, like an initiation.

And now in the middle of my life, I am learning a new business philosophy. I am inspired by situations and people around me, and I strive to be of service to our Earth. I grow slowly into a different person, and business is not my priority anymore. So I restrict my business expansion for the sake of my personal freedom. I do not have to live the "bigger is better" thing that drives our economy. It is so tempting. But I had to ask myself for whom I worked so hard? This is new for me. I see myself changing to allow soul-wisdom to rule my decisions. So I would say that the encounter with my deeper, more-spiritual self has become the new path. I listen to my soul, and it speaks to me.

That is my new way of living a creative professional life. I always headed toward a goal, and if I wanted something and it felt right, I went for it and usually reached it. That feeds the ego—but not my spirit. I am now building and following new values and visions. I had not been able to think that way before. I am in new territory. Before, my basic desire said, "Being successful is having multiple stores and creating a national brand." Now I shape that path differently. I build only one store in the way that it feeds me and brings income. And since I am an accountant by trade, I see that can be done. What would keep me from following that more-peaceful direction? Only because it looks more successful from the outside? And I notice that the people around me get nervous, asking, "Will you not lose when you shrink instead of expand?"

Oh, I had to calm myself down. Yes, I knew how I would do that. I live and breathe that stuff and understand business very well. Even with this new freedom, I am not just floating. I have a solid plan how to simplify.

So I reflected and realized that the first step would be to prepare a sacred space for this change to happen. This reduction of business space will be a big move for me. The space needs to support the flow of energy in my business. So much of flow in creativity is dependent on the space where it can live and unfold. I am good at creation of that space. I make it soul-space.

CHRISSIE ORR

In my world as a young artist, before my awakening, I had a sense of innocence. I loved studying the arts, and it was wonderful.

After college, I was living in a tiny apartment on Royal Mile in Edinburgh, working in the evenings as a barmaid. I was creating my art in this small space. I was a successful artist, had a couple of one-woman shows and people who were collecting my work. And then, everything changed for me when I had this epiphany: One of the collectors asked me if I would want to come and visit his apartment to see how he had placed my work and look at the other works he had acquired. "Yes," I said, "I would be delighted to do that," and I remember how I came to his flat—you know, in Edinburgh, most people live in those very small apartments—on the fifth or sixth floor. So I arrived at his door and knocked, and he opened it and I looked at his apartment, and then I got this huge hit, and it hits me in the center of my being as I realize: "This guy has the worst taste in the universe!"

My mouth just dropped open, and I was speechless, did not know what to say or do! I remember leaving and going back to my little flat and asking: "What is this art world about, the one I was trained for as an artist?" I realized that the artist's work had no connection to anything around it. It might hang in a gallery but had no bond with real life. And somebody buys it, and I can't see the threat that's coming from my soul to them. I mean, if you are a creative being in this world, a really creative being, your work comes from your deepest self, exposing your naked inner depth— oh, I thought, I do not want to do art this way anymore. Ever. I don't want to create any more art which goes out and I have no connection to it.

So that put me into a huge dilemma. I had finished art college and was doing well, but this experience pulled the rug out from under me. I remember going into the bar where I worked and speaking to my colleague and saying, "I don't know what I am going to do! I am really lost now."

And he said, "I heard about this workshop just around the corner. There are lots of different artists working there, and they go out to communities with their work. I don't know much about it, just a gut feeling that you might get inspired there. Go and look."

This started the next stage in my life as a creative person. I did go around to this place. I met the director, and basically we chatted for two hours, and he told me that, Yes, they had theater people and musicians and visual artists and writers working there together. And they would go out into the street and work with community and community issues, building community, using the arts as a way of activism.

And he said, "Why don't you go and dream up something." He took me on. There was no money in the beginning. I just went and joined. As one of the first things I did with him, we went to work at a school for the blind. And that was a new beginning in my life as an artist, and I have never looked back.

This involvement with community has taken many, many different forms, and I tried to give it up—but I stuck with it and basically gave up any kind of work in the studio. Today it has shifted so that my work straddles a bit of both sides. Because I feel now that you really need that, you need that reflection time in the quiet of your studio besides the work in teams. I can't do the community work all the time, like when I was younger. That had a sense of urgency that drove us to be activists. I learned a lot on my feet. But it took several years for me to look back and reflect. That's where I am now: one foot in community, the other in my reflective private space. I have integrated both, and I am still seeking and changing.

Chapter Four. Place and Time

I note the echo that each thing produces as it strikes my soul.
—Stendhal

*I reach and have reached
the timeless moment,
The pure suspension within time,
Only through love*
—May Sarton

The Intimate Substance of Time

As I age, I observe that the invisible stuff called Time has become a lively companion at my side. It nubs and pokes me and whispers into my ears. Time has personality and a distinctive character of its own, with dark and light hues. My relationship with it is like being in a marriage: I love it, and occasionally I despise it. I encounter it like a favorite old companion who spoils or bugs me. When I read an ad in the paper for suggestions on "How to kill two hours in Las Vegas," I shudder about the obscenity of this expression. Who would truly want to *kill time*? I hold it in my hands like a pearl, rolling it around in my palms, admiring the muted radiance.

I want to create art out of the substance of my life. I want to honor time, the time of my life. It is truly mine, as much or little as I have left in my account. I want to live creatively, every day. I embrace the small things of daily life and the use of my senses: I smell the vegetable soup as I add parsley and garlic; I touch the furry skin of the peaches I harvested, listen to the purring of my beloved cat, Daphne, a thirteen-pound Maine Coon, gray with white socks on. I built a mosaic out of the tiles I fired in my old kiln. I paint my garden furniture purple and yellow.

Creativity is action, and as that, it is always placed in a container of time. I am a snob about my time, being very selective in how I use it with people, activities and events that bring the most return in value. I do not want to waste the intimate substance of time but instead extract the most blessing and joy out of every moment. A dear friend died last week, and my heart is heavy with sadness. I am reminded, at an age beyond eighty now, that my own span of life is dwindling.

And so, I delight daily in the sheer fact of breathing and being alive. This morning, after having brewed a mug of tea, I sit on the porch bench to wake slowly to the new day. The gentle New Mexican desert wind touches my cheeks like velvet. A monarch butterfly sails by and reflects the light on its wings. *Oh,* I think, *this might be the best morning of my life.*

I nestle the mug between my palms and observe the steam emerging from the black surface of the tea. It swirls in little circles around my knuckles and then it evaporates into the breeze, as if time itself has turned into a delicate substance that dissolves into open spaces.

Brilliant morning light strokes the purple roses and the heavy phlox blossoms in front of me. I know about them in the biblical sense of physical intimacy; the poetry of their beauty vibrates through my whole body. Yellow tiger lilies lean their heads toward the sun, their petals spread open like seagulls' wings soaring in the wind and teasing the law of gravity.

Minutes dissolve like chocolate on my tongue, and I marvel how long time stretches when consciously tasted and cherished. Every breath carries the substance of time into my body and releases it again when it leaves through my open lips, connecting my own chest with the rhythm of the great oceans and the tides of the moon.

Creative life happens in such a place of gentle alertness.

I am deliciously happy.

When we have listening ears,
God speaks to us in our own
Language,
Whatever that
Language is.
—Mahatma Gandhi

Angel in York

Traveling from Edinburgh to London, I arrive in the medieval town of York, in northern England, at dusk. The faint evening sun covers towers and gables with a golden hue. This historical place is famous for its beautiful old stone houses, narrow cobblestone streets, and the medieval wall surrounding it in the form of a circle with four gates. But the pearl in the heart of town is the enormous cathedral, called the Minster. The roots and foundation of this building are deep, reaching back into ancient history.

A ceremonial center of a Roman fortress had been found beneath the Minster building. It was in the year 627 that the English King Edwin accepted Christianity and a first building was erected at the site of today's Minster. And thus, York became the northernmost official outpost of the Pope in Rome. These fascinating historical facts are telling us that for more than 1,400 years this place has been a flourishing gathering point for worshippers of Christian belief and its sacred images: Christ and his mother Mary, and God the Father, surrounded by angels and saints.

The town is bustling with tourists when I arrive. I am lucky to find a small room in the attic of a tiny old hostel nestled into the folds of the Minster; I fall easily into a deep sleep, happy to rest after a long day of travel.

And then I am gifted with a visionary dream.

I experience myself as lying in the actual hostel bed, my back on the mattress. Above me, the roof is wide open. My gaze expands beyond this building and beyond the colossal cathedral; it reaches above town toward a shimmering black velvet night sky.

And there, stretched from east to west and curved into eternity like the Milky Way, I see the most beautiful and shining vision of an angel. Her contours and form are sprinkled onto the dark sky by millions of stars, like a dense celestial constellation. The vision is very clear, each detail shaped by great artistry; her enormous wings move slowly, and her flowing gown glimmers in the dark. She has her hands stretched toward this planet Earth, blessing us and offering serene signs of grace.

I am in the dream but lucidly awake in the same moment. I am conscious of the Minster to my right and my body in this bed and in this hostel room. I find myself in this reality and also in a richly expanded space. I am aware of a deep and saturating bliss that vibrates through my physical body. This angel blesses the whole globe, including me as I am adoring it, struck by its beauty and might.

I wake and lie silent in the dark. As I muse about this dream, I receive the gift of an insight that has guided me ever since. I realize that there is an orbit of energy around this historic place that is filled with the visions, prayers, and longing of thousands and thousands of pilgrims. They have been gathering here for centuries! Their prayers and images are an invisible force that creates in and above this sacred place the reality of the divine beings toward whom those prayers are directed!

This dream or vision teaches me to be aware of the energy in places where we humans have celebrated our divine or demonic gods. In those places, we are not only visitors but are also active participants.

I leave York the next day with the new insight that the invisible power of *thought* carries a real energy that creates and shapes our world and us. What happens around me every day reaches into my psyche and into the "private garden" of my soul, for good or ill. My mind and imagination creatively weave the story of a place into my dreams.

I am part of that energy and influenced by it, may it be in a cathedral or on a battlefield or inside a concentration camp. A place has a character that is alive and can express itself. Past, present, and future all exist in this very moment and place, creating reality. The place I stand on and the earth I walk on radiate their history and leave their traces in my heart, mind, and body.

A Creative Perspective on Time: The Vision Quest

Is *time* a gift or curse for you? Are you pressured by telling yourself that you don't have enough time to do all the things on your list?

I want to tell you about a new encounter with time that changed my relationship with this strange being that does not really exist.

In September of one recent year, I decided to go on a Vision Quest that contained, at its core, four days of fasting and solitude. Hours after leaving Santa Fe, I settled in my vision place at the edge of the magnificent Canyon de Chelly, and there I spent most of my solitary time as in a sacred container that allowed deep introspection and encounter with mystery.

I sat on a mighty rock and experienced physically and with all my senses how the sun moved from east to west, from my right shoulder to my left, from my right hand to my left—and that lasted for hours and hours, days and nights. The sun circled and painted changing shadows on the canyon walls across from the place where I sat and observed the turning of this cosmic wheel. I felt how the rocks and trees and squirrels and bats were conscious of my presence in a similar way as I was feeling them, breathing in the rhythm of nature and of the planets. The pulse of life itself was rhythmically flowing through me, and I merged with stone and trees and the bats at dusk. Silence surrounded me like a cloak.

And then it happened that Time exploded out of its small containers of human imagination. Time communicated with me: "I am Time. I am not contained in those human-made capsules of minutes and hours and days and years. They are the products of men's imagination. I am big; I am in between everything and fill all empty spaces in the Universe. Every moment, I am dissolving and I am newly born, endlessly. I am the vast space of the cosmos where there is no beginning or end."

I sat on my stone, and the stone seemed like the center inside this cosmic space. I had no more boundaries or edges or skin to define me as an object that existed in this very moment and in this precise space. This rock and my skin were not separate; we all were one being, knowing each other and weaving into each other's story. The rock was electrifyingly alive. It had been sitting here for hundreds of thousands of years and was part of movement as well as of stillness. Stillness was full of time; it was not the end of time as we define it. It was in constant beginning.

Since this Vision Quest, my relationship to time has been awakened in a new way. I am aware that there is a lie about time, the lie of measurement and loss and gain. Time does not really seem to matter much for me anymore. Yes, you need it to manage your days and do your work, to meet your friends and hug your kids and cut carrots and make a salad or dance and sing at a specific time, but your dance and song and salads are all part of a big body of something we call time that is always there and has been existing since long before we made little pieces out of the idea of time: minutes and hours of a day, and the piles of these little pieces built the years of a life, like the bricks in a wall. Those bricks build our lifetimes so that they can be named and counted. But in reality, time is an illusion. We try to cut eternity into measurable units, but that's just a creative game we play to hide our limited perspective.

I am seeking. I am striving
I am in it with all my heart
—Vincent van Gogh

Place and Time: The Interviews

ESTHER MARION

Oh, place matters. It matters if you are in a culture where your art lives, where you hear flamenco music everywhere. A city can be cold or warm; it's a question of tradition and geography. The ground and environment where it is located influences its energy and artistic expression. Living in a country like Spain, which contains flamenco music and dance wherever you go, is different than living in cool, northern Seattle. It's more difficult here to keep the fire going. In such a case, to survive artistically, you need to draw friends to you who support this art form. I long for a cultural influence that is not available here; that's the burden I bear by living in the American Northwest.

I am European. I traveled a lot and saw different countries and cultures. I see my origins there. We are under the influence of ancient and new creativity. I went to the North and lived in London, just to learn the language, but going South was the pull; that's where my heart calls me. Even our family is tied into many different cultures. That's fascinating. All of us are explorative; we went to Greece, Italy, and Spain. Being European means to be familiar with other cultures. Visiting those places really opened me up to variety.

Yes, the place and time of a creative endeavor has a deep influence on its style and final result.

MICHAEL BROOME

Place and time play a role in my life mainly as far as distraction and interruption move it. It's harder and harder in our time to keep yourself off all the—mainly self-imposed—treadmills. There's the email account—it's a treadmill, you get a letter and write back, and it gets going for more exchange. If I got on Facebook, it would ruin my creative life, it would eat away my time.

When I was young, just out of art school, I lived in London. That was the great center for art in the '60s. I had a whole library of my photographic work, and in those days, English photography was sold all over the world. My agent would sell a lot of stuff to Japan because they desired images of the culture in London. It was very attractive and sold easily. London was at that time the center of what was happening, and I happened to be there and worked as a photographer in the 1960s. Timing was crucial: London was hip and I lived there.

But then I went to Wales, and the life in Wales altered everything because I got involved with painting, a new art form for me. And I realized that, "This is difficult and demanding." I had studied photography. Painting was different. I knew nothing about painting. Being in Wales seemed to change my molecules; it got me onto a new path of creativity.

Making art is basically a fun activity. It's joyful to push yourself to the limits and find out what you know and what you don't. All those deep questions come to the foreground. Art is a place of questions. You don't know what things really mean; they reveal themselves later, below reason. Reason did not invent art. That's the interesting thing about doing art. You see yourself as outside of yourself, and so art can be very humbling for the artist. People are afraid of putting that first brushstroke on the canvas because it's a very daring thing to do. The canvas then becomes a place of meeting yourself. So all those questions of self-image are quite important for the artist.

It's good if you spend a lot of time meditating. And that's another art in itself. It's a place of being. It's an art without producing anything. When you meditate, you can either enjoy that self-exploration or you might hate it. If you enjoy it, it's very rewarding. Coming out of long stretches of meditation is like landing in a place of creativity, a no-man's land. Timeless. I love to hang out there.

TONY JUNIPER

Living here in the U.K. in the ancient town of Cambridge—that's important for me and my work. We've resided here now for about twenty-four years. I came here by accident, for Wildlife International, just down the road from my home. It's a place of connections with this massive environmental community that lives here: organizations and academics and so on. It's close to London, a very good, strong place to be stationed and to be able to do my work. Ideally, I would love to live in a forest on the side of a mountain, somewhere quite far from all of this. That is not really practical, a dream. So I live here, with a small garden and a fountain and the sound of water gurgling in it.

I get a very, very big feed of information that includes my life here in Cambridge. A cauldron of intellectual richness is cooking here.

Yes, I teach a bit at the university; a sustainability leadership program. It is mostly focused on executives. For example, you have a big company focused on mining. Its work is unsustainable from the point of view of impact on the environment. So the question is, What are we going to do about it? That is a highly creative process actually. What is the answer, considering that we are dealing with consumer goods here? We have to look at every side involved. That is very complicated. In teaching, you build up experience, and it's worthwhile to give back to people through that channel. I do a lot of lecturing and talks in different places of the world.

There is no one right answer to those vital questions, and you have to be very creative in your approach to see what is possible and what is workable. How can you deal with all those different influences? The shareholders want this, the non-governmental groups want the other, your internal set of incentives say this, the technologies you've got allow that, and the government thinks something else. What's the pathway through here? And is it the right path, or a detour and new trajectory? So that is a highly strategic place to think. It requires much creativity in that process. There may be seven or eight plausible answers.

I have been involved in that for years and years and heard the arguments and counter-arguments, seeing what works and what does not work. I have developed an almost-instinctive sense to see where these things go. I probably have got a slightly entrepreneurial approach, asking how we best use an opportunity, determined to make something out of something that offers itself, sometimes by turning a small thing into a big thing.

The time is ripe for creative change. The place where I live is saturated with new and bold visions. I am lucky to live here.

CAROLE WATANABE

When I was three, I fell off a building. A little girl of the same age pushed me off the stairs. She wanted to sit where I was. I fell down three floors and broke my coccyx. And I remember how my dad reacted: He made me a little easel. He must have known that I was creative. It was placed in such a beautiful, sunny golden place on the porch. I remember all of it, the warm red colors. This place was my creative home.

And then there was a teacher. At the end of the school year, she always brought me a big box full of all those leftover painting materials. Between her and my dad and a grandmother, I was supported, and I healed. And there was Mrs. Roselle—she came for Sunday dinners. She was a buyer for this elegant store in San Diego. And she went every year to Paris to select those wonderful outfits, hats and clothing. She would show up like Auntie May. She always encouraged me. She taught me how to make my own clothes. She was a role model for me—very elegant!

When I was eleven, we bought a beach house and would go there every summer. Across from us was this wild, creative woman, Elly Katz. She went into the neighborhoods and taught people how to build parks and gardens in derelict lots. She would take me along and showed me how to put all those colors into the cement. We would pour bike paths and make mosaics on big surfaces. We'd get the whole neighborhood involved. The place was buzzing.

Elly was really an important teacher for me. She was just this wild woman. She said she had a doctorate in "play-ology." She taught me how to inspire and involve whole neighborhoods and get all the kids involved. We created and lived in a magical place.

My favorite painting that I have ever painted emerged at a time when I had great emotional pressure, during my first show in Paris—I never had one there before. The theme was a maritime scene. It was for a gallery that was huge, and they wanted really big paintings. So I painted big paintings of boats and water, and was not happy with that at all. I was very frustrated; it did not come out how I envisioned it.

And here came my son and suggested going to a quiet retreat. I waved my arms and said, "No way, I don't have time. I need to paint!" and he said, "Yes, you have time. Come with me." And we went: ten days' quiet meditation, sitting every day. And the first painting I painted when I came home is the best painting I ever created.

A person in a boat, with oars—you cannot say if they are coming or going, if they are lost or have direction. It's my Buddhist spirit that is expressed; it is Buddha in the boat. And a winery loved that image and chose it for a wine label.

CATHY ATEN

Three years into my diagnosis of multiple sclerosis, I realized that I had no idea what to do with my art, my work. I stopped creating, but nothing was coming through. What I did was flat, not good, so I stopped and hiked around in the mountains a lot, and prayed. What shall I do? And that's where I received the message: If you love the land so much, why don't you use the materials of the earth in your art? So I gathered the actual earth of the desert, the red dirt. I got inspired by branches, shadows, the place itself, nature. That's where I go for my inspiration now. I am a wanderer and watcher. I feel drawn to magical places. I listen patiently.

I am from Michigan, but that was never my place. I had never gone west of the Mississippi. Then I got here to the Southwest and never went back; it was home, it nurtured. This does not happen if you are not in your place. For me, place is vital!

I allow a lot of silence, and I am not tolerant of superficial encounters.

Silence and nature provide source energy for me. So do talks with people, books, music. I have the luxury of spending a lot of time by myself. I indulge in silence and solitude. Many people never experience or choose this luxury. Look at the view outside my window, the mountains, the clouds, the birds. I take it all in.

I can hardly walk, but I have all this space and beauty and time. That's a luxury. People think I am navel-gazing, but I like this contemplative place and don't have apologies for it. I live in the space that is shaped by me and my fate. I live my life how I choose to, and that is true luxury, as it is luxurious to have time for reflection and time for just being. You see? My illness carries some pearls in the oyster for me.

AARON STERN

I travel a lot and find that I am humming the tunes related to the land where I am. In Denver, I sing Native American melodies, but when I am in the Black Forest in Germany, that would be the last thing to hum and think about. It has something to do with the folk souls and the land and the atmosphere that is present there. New York is very different for me than the high desert of the Southwest. Location matters. It sparks the music inside me.

I will tell you about one of the fateful moments in my career, when I decided that I had to turn away from being only a musician. By then, I was a performing musician, a composing musician, and also the dean of a music college. I was at Carnegie Hall, and there was a performance of Mahler's Second Symphony, which is his great testimony to brotherhood and sisterhood. Bernstein was conducting, in this excellent building made all of wood, so I joined him. I was at that time always with him, and this was one of the highlights of our lives together.

I sat in the front row of the balcony, and when it was over, the audience went wild! Of course, it is the celebration of humanity, our possibilities, like Beethoven's Ninth. For this one moment, we were united as humans. There was coherence and aspiration; something like this can happen in music. And there was beauty and order, all of this in amazing perfection. But then, within minutes, when all the curtain calls were over, you could already feel the change of spirit, people were anxious to get out, pushing a bit, shoving to get out and get a taxi.

I realized in that instant that the place itself had inspired the people to still themselves and to devote their attention to the music and the moment. And when they left, they moved to the place of a noisy city. Place has power and purpose. Place can help or hinder.

Here, in this building of the Academy of the Love of Learning, it's very objective. This building expresses ideals. It's built especially for music and listening to sound. Some say it's too white and light in here, and others say it's so good that there's no color in these rooms because it leaves me to imagine whatever color I prefer. I wanted this place to be very pristine and calming, I wanted the sound to have a specific quality. I spent a lot of time on sound. Intention infuses this building. That's a very important part of it. I mean every detail; every detail is given thought and attention! There are things here that have very specific purpose. I could tell you something about every detail. I can tell you chapter and verse about each corner and why it is the way it is. So I see it now on a subjective level, and sense the feeling of love I have here, because every detail came from a place of love and is reflected back.

I think that Leonard Bernstein's spirit is active between these walls. Once we were preparing for a performance with the Vienna Symphony, and we were in Spain. We were intending to meet Salvador Dali, and Leonard took me to the place where Dali lived, called Figueras, an incredible place, magical. A place of explosive creativity.

We were there in November 1983, and that's where I understood the power of place and environment.

Anya Achtenberg

Time and space and location have a very important influence on me as a writer, yes! Look at New York; it is such a soup of language, of ways of speaking English or other languages. There was always an understanding for me that whatever I expressed meant something different for the other person. I also think that the rhythms of the city affected me—living next to a story, under a story, or over a story. The question of meeting people, seeing people, without knowing them, watching how they hold themselves, envisioning how they got to the place they were.

And then the train, all the public transportation in New York. One is locked in with other people for hours and hours. In New York, there is always music and building and construction sounds, smells and temperatures typical of this city. Some things made me feel included, others excluded. So place affects my story and my sense of belonging.

ELIAS RIVERA

When I lived in New York, I walked around for hours to observe and sketch people who took their time to talk and listen to each other. I hung out at Forty-Second Street and Grand Central. I would study them and sketch their faces and gestures. I followed those people. I am deeply interested in them. I never forget how I did a painting of one man, because there was something about him that intrigued me. I did a magnificent painting of him.

But then it happened that Sue decided to go to Oaxaca in Mexico, and I joined her. And that's when I discovered a whole new world full of colors and lively customs. And then Peru. That did not work out for me. The hats created too much shadow in people's faces; I could not paint them. Then I found Guatemala, and it blew my mind as an artist and lover of people. I traveled there for years and years, and it brought me great success as figurative painter—such a blessing for me. It's a wonderful thing to travel and discover the world. Yes, New York has great art and museums, but Guatemala is a different world, showing a different humanity. Those beautiful beings grabbed and nurtured my heart.

I can't easily travel to Guatemala anymore. I am fragile now. It takes strength to travel, especially to that world. I am so grateful that my art has directed me to such a beautiful culture. It's healing, and I receive it, and also give that back to the world.

I grew up in New York, but the city that had encouraged me all my life began to destroy me as an artist. I entered the world of art in New York at the wrong period. What it was then had nothing to do with my style of expression, which was not timely for that place. I am a figurative painter. So I was hitting too many brick walls. When I came to Santa Fe, I approached the town and looked down on it from a hill, and I fell in love immediately; I am still in the quiver of that love. Here is home and a place that inspires my art.

YAEL WEISS

I was born in Israel and lived there until moving to this country when I was seventeen years old. That was something I knew I would do since I was seven years old. At that time, American musicians came to Israel offering master classes. I was a kid but allowed to participate in those master classes. It was a privilege to study with those famous artists. I met Leon Fleischer and studied with him. I remember that I barely spoke English, but in that one-hour lesson, he transformed my life. He left a very strong impression on me. So when the time came to make a choice, I knew that I wanted to study with him in the U.S.A.

I think the other influential experience was that I decided to participate in the Marlborough music festival, a great event for young artists, directed by Rudolph Serkin.

This festival is very special. There is no separation between teachers and students; everybody is equal.

How they structure it is that everybody is invited into small chamber music groups, and one of the group is what they call a senior member, who could be fifty years old or a very accomplished twenty-four-year-old. This person is leading and also like a member of the group.

Do place and time influence the musician? I am sure they do, but the score is the score, and it is the same everywhere. There is for me no question that my physical state and environment influence the quality of my performance, but it's not something I will use in my interpretation. It was the atmosphere in Israel that supported my development as a musician, and it was a time when there was a great urge to shine, internationally. Being born in Israel and growing up with so much support from family and institutions shaped me as artist. I feel very grateful.

UWE WALTER-NAKAJIMA

I live in Japan but was born in East Germany. That's a big change, and it leaves me transformed. I am this and I am that; place and time are continuously working on me.

The culture in Japan is a matriarchy. Japanese men have their own society. They are very close, they laugh from their hearts, they are bonded. I have many close friends there, almost too close. They walk into my home at any time. I am not the white man anymore. People forget my origins because I speak their language fluently, even their dialect. It's like in music: not the sound is important but the aftertaste. There is much said in the in-between spaces, in what is not said but is hanging in the echo of the words. You are not making it up; you feel it. The silence in between the words is important to so that you can check out what the other really said. And then the cup of tea—it helps to connect on a deep level. There's an expression that says, "You can read the air." We are connected, not only you and me but throughout the Universe. That's the real meaning of a cup of tea. It means, "We are from different cultures, but we are connected; we have tea together. We can meet without fighting, so we create peace by having tea together." That means having time to be quiet together, listen to each other, enjoy each other. The place of bonding is created through ceremony.

The Japanese are very sensitive. They see the universe in a cup of tea. It may take half an hour to have one sip. I love these people, and I am at home there. The place feeds my creativity. The Japanese arts have deeply imprinted my way of life.

Tim Gosnell

My place is with others. Much scientific endeavor is grounded in self-focus; it's self-directed. And that creates conflict and envy with your colleagues: who gets credit for what? And I encountered that at LANL [Los Alamos National Laboratory]. I am not skillful at that struggle. I became less and less interested in that self-directed kind of work. That's when I began seeking work in small companies, because I was in the wrong place. I understand that business is part of science, plus a salary, and I consider the collective endeavor a great accomplishment. I am a team worker and less and less interested in personal achievement. I did that in the past. I was very competitive in school, in my career.

When I began high school, I was very interested in drawing. It's one of my unlived lives. I did a lot of that, but it kind of flamed out. I took one year of art in college and left it behind. It was not rich enough for me, but science was. I had a resurgence of it in grad school, but science won. I burned out on art; it did not hold my attention. I was interested in abstract art, but it was too academic and intellectual. I wanted a more emotional experience in my encounters with art but found myself again in the wrong place at the wrong time.

For fine artists in this country, suffering is common; art is not rewarded enough in the American culture. I have so much admiration for people who just have to live their creative impulse and inspirations. I wish I had that kind of inner force. It's easy to go into science, compared with art. I had a totally free ride: Either the department or my professor paid for everything. I went through my entire schooling debt-free. For that, I was at the right time in the right place.

I encountered some remarkable physicists of our time. I had a certain amount of success and found out that being a physicist is not an easy task. You cannot do this unless you have a level of talent. Even among the physicists of the University of California at San Diego where I was an undergraduate—you have to be pretty good to be admitted there—from twenty-five guys and a few girls, two or three of us got into the top schools. This is after you have already earned a physics degree in college. And even then, you get filtered down to a few to get to the top places. It's a place of enormous competition. And then there is another filter after that, and after that. So you go through all those filters and work in the industry and do research. That's not easy to do.

Nonetheless, most of us work in obscurity for most of our life. I have this notion of writing an autobiography of an average scientist, because most of what we know of the lives of scientists is written about those superstars. There is this whole different experience of those who never rose to those public heights.

JERRY WENNSTROM

Lao Tsu says, "Grow old and be renewed."

Old age brings the ultimate knowing about *time,* because we are daily aware that it is limited. And we all deal with old age with a certain amount of kicking and screaming. We don't want to go there. I find that there is a kind of efficiency that takes over: You get better at the craft; you are doing more with less energy. So you developed all sides of your craft so that you—as you get older—watch how you invest your energy. As you grow older, your creativity becomes naturally more efficient and you are more aware of the flow of time—whereas when you are young, you have so much energy you can waste a lot.

And you can get more inspiration with less activity. I am not old enough to know where this is going, but I feel already some limitations. I am just being with what is, and there's enough in what is given.

When the arms and hands don't work well anymore, I trust that creativity will be given in some other form. If there's anything that duplicates the limits of old age, it's having and doing nothing, as I experienced it in my life after giving everything away and having no place that I could call home.

A nurse told me this beautiful story about a young man who fell out of a tree and was completely paralyzed. He was just there, could not speak, but everybody in the hospital came by and visited, because he glowed, his presence beamed. There's old age; we can just sit there and complain about our limitations, or we can glow.

Yes, we can just glow! [He laughs and laughs.]

VIJALI HAMILTON

I need to be grounded on earth. I surprise myself now, sitting here in this place, in Santa Fe. Yes, I am missing my raw place out there in the high desert of Utah. I lived there for seventeen years out in the wilderness.

That's when I wrote my book and wrote poetry. I had a cave on the land for meditation. There's a very profound depth that comes with such a solitary life connected to the earth. I lived there for five years before I started my World Wheel, and then I was called. I had a dream. I was called out of my solo retreat and guided to go into the world and to do the World Wheel. That's how I stretched beyond myself and started to travel for the global work. Next, I will go to Georgia.

I have a desire to go out and create peace altars, because of what is happening in the world with all the turmoil. I'll go and ask people just my three questions:

- What is your essence, your deepest desire?
- What is your problem? What keeps you from living that essence? How is that affecting you and your community and the planet?
- What do you see as the solution? What could bring you and your community back into harmony?

So now, after I finished my first journey around the world, I am planning to ask the political leaders these questions. I am trying to get in contact with the president of Georgia. And then to India next year, asking the Dalai Lama those questions. I am getting together with my artist friend Dominique, defining my next goals and steps. The World Wheel is my strongest tool. I am feeling like an interloper, taking a deep breath. I am hoping that the wheel will change the planet, just by asking the leaders these three questions.

I'll video it and make a feature film of the world wheel with the leaders answering those three questions. My already-existing twenty-seven-minute video will be a trailer for the longer film. And yes, it does include the president of the U.S. This is my real work, the World Wheel. And that's my contribution for this time of non-peace and chaos in the world.

I am on the second wheel, but this time, I have a base in Santa Fe and can come back home in between the countries. It will take years, and I will probably do a third one. I will be going along for the rest of my life—yes, the rest of my days [laughing], using my artistic skills and the time of my life to create peace through art.

I think a place has its own energy. The spirit and imagination come from the earth and sky. I am missing that here in town. Yes, I am so grateful that I have this place here in the senior complex; I could not afford normal Santa Fe rent. But Thursday, I am going up to Abiquiu to look for some land. I don't have the means to build something, but if I could just go out to be on the land and spend some nights under the sky and meditate. I feel that's so important; there's nothing that can take its place. I will fill myself with that earth and sky energy and bring it back to the city, I need that shot of nature.

AMANDA MCPHAIL AND WESLEY WEST

Wes: Yes, place is important. My creative process always starts out with cleaning. I could never go straight to my ceramic studio and begin working. I'd always have to Hoover-up or sort things out. That's part of my ritual. Some of my friends work in a complete mess. I can't do it; I need to first get my act together. And then I clear my bench, and then—pfuittt—here I go.

Amanda: Me too. I always have to do the washing up first. I remember listening to the BBC station where an artist was interviewed, and she said she is doing anything first, to avoid that moment when you have to actually get down to what you meant to do, which was for her to sit down and write. She said she had a needle book, and she would even rearrange that needle book to avoid the start of her writing. So now, when I am fiddling around before I dive into the actual work, I always think of her needle book and that I am doing it, too.

Wes: I leave my studio and go over to the house and open the fridge and roam around in it, and think, "Can I not just get on with it?" and then I argue inside, "But I am not quite ready right now," but when you get finally into it, and you don't want to stop or have anybody interrupt you. The preliminary fiddling is like foreplay; one cannot just drop into it and begin.

Amanda: I need to have one space which is solely mine. I have to clear out everything that's not related to me and my work. That's very important, this one space, my studio.

Wes: Yes, I do that too, all for myself, all my stuff. Like my office, where I have all those funny things hanging everywhere, things I have made. So when I lean back and look around, it's inspiring and it's all geared toward my imagination. If I would be sitting in another room where others left their things, it would not work so well; it would be distracting my mind.

There's something strange about creativity: You can't just kindle it, you have to court it; yes that's it.

Sara Warber

Place is essential for me. My home is such a haven, where I can be. I am right now—as I talk with you—in my creative spot on the couch, looking outside over a pond and the trees around. I track the sun as it goes across and changes from summer to winter. It's a quiet house. My husband plays music, and we talk occasionally. Otherwise it's quiet. All my creative work comes from this place;

it's like a nest. Otherwise, in the clinic, the place is not as important, but I am very, very present in my relationship with the patient.

I charge my creative batteries in nature. That's where Spirit is, where reality is, where I check into refined states and find balance, let go of the trivial and disturbing. It charges me as human being and as physician. I go into a prayerful state in nature when I am really struggling with creative work. That often means writing; that's where the struggle is. I am describing here somebody who needs to be alone a lot; that's true with me. The way that I construct my day is to be at home in the morning for my work. In the afternoon, I see patients and feel generally exhausted after that. I have to go home and curl up in my place here on the couch to recharge. I will be mindless for a while, but next day I am ready again.

RUTH BAMFORD

I think that my intelligence capacity is related to the fact that I am dyslexic. I have been talking to other intelligent dyslexics who have managed professional careers, and found that we all have the same quick leaps of understanding, a comprehension of the whole of a situation as opposed to its detailed parts. But what is obvious to us is not seen by others. As a dyslexic, I perceive the world through my senses. I perceive the place where I live or work or observe the activities as one whole.

I remember situations as unified experiences. I am aware how much light was in the room. I recall the entire sensory experience, not in micro detail but the full feeling: the sound of the water in the fountain, the pleasantness of the temperature, the walls of the building—like right now as we sit here. Using all my senses activates my brain and captures all the elements of the creative moment. That's why I can do physics. It's not about the details but about being fully conscious: What do I want to develop, and what are the steps to get there?

I am a creative visual thinker. Space is very important to me. I see pictures in my head and translate them into words. I manipulate objects with my imagination. Even in math, I can see the pictures of equations in my head. I don't write them down.

There are scientists who can't live without being creative. There is no difference between creativity as art or as science. I think it's a perception by many artists that scientists are not artists. I say they are!

I invented the deflector shield for space exploration: a way of having a protective umbrella in space, a force field that will keep humans safe from cosmic rays outside the atmosphere that protects us. This active magnetic shield is a portable protection outside the spacecraft. We are using its own nature and energy against it.

To concentrate and work well, I just need a lack of distractions, no disruption. Not easy because I have two small children. It can take me a while to get into the creative zone. I call it focus. These are practical issues. As mother and scientist, I need to adjust to those. When I work, I put music on—music sufficiently good to be not annoying but not so good that it takes the attention toward itself. I can't put Bach on, but Mozart is perfect. I can't listen to something too passionate or soulful. Elton John works well.

Peggy O'Kelly

Nature is always the place for me to get inspired, or in my own office, or in my stores. There I feel the creativity and joy that inspired it all.

And there are special places that highly nurture me: the beauty and the energy of New Mexico. I gave myself a sabbatical and I lived in Abiquiu, where Georgia O'Keeffe settled after she fell in love with the harsh beauty of the land. I think a lot about it, especially the magical White Place and the Chama River— ahhh! I long for that. And for the people. You run into so many interesting people who are doing life in a different way than here in California. It was so very comforting and inspiring for me. I found my tribe here, kindred souls.

If I am down and have a hard time, I give myself twenty-four hours to feel sorry for myself and do what I need to come out of it. That means a lot of self-nurturing. And what always helps is when I walk into one of my warehouses, and I come out and feel wonderful that I have created this place. The store is totally my creative outlet and product. It's a place which is part of me and my personal expression. I go in there and re-merchandise it, and I feel as though I am in heaven when I do that.

And I am always amazed how I regularly have what I need in my life, without even planning for it. It has an internal logic and energy—miraculously!—because I always can take an object and make it what it needs to be. I invent all the time, naturally. It is so much fun and charges me to enjoy life. Creativity is magic.

I don't use anything traditional for the display, but it always works all the time, and it looks great! I might even completely revamp the exhibition, the colors and materials, but I don't plan it. It just emerges out of my involvement in the moment. Women love the stores and tell me all the time about that. We are a high-class store, but I just improvise those displays and love it.

I write blogs and my customers really read them. They know about my private life and care about me and my two daughters. The more I allow this playful side of myself to emerge, the stronger it gets. I focus part of my energy on my soul self. I train in Reiki. I meet with my coach every week. I meditate. I care for my garden, my dogs, my chickens. I eat very healthy and keep my body in shape. Oh, and I am inspired by my two daughters; they are grown women now, and they are very creative.

I am changing and growing. Four or five years ago, I did not live in this manner. It took me some time to let go of old patterns and live my life more in accordance with my spiritual self.

CHRISSIE ORR

Time and space and location are not really important for me, but I love new and surprising experiences. I love to travel, to be in new places which are unknown, in a new language which I don't speak, encountering groups of people with whom I normally would not hang out, being confronted with the unknown. That's different from my day-to-day place and timing.

I have traveler's eyes. I love being inspired this way, maybe even being a bit uncomfortable. It's an edge where I like to hang out. It charges my creativity batteries. If I get too comfortable in my own patterns, that's not good for me.

Theodora Capaldo

For sure, I definitely put on a different coat for winter than for spring; that's my favorite time. Fall is my melancholic time. I have moods, and they affect how creative and passionate I am, or not. In the fall, I am like a squirrel, getting everything ready for winter. That is a creative act, the way one lives with the seasons. I have a biorhythm related to time and location. I grew up in New England and spent my entire life with four seasons. There is a cyclical quality to my energy level.

Place? Yes, I enjoy the inspiration of the big cities, like Boston or New York, but then I feel urgent to get out of there, had enough, want to go home. I need natural beauty, not just man-made beauty. Reading Cormac McCarthy's book *The Road*, I thought if we ended up like that, everything destroyed, I would want to die. I cannot be without nature. I always lived with big fields in the backyard, cows and yards, loved it. My greatest ally as a child was nature!

I am reminded of the Rumi quote, that the longing itself is worthwhile, as much as the fulfillment. One has to be careful of that reliance on passion and longing, because I like those emotions, and that involvement makes it harder to be still. You have to step back and really look, because you might be longing for what you already have.

CHAPTER FIVE. THE SOURCE OF CREATIVITY

CONTAGION

Women have sat indoors all these millions of years, so that by this time, the very walls are permeated by their creative force, which has, indeed, so overcharged the capacity of bricks and mortar that it must need harness itself to pens and brushes and business and politics.
—Virginia Woolf

RESPONSE TO A QUOTE BY VIRGINIA WOOLF

Reading is a source of creativity. Reading offers fuel for your rocket of imagination to lift upward into space. Reading another writer's creative expression might ignite a fire in you. Stepping into another writer's space of thought might crack open the access to a similar space in you.

- Creativity is contagious!
- Creativity is charged!
- Creativity triggers change!

Another artist's expression can be a deep well of inspiration that pours into your own soil of thought and manifestation. The quote above from Virginia Woolf makes my heart beat faster, urging me to give expression to feelings that had simmered for a long time.

Come out, women! Come out of brick houses and caves, palaces and favelas, tents and prisons, gardens and offices. Come out and let your voice crack those walls and windows. Step out and speak or write, even if you are irritated or bitter. How could you not be angry after the thousands of years that your voice has been subdued?

Blow into your inner fire. Set your talent ablaze. Allow it to burn. Better you go off in flames than smolder for centuries to come. Your fire will spread and light another artist's talents and courage. Be a conduit; risk the heat of enthusiasm. We women itch with creativity, we boil with insights, we tremble with knowing and light up with our creative impulses.

Are you an artist? Do you have the heart and vision of an artist? Do you have the curiosity and tenacity of an artist? Risk coming out, risk looking foolish and naive. It is okay to be afraid that you might not know what to do, how to speak, how to get up and stand tall. Yes, be afraid. *But act anyway*! Like Joan of Arc, hold your banner high.

Oh, we women know well how to comfort and console. Our feminine ways come from the earthy ground where we have firmly planted our feet. We nurture each other. We sustain our strength this way. But, familiar with hiding, we are still hesitant to step out into public places, hesitant to be seen and heard. We place ourselves with reluctance in front of groups. We listen rather than speak; we know how to make and create space for others. We swallow grief, we eat tears, we are vulnerable in the softness of our female bodies. We gasp under the weight of what we know about this world, but still too often, we hold back and hold in.

The creative force that glows in us is without gender; it is driven by life's longing for itself. It wants *you*. It needs you to be a channel for its furtive, forward-rolling force. Creativity is demanding and ruthless in its urge to penetrate, sprout, and expand. It courts you with sweet whispers. It triggers your vigor and arouses your body's longing to embrace, to multiply, and to burst into many.

The creative force needs you as a channel to express the mystery of the universe. Creativity is by its own nature harnessed to the body; it wants your hands, your eyes, your mouth, and the soles of your feet. It electrifies your brain, heats your muscles, and penetrates your womb. Let it crack you open. It is the time now, woman, to be ungraceful, to howl like a wolf, to stomp your feet and clench your fists. The wounded Mother Earth needs our courage and action because we are witnesses to her suffering. Don't ride on doubt or shame; don't allow hesitation to hold you back. Don't allow "legitimate rape" to impregnate your mind.

Woman, come out from behind brick walls and harness yourself to pens and brushes, to business and politics. Your name might be Hillary Clinton, Jean Houston, Arundhati Roy, Natalie Goldberg, Toni Morrison, Jhumpa Lahiri—or just plain yours.

And yours, man! You are required as partner in this creative endeavor. We need you! And we want your action!

Let's light the fire of creativity and courage in each other. We are allies. We emerge together, or not. We are standing at the edge of great change; let's hold hands as we march together.

If you are a writer, sit down in the chair in front of your laptop or pen and paper and write; stay in place until your voice has shape and form. Step into chaos and wrestle it into structure. Don't allow excuses to distract you. Don't abandon your seat! Don't leave your room-of-your-own before you finish your statements.

Speak your truth. Share your knowledge. Look down, woman, into the abyss of thousands of years of silence—and speak. Look down into the valley of fear—and speak what you see. Look down into the graves of hundreds of wars and speak against killing. Look down into the well of grief of mothers who lost children and husbands—and speak against guns. Look down into the oceans, cluttered with trash, and speak against negligence. Look up to women and men who inspire you and spread their fire, carry it out to the favelas, palaces, and offices. Look up to your own mother and daughter and partner and son; look up to your sisters and brothers, and to yourself.

And then, walk to the podium with shaky knees and open your mouth to give testimony. Sit with the committee and say *no!* to business that harms this earth. Walk your protest in the streets. Write a poem that expresses your love and joy, and read it when your family gathers. Write a poem that contains your fury and horror, and read it to your friends or colleagues at the rally. Hold your children in your arms and teach them how to compose the message of creative peace and how to dance and sing this vision. Teach each other how to emerge from bricks and caves and offices and favelas. Your children will learn from you to claim their place outside the walls.

And, women, reach out to men. Men who use their smartness to prove that there is no God or Goddess. Men who misuse science to prove that there is no change in the climate. Men who apply their power to explain why war is a legitimate political tool. Invite them to listen to the feminine voice; invite them to be partners. Support the seekers of justice—because we are all seekers, yearning to make sense.

And you, man, embrace your creativity; it is a living force without bounds. It is ravishing and vigorous. If you lock it inside your mind and body, it will break you and wipe you out. We need you, yes *you*, to express the mystery of being human and the mystery of being woman and man. Your creative force cannot be tamed or imprisoned without damage to yourself and to the world. You are being called to participate in its emergence. The creative force leaks out of walls and bricks, and it might become a flood that will destroy us if not applied to life—to your life. If you don't open your mouth and heart and mind, your voice will be missing in the family of all things.

Harness yourself to pens and brushes.

Harness yourself to the Muses, the forces of creative manifestation.

Harness yourself to your heart's desire.

Develop your skills and talents.

Be disciplined.

Be devoted.

Sweat and get tired.

Sweat and get energized.

Resist negativity.

You, woman and man, you are being called to apply and shape the creative force. To speak and write it. To breathe and dance it. To paint and sing it. Woman and man, come out! In this twenty-first century, life on our globe will not continue if you don't join your voice with the song of the Earth.

God dwells within the heart of the artist, and the artist draws God out of her heart when she is at work.
—Matthew Fox

It is not that language is merely a tool of communication, or that we only use language to express our ideas; it is just as true that language uses us.
—Rollo May

The Magic of Words

I revere words and their power. They are the bridges and tools for connection with others. Words, these mysterious, small beings made out of letters. Words emerge from your breath. You inhale, and when you exhale, you form sounds with your mouth and your breath creates words as it leaves the confines of your body. Personal language comes from the core of your being. And your breath is the material and tool that facilitates audible communication.

As a writer, I love words, and I often wonder: Where do they come from? Who invented them? I imagine that somebody, somewhere in ancient times sat under an apple tree and held a juicy, red or yellow fruit and took a deep bite and then vocalized a name for it: *apple or pomme or apfel or manzana.* A different word in different areas around the globe naming the same object: *apple!* And that word became a common good. Hundreds of years later, you hear the word *apple* and you imagine your own version of this round creature called *apple*, and saliva builds under your tongue because the word is alive and interacts with you, your senses, and your imagination.

Words are magicians of great power; they trigger our imagination. Look what happens under their spell: When I say *honey*, you may taste sweetness on your tongue.

And when I say *wind*, do you feel the air tangling your hair or see the branches of the trees swaying? And when I say *green*, you might imagine a mountain lake's transparent turquoise light playing across pebbles. And listening to the word *hummingbird*, can you see the whirring wings or the tiny feet dangling in the air or hear the sharply buzzing sound? I say *chile pepper*, and the word might trigger the memory of a dinner with friends under New Mexico's wide skies. The tang of the hot spice on your tongue represents the real thing. Words follow an unspoken agreement to communicate about our world in all its appearances. The abstract words have the power to contain—like a seed—the physically experienced real thing. Most of the time, we don't even think or absorb what a word means. That's where poetry helps to awaken the imagination.

> *Honey . . . green . . . wind . . . .*
> Green honey in the wind . . . .
> Windy green inside the honey . . . .

Poetry resides in the landscape of words and sensations. It dares to scramble them and to shift them around, and so to reshape the experience and shock the reader's imagination.

Words, those small, abstract wiggly beings, connect you and me in an agreement about the world and life itself. Or, to the contrary, they may reveal our opposing points of view and estrange us from each other. Words disclose to others who we are, what we feel and think and love and hate. Words open doors from your world to mine and back to yours. Words are the main carriers of information between you and me. Words are the threats that weave our stories and relationships. Words are, so it seems, a uniquely human and intimate form of expression. Words neatly ordered in lines tell us about the life of the writer.

The Source of Creativity

When you write, magic happens: Invisible thoughts walk through a door inside your brain and step forward. They become visible, audible sentences written on paper, projected on the screen or carved in stone. Emotions and sensations inside your imagination turn into an outer product, like a booklet that you can touch, hold, read, and put into your pocket. The carriers and tools for this transformation are words—mysterious, small beings made out of letters.

We communicate and speak to each other through the process of turning signs into sounds. That way, they become a bridge that spans from me to you and from you back to me. The little synapses in our brains connect us with meaning in the same moment that the word appears as a sound or a letter printed on paper. Isn't that magic?

Is this creative exchange uniquely human? Or are there other ways to communicate?

Maybe. Look at the herons. They perform majestic dances to say, "I want you, I love you" to their lady. And nightingales string their elaborate songs like ribbons in the trees. Birds build exquisite nests and decorate them with pebbles and moss, signaling that they are ready and able to nurture a family. Gophers dig solid walkways underground to say, "This is my territory." Sunflowers turn their heads toward the sun following its path from east to west. Is that creativity or instinct? Or is it simply the language of living beings without words but with magnificent creativity?

As writers, we risk being seen and heard and judged—and we long for exactly that connectedness. If we imagine the long path from sound to word to written language, we find ourselves in awe at the ingenious capacity of language. And if we consider the effort we might invest in learning a foreign language, we understand our longing for a deep level of connectedness beyond borders. Creativity builds bridges made out of thoughts.

> *In nothingness the heart of the world has space to spin,*
> *has silence to sing.*
> —Rumi

Nothingness

The great principles of spirituality don't mean much to me if I don't understand them with my whole being, my whole sensual body and awakened soul. Here are two of those principles that I have been struggling with for years; I hear the words but they don't lift the veils that shroud those principles.

Those principles are One-ness and Nothingness.

It happened very recently that one of those principles revealed itself to me, like a flower or like the moon suddenly appearing above the mountain. I felt its truth melting inside and penetrating my heart and mind, energizing my whole body. This truth was like a living being, giving itself to me, reaching out to me with hands full of gifts. And this is how it occurred:

I was at a retreat at the Golden Sufi Center in Point Reyes, California, sitting in the simple and magical garden behind the house. A tiny fountain whispered its fluid songs, and two goldfish flashed their color between the lily pads. I was reading Lao Tsu's poem about emptiness in *Parabola* magazine, and there I found this Rumi quote:

> *Stay quiet like a flower,*
> *so the night bird*
> *will start singing.*

In that moment, a memory grabbed me, and I relived that event with all the sensual details: In 2005, I had spent the whole month of April in southern France, in the Montagne Noire, to edit and complete my memoir. It was springtime: tulips nodded their yellow and purple heads under the weight of bees landing and leaving, and the wind whirled wild cherry blossoms through the air like snowflakes. I was at La Muse, a retreat inn, and occupied a room in the old nunnery. "1643" was carved in the wooden beam above the door.

One night, I was awakened by a nightingale's song from the

valley below. The sound floated in the velvety darkness outside like leaves in the wind. It pulsated in mysterious and indescribably beautiful patterns. The bird sang in changing sequences, like operatic arias.

I got up out of bed, put my sneakers and jacket on, and left the house to walk quietly into the night and into the song. The pauses between the different sequences were filled with the most luminous silence. Sound and silence held and shaped each other. They belonged together in a love embrace. These silences between the arias were empty of any human noise, empty of substance, and empty of things. No-thingness was contained in the song as the potter's vessel holds empty space inside.

It was out of this emptiness the song of the bird emerged, and the song made nothingness possible by being there and then not being there. The rhythm of song and silence created a space where nothingness became the birthing place and container for the beauty of sound.

I walked into the darkness all the way down to the bottom of the valley until I reached the brook, where I sat on a big rock covered with moss. This was one of those moments when life offered its mysteries generously and with radiant joy. I believe that my presence was part of the magic; the silence knew that I was listening, and the nightingale knew it, too. I sat in the center of emptiness and knew it because I heard the edges of it shaping themselves around the song of the nightingale. The source of creative gestation pulsed inside this emptiness. What was *not* there gave shape to what *was* there, and it all emerged out of emptiness—and left me with ecstatic happiness and endless longing in my heart. What was *not* there gave shape to what was there.

And I knew at that moment that this longing was a source of Creativity and consciousness. I knew that both are present in our daily, ordinary life, and we may hold it at any time in the palms of our hands like a living being.

*We put thirty spokes together and call it a wheel;
But it is on the space where there is nothing
that the usefulness of the wheel depends.
We turn clay to make a vessel;
But it is on the space where there is nothing
that the usefulness of the vessel depends.
We pierce doors and windows to make a house;
And it is on these spaces where there is nothing
that the usefulness of the house depends.
Therefore just as we take advantage of what is,
we should recognize the usefulness of what is not.*
—Lao Tsu

*Blow into your fire.
Embrace education,
it's a source of creative
thought and action.*
—Amanda McPhail

The Source of Creativity: The Interviews

ESTHER MARION

The sensuality of nature stirs images and offers a wellspring of ideas for creative actions. Sometimes I smoke a bit of marijuana; it comes from the earth and wants to be used in a sacred manner. It enhances the archetypal images that want to be expressed through me, and so does powerful music. Melodies trigger deep, dark visions, leading the listener into her own process. It might take me years for a new dance to be ready for performance. But I cherish the process of gestation.

In our time, there are many ingenious people around to motivate and inspire—for example Jean Houston. She is an amazing thinker and opens resources in my mind and body. She travels and shares her knowledge generously. Her spirituality is contagious.

There are creatives whom I study all my life. One of them is the guitarist Paco de Lucia. I never get tired of his music and virtuosity.

And the artistic fire inside my body is sparked by my sexuality. That changes as my body changes. My sexual self feels bonded to my dance. It takes on different shapes; it is as cyclic as women are. It's like other forms of art in my life, like creating a beautiful table for a feast with my friends that is erotic, colorful, artistic, and sensual. Sensuality and sexuality are wellsprings of energy for my art.

And there's "Art Magic," my work with children. I take them into nature. We settle beside a brook, under a big tree, and there we write and paint and celebrate rituals. We go on journeys together, and nature is our teacher. It's a creative learning process, different than normal school. These elements of nature are so neglected in the classroom. It pains me deeply how children lose contact with Mother Earth and her generous gifts. Children today are tuned into those small electronic devices and don't even know what they miss out on.

I am surprised how many of those source-moments happened in my life. I have been deeply transformed through specific performances, like the Japanese butoh dance in my youth, or a powerful flamenco performance in Spain, or a sexual encounter with a lover. That's like awakening the artist within and giving birth to my creative self, sinking deep into the mystery of life and art.

I am not following a specific religion, but I am spiritual.

My exploration of spirit is not a study through the book, but through the Goddess. I feel her inside. I am very matriarchal. It's in my bones. My sources lay in ancient Europe. I am nurtured by the Great Mother. My creativity is sourced by her and by my dreams.

I was brought up Catholic, but I was also deeply immersed into native spirituality, without giving it that name when I was young. I lived both paths parallel, without much difficulty, like native people do today, being this and also that.

The Catholic Church revealed to me what I did *not* want. It made me furiously angry. It fired me up and lit my rebellious side.

So it helped me to become very clear what I wanted and what I did *not* want in my life. I don't follow certain rules and rituals. They occur naturally for me; they emerge from deep inside, like an old memory and song.

In our family, spirituality has different names. We are not religious people but we live spirituality in our daily lives. We let each other be, in the closer and wider family and in the circle of friends. It helps to dedicate yourself to a path that has existed for a very long time. For me, the Goddess has such a long tradition, especially in Europe.

I am influenced by the books I am reading. They affect my dancing and charge my creative batteries. I read *Island Beneath the Sea* by Isabel Allende, and it became a source for my dance and my song. It influences me energetically and emotionally. I am fully present in the moment of performance and I am also ahead, envisioning what evolves next. I surrender to the genius of creativity. It's occurring in the highly focused state of performance when I receive knowing from deep sources. If you say "yes" to that source, it feeds you generously; it's ecstatic.

While I am dancing, I experience deep moments of harmony and power, and I wonder sometimes if that is unlimited and can happen again and again. It's like a gift given in that moment; with my dance I am creating the space for it to occur.

When you have a passion for something that sets you on fire like that, with music and dance and a sense of community, and life in all its cycles—that's my religion, that's my way of finding God. It's a prayer; at any time in my life, I try to be in a state of prayer. I keep on longing for that space. And I move into it incessantly.

MICHAEL BROOME

What motivates art? I think it is frustration. We are not satisfied; that drives us. We want to make a change, leave a mark, want to make something new. We want to create something that is an agitation. And when you allow the gestation of it, the calm settles in, the frustration goes. But remember what gets you going. If you were satisfied, you would not do anything. I admit it's a little obsessive; making art is obsessive. What are we obsessed with? I think it's the urge to avoid dying. Art will definitely help me not to die. It's not the ending of life, it's the ending of this moment we want to avoid. It's much closer. It's not there; it happens right here. It's boredom, boredom. We can't stand boredom, so we have to fill the moment.

Yes, we could fill that time with many other things, like baking a pie or driving around in the car, but art is the much better activity to avoid boredom. If we have to live with this neurotic creature we are, let's do *art*—because it's a great way of knotting a true relationship with that obsessive energy. And then, you get a lot of satisfaction out of it. Once you start the doing of art, you are in the motion of change. You are in the real nitty-gritty of life, which is change. Every moment is changing. The artist grabs the moment of change, and then he is changing with it. He is conscious of the change, conscious of building his painting or pot. He is there with great concentration. He is hoping to give that painting some sort of life that continues. That's what art is about. Art is basically movement; it moves with life's energy and contains magic. Even found and rejected objects can become endowed with magic energy. They carry something inside that moves you when you are feeding on the sources of creation.

We are working with the force here. We artists call it *divine* because we don't know where it comes from; there is no other word for it.

TONY JUNIPER

My inspiration comes from reflection and thinking about things. That is kindled in the work I do. It means I have all kinds of varied experiences through my activities. That is something I found out since I stepped outside normal work and stopped having a proper job. I am more independent and flexible, so I get to see things from the point of view of big companies, from the point of view of academic organizations, from the point of view of international agencies, or from the point of view of community groups—and from my own point of view as a long-serving campaigner. When I am in that configuration of influences, I find it to be highly stimulating. That feeds me, and I can process all that through reflection. This inspires me to work toward a better future. So that's stimulating for me.

Through my international connections, I get a very, very big feed of information that enthuses me, including my life here in Cambridge, because a cauldron of intellectual richness is cooking here.

That's something I got used to with Friends of the Earth. We need that because we've got very small resources. But it's about big things, and we come to these subjects with passion. You realize you have to think out of the box to get to what you need to do. We look at an opportunity and how we can achieve results. We inspire and feed each other—the colleagues and this environment. They are contagious and spark the vision. There's no shortage of ideas and inventions here.

Carole Watanabe

The source of creativity is Chaos! I visualize my studio: I have all kind of art supplies, totally chaotic, but it's this rich stuff to choose from. With playfulness and that chaos of materials, the colors, the textures—that's what inspires me and gets me going.

I trust that I can make something out of nothing, or out of all-things. Somebody might walk into my studio and think this is just a bunch of stuff. But I pull from all of that, from everything. I play and live with my senses on alert.

Cathy Aten

Creativity wears many more costumes than I thought in younger years. The source of Creativity for me is the thing that I call God. My creativity is dependent only on me getting out of my own way and silencing the critical judge inside. Then a channel opens and creativity flows easily. I feel it in my body, like an electrical charge, something of substance—like it is right now passing between you and me.

I allow a lot of silence. I am not tolerant of superficial encounters; they drain me. Silence and nature feed my creative source energy, talks with people, books. I have the luxury of spending a lot of time by myself. This solitude is a deep source of creativity for me, a luxury and a gift.

Everybody has some sort of genius. My gift in this lifetime is to be a voice and a way-shower. The right side of my body does not work at all. So action is reduced to one side. My illness has segued into my life as my work of art; no distinction separates them.

I pay attention to the people I am with. I watch what I think, what I eat. I pay attention to my thought, to what I write. I nurture my relationship with everything on a much, much deeper level than ever before.

I cherish my relationship with my dog, my home, myself. That means constant alertness. I am moving toward life, but when I'm lazy, I disconnect. I have this fierceness of a lioness. I am not afraid to give voice. I honor myself for the choices I have made in my life. I worked hard to get here. I was repressed. Now I have some substance. I feel like if I can do it, anybody can, and if you are not interested in this intensity, I don't want to hang out with you. M.S. restricts me, I can hardly walk, but I have all this space and beauty and time. That's a luxury. People think I am navel-gazing, but I like this being able to hang out with life, and don't have apologies. I love my life with all its limitations and flaws.

The biggest thing I have done to cultivate and feed my creativity is to allow a soft heart, to be undefended! And I feel that our culture is so defended. We are all so shielded; creativity cannot get through. The more I take down my own armor, the more God's voice is there.

AARON STERN

The question of inspiration and influence is an interesting one. I could enter it in the frame of education, or where I grew up, but since the topic is creativity, I could enter into it as creative biography. And what comes to mind to me is the time when I was a kid, very young—I would say around six or seven years of age.

I remember vividly that I would sit at the piano and create thunder and lightning storms. I would create whole symphonies. They had different moods. When I later understood about how music works, I would say all of the components were present already in the beginning of my life and career. For example, what I mean is contrasting loud and soft, and fast and slow, and light and intense, and repetition and absence of repetition—and so expression with the form of time and space. Those are my earliest creative memories. All that was naturally inside me. The source of creativity was already waiting to be used and activated.

Through the play with music, I was trying to make sense of the world we are in. In other words, I was creating a narrative that accounts for the world we live in. Where I grew up, there were some very challenging stories in our family, very painful and explosive, deeply unsafe. Finding a narrative in the middle of an unsafe family situation is also a creative act. It created wholeness and a sense of rightness in the midst of chaos. So the source of my creativity in childhood was chaos. There was explicit and implicit support, and also the opposite. I felt that my mom had some fundamental belief and love for me. Explicitly, in a classic Oedipal sense, the message was mixed. She was not successful defending me in the presence of a very violent father.

A dear friend of mine says: Impression without expression can lead to depression. That principle is at the basis of many of our programs here at the Academy for the Love of Learning. That simple principle is: Becoming aware of the impact of experience and making meaning out of that by using the arts. We rescue ourselves from depression and do this in the company of others, in community. We do it as a collective experience. So I think if you do it as performance, that adds another dimension to it because there is an audience.

And here is a family story as I was told it: We had a piano in our house. I was four or five years old, and had not played much prior to this event. Piano was not yet familiar to me, but there was a magical moment, and we had gone to a performance like *The King and I* or *Camelot* or so, and our whole family went to see the film made out of this musical. We had a babysitter at home, and I sat down at the piano and played spontaneously all the melodies from the musical that I had heard before. My musical memory was enormous at that age, and my capacity to bring it onto the piano was natural for me, so I knew how to do it. When my parents came home, the babysitter asked my parents, "Do you know that your son knows how to play the piano?" And my parents were perplexed: "Really?" And she said, "Yes, he was playing all those songs from the musical, and I recognized the melodies."

That was part of the confirmation that I knew how to hear and create music.

And in later years, when I was the dean of the music college I taught at, I was first in the faculty for about eight years and then became the dean and the vice president for about five or six years. All of the curricula that happen here at the Academy have grown out of that first childhood experience. I wanted to encourage the innate musicality that lives inside to come out of people, in a world that is primarily teaching by pouring in. When I taught, I had two groups of people. One was a band that came out of inner city Chicago. They had no training as musicians, but they were passionate music lovers. They were free to compose and improvise in the moment, fresh and daring. Those encounters were full of inspiration and creative life.

And then there was the other group, students who would apply for admission to the conservatory. They could play all the usual exercises and scales, very mechanical, and there was no innate musicality, no risk-taking. For me, that is an ongoing question:

"How do you keep the risk-taking alive as you learn the basic skills and craft? Risk is a breeding ground for the unexpected and new; it's the muse of courageous invention.

ANYA ACHTENBERG

I saw that the piece of reality that I was born into didn't satisfy me. On the contrary, it frightened, unnerved, and annihilated me. As a child, I felt a yearning not to be a little person. That was my daily prayer to Spirit and God as the source. It was my worship to connect with that source because I was born into a society that is basically ready daily to kill you. Born as a baby, you are vulnerable, and that's "unacceptable" in that kind of environment. It was dangerous in my home to be a child and to be myself. As children, we deal so much with what the world tries to do with us. We urgently need expression in the form of art in some way to keep us sane. Art is a healing force. And God is the source.

What is important for me today is related to what I was missing in my childhood in my immediate environment. What I later found as my path had originated in a unique impulse—the impulse for beauty and vitality, the search for what was truly and deeply alive and what propelled and nurtured growth. I yearned for truth. What I do in my work today and what propels it is to point to the fact that truth is being stolen and hidden, distorted. And children sense that, that something is not being said because they are small.

So you think, "Maybe they don't speak truth because they don't know." I remember understanding that people are going to die, and I imagined that my parents quite didn't get that, but indeed it happens, and it will happen to them.

I grew up in Brooklyn in a housing project. You heard everybody else's drama through the thin walls.

When I was five or six and had words in some order, I started creating poems. The environment inspired me to express what I observed in this harsh world around me. So this world became the source of my first poetry.

I got read to occasionally but very rarely. I remember that books were making me happy. My imaginary world was supported by them and by movies. Both were a source of inspiration, a view into the lives of other people. There was no richness of life in my house, but a lot of silence. Reading softened the silence.

Elias Rivera

My teacher, Frank Mason, was a brilliant artist and pedagogue, a source of inspiration for me. He brought music and literature into the studio and filled me with passion for the arts. I personally never wanted to be a teacher. I did every possible thing in my life to work and make a living as an artist. I have done everything: dance instructor, carpenter, including what Charlie Chaplin did in *Modern Times*—I worked with machines. I have done it all and was willing to do that up to a point. And then I jumped into art.

A lot of times when I am painting, I kiss the canvas. I thank the universe; I thank it for guidance. It's essential to me that I never lose sight of that energy and its source; it feeds and inspires me. It is Divine.

I grew up in New York and started working when I was ten or thirteen, taking out the garbage in the building where my father worked as a carpenter. I got sick when I was ten: I had rheumatic heart murmur. My mother bought me some clay. I played and worked with it, and in that moment, I realized that my destiny was in the arts. So I learned painting and created pretty good images. When you are a figurative painter, you always think in form, so it's easily translatable from clay onto a canvas.

The mornings are better for my inspiration and work. If I have a show, I stay disciplined and totally devoted. I learned very early on to listen inside. The art took me to extraordinary places. I feel very grateful to have this special talent. I was a decent cabinet-maker for many years, but then I learned that I could take my craft to a special place, and that I can take people to those magical places where they get deeply touched by my paintings, and that is very satisfying.

When I paint, I leave limitations behind. I go where the soul expresses itself. The source of creativity is in my soul.

Yael Weiss

I was teaching, was a professor of music at the University of Indiana for six years. A year ago, I decided to move back to New York because this city is a place and source of inspiration for me.

I needed to settle. My life had gotten a little too crazy with performances and travel. I did want to focus on projects that I always wanted to do. Being in New York helps me to focus.

I started concert playing when I was seven or eight years old. Coming from a family of musicians, that was a natural thing to do. I performed solo recitals and orchestra pieces. And yet I grew up going to regular school in Israel, experiencing a normal childhood, and interacted with all kinds of kids and adults.

My mother and uncle are musicians. I don't think anybody in my family had been as serious as I was. It was something that was greatly encouraged. Growing up in such an environment provides much reinforcement.

The source of creativity for me is silence. That might sound strange to say for a musician. I think that, besides this silence, there is nature as a source of creativity. Many musicians are trying to create from this place in the country or near the great oceans, whatever their favorite and most inspiring location might be geographically.

Many composers are inspired by that place of stillness in nature and the mystery of wilderness and beauty.

Uwe Walter-Nakajima

I was born in East Germany and my father participated in the rebellion of June 17, and he was consequently shot to death. So my mother escaped with us children to West Germany, and we grew up under extremely poor and rough circumstances. There were gangs around me and street fights and much aggression. All of that was not an inspiration to turn toward art and creativity, but at the end, it saved my sanity to walk the path of theater and magic. Performing arts have always been a source of mental and spiritual healing for me and others. Yes, I felt yesterday, during my performance in Santa Fe, that I am able to open hearts with my art.

In younger years, when still in Germany, one member of our group got money and invested it into buying a circus, and so we traveled with it, stayed outside the cities, lived with the gypsies, performed street theater. I have seen a lot of life and studied human behavior. Life itself is such a source of creative inspiration.

This world is so strange that I sometimes laugh out loud. I love to be amused by this world and us people on it. With my shakuhachi flute and songs and stories, and with my funny performances, I make people laugh giggle and laugh.

I have now lived in Japan for thirty-four years, and I am still looked upon as white and Christian and as one who still does not know much about Japanese ancient culture. So I pack my sleeping bag and go up there into the wild mountains and call on those ancient gods: "Come out, I want to meet you, I want to know you!" I look for direct encounters, direct exploration of the gods of the mountain—not books and studies, but meeting the energy where it comes out of the ground. My creativity emerges from the ground—it is very sensual and tactile.

When I still lived in Germany, I had studied pre-Christian cults and culture, exploring shrines and caves. Being in Japan helped me to look back and find my own roots in Germany.

My son is an inspiration. He studies for his Ph.D. in astrophysics. We have long discussions when we meet. I feel energized and understood by him. Art and science are very close, depending on the angle from which one looks.

TIM GOSNELL

One of my greatest inspirations came from my professor in graduate school. It was one of those magic moments that I will never forget. I didn't feel so accomplished that day, when my professor said to me: Look around here: There are all those guys here with straight A's, looking accomplished, proud about good test scores, but there is a thing missing. It's called being a researcher; it's intangible, one can't touch it, and—you have it! "

I was completely unaware of it until he said that.

I got a performance report at LANL, one which said, "He is an out-of-the-box-thinker." That is another one of those moments when somebody on the outside looking in finds something that I did not really recognize in myself. That's one of the more rewarding things I have been told. These are encounters that set me on fire. I think that we are all geared toward others' approval and feedback, hungry for recognition.

The main thing that works as a battery charger for me is doing something *new*!

I never end up being really good at one thing, because I try so many different things. That sparks me. The early phases of trying are full of creative sparks; there are no restraints. Everything is possible. Eventually that evaporates. For example, I went to work for this company in San Diego. I had this enormous number of middle-of-the-night experiences, solved problems, and had new ideas at a time when I was not yet informed of what had already been done before I came. You never know when you go over the same and known ground repeatedly. There was this huge burst of creative activity going on in me, individually on my own and also collectively between the three team members. The synergy was strong. It inspires me to work in a team, looking at others as a source of ideas and creativity and unfurling them together. Teamwork is synergy: one and one is three.

Jerry Wennstrom

Inspiration takes incredible simplicity. Picasso said he spent all his life learning how to paint like a child. We just pretend to construct art with such intelligent strategies. We follow trends and traditions. But the most frightening moments in life are those when you are totally alone with your creativity. That scares the heck out of us, that emptiness and aloneness.

To be a unique individual is the most terrifying thing in the world; that's why there are so few of them. We hold on to our life preservers. We all do that; we seek life preservers. Look at the pressures we put on ourselves to demonstrate conformity.

If you have found a way to communicate with your own god, you will also find a way to support your creativity, by taking those risks and living them and showing how it pays off. It needs results. We look for boons.

We risk and produce, because there has to be some kind of product, even if the final outcome is a miracle. If the miracle did not appear in my life again and again, I would not have the courage to live further. Always, and in my darkest hours, the miracle came through and I knew I was held in God's hands. I trust, and God is the source of my trust.

The source of my creativity is freedom. I lived freedom the best I could. Freedom allows great risks to create something new, to fly and be unencumbered by outer limits and conventions.

Live your passion to the max and then leap. Great movements in art, or the invention of the light bulb, often go on in different countries at the same time and the creators don't often really know about each other. It's just happening. Inspiration comes and goes. Sometimes the time is just ripe and the creation explodes into being.

I think that we make too much out of our art as creative act. It's like Russian roulette to have something happen. We grab it when it appears and hang on and go with it, fly with it. Inspiration needs a landing space; stay open to be the target.

Vijali Hamilton

Artistic inspiration comes to me through simply living ordinary life and doing it very consciously. That's really the most important thing, how you do your daily chores. Everything that appears needs you, and that counts more than isolating yourself. Ultimately, to live an ordinary, normal life is the greatest task and a piece of art. You have this stillness inside of you, and no matter what happens in your life, that is what it's about, to be centered and conscious.

I decided to enjoy all those little practical tasks. For example, I scrubbed my kitchen floor this morning, and—wow—it looks so good and I enjoy it so much I think that's spirituality, how it's lived and integrated into ordinary life. That ordinariness is a source of inspiration.

And I think it's important to keep your life as simple as possible. I have always done that, have always lived my life very modestly.

A lot of my time is responding to the demands of the practical life around the art itself. That includes all the emails and contacts I make, my responses to people I met along the road, maybe my financial support of them. That takes up much time and is part of my work.

I have certain principles: I have never been in debt, have never asked anybody for money, because I think you would sell yourself to them. Even having a mortgage, we are in debt and part of our soul is tied down. I always lived with whatever I have. Then there's no bondage, no pressure through finances or debt.

What inspires my art? For so many years, I concentrated on environmental peace work and the World Wheel.

What inspires my art is that real part of myself, when I am in touch with it. That real part is connected with an infinite source of possibilities. I do feel that the artist has responsibility to be true to that and let the work represent who we really are, not what society expects. We are called to represent this essence of ourselves. It is universal but comes through this personal voice and has its unique story. Art is where the two meet. When the universal and the personal meet, that's where art manifests. These are powerful energies that flow through us all the time.

WESLEY WEST AND AMANDA MCPHAIL

Wes: I went to Bath Academy of Art and studied ceramics and pottery and three-dimensional design—not because I fell in love with clay but because I fell in love with the people who taught me clay. They were a source of enthusiasm for me. And I still see them now: Blake Mackinnon and Ed Harvey. I wanted to be like them. So that's why I chose ceramics, and now I don't really work in clay anymore. I use lots of different media. But those first teachers—they inspired me and started the fire inside.

Amanda: The source of creativity is sensual perception. It's looking; it's visual! And hearing too. It's in us human beings. I am a bit dodgy about any "higher source." I had creative ancestors and it's just inside me. Something has trickled down. I love making and doing things. Look what you, Shanti, have created here in your house and garden—you must have an enormous amount of energy. It inspires me to go home and do. It's contagious. Walking around here in your house inspires me. You painted a tree golden after it had died and splashed red color over that chicken in the tree and set a black raven into the ground and mosaics everywhere. And there are some sticks indicating directions in the wilderness, going this way and that way. You use what's around you. In this place, you are my inspiration. It feels playful and joyful. I will carry these ideas to Cambridge.

Wes: I was a teacher and always worn out in the evening because good students make demands on you. You have nothing left and can't even go into your own studio. I used to teach three days a week. Can one teach creativity? I think, yes! Part of it is attitude, teaching attitude toward your art, your work. Teaching can get a student into the right place, instructs them how to see and look at things. I teach because I was taught well. The enthusiasm of my teachers was contagious; it lit my imagination.

Amanda: It took me some time to catch fire for the arts. In my teenage years, to the horror of my parents, I just did work, made money, traveled, worked on a barge in France, came to America and climbed into a Greyhound bus, traveled the States, and finally, at the age of twenty-four, when I was in Mexico, I decided to enroll in art school. My father was furious, my mother too, but at that time, I could not care less.

I applied from Mexico, and had friends who lived in Cambridge. I had no money in Mexico, only one sketchbook, and sent it off to apply for admission to college. When I came back to the U.K., I went for an interview and was accepted into the foundation course at art school in Cambridge. I did a year there and applied to Bath Academy of Art and got accepted, and that's where I met Wesley. I was about twenty-five and Wes about twenty-seven.

I remember that I went for an open day and saw Wesley's pottery before I met him. I saw his works and thought, "My god, they are fabulous! This person has talent!"

I taught for eighteen years, graphics and illustrations. At Cambridge Art College, I told my students, "Start thinking and start drawing or painting. Get moving, throw yourself into your work. Blow into your fire. Embrace education; it's a source of creative thought and action."

Sara Warber

My parents were extremely supportive of my creative endeavors. I can't remember a time of *not* living in the creative world. That's how much my parents supported me and lived creatively. For my mom, art was creating a beautiful home. She was very ingenious about that. It was always important for her to create, helping me in writing, drawing, revising papers. Dad typed my writing beautifully. Music was important. Everybody in my family played a musical instrument. During holidays, we were a whole orchestra and played together. That was my favorite childhood memory, that playing.

In college, I did not start out as a med student. I was inspired by the performing arts and stage settings, and so I studied and apprenticed in theater and tried to make ends meet. I became radicalized, completed undergrad school with a BFA in fine arts and drama. And then I encountered a key turning point: To make an income, I worked in a hospital, and there I found I was as intelligent as the medical staff, so I decided to learn more and trained as a nuclear medicine technician. But then I realized that this was a glorified form of photography. I did this for a few years, but it was a dead-end-job. So I decided to go to medical school. That's when I met my Native American teacher. She inspired me for the rest of my life.

The Native American and shamanic wisdom about healing with natural means has always inspired me. I was the cofounder of the Holistic American Medical Association and taught at Michigan State University. Nature teaches me; nature nurtures and inspires me. A major focus of my research work has always been related to the healing power of nature. I am working right now on an international research paper about the healing effect of green spaces in inner cities. And still, I feel drawn to the arts, and sometimes I wonder if I should have become an artist instead of a physician. Art is a great healer, and active creativity creates well-being.

RUTH BAMFORD

I am inspired by new challenges, new ideas, and daring solutions to problems. I am inspired by the unknown, to make it familiar and wrestle its secrets from it.

Science is not just the equations; it's the concepts. And that's born out of imagination. I had a choice when I was about sixteen to pursue fine art or science. I only stopped doing art because there was no university offering both. I had to restrict myself and choose one. I still make a lot of drawings about my projects, and I do photography. I love that. It's very artful photography, like the edge of an object with snow along the surface, portraying rather abstract shapes and views. I see the world a lot like that, lines in specific angles, light and shadows. Light in Oxford during spring time is gorgeous. So you see details and contrasts that are very artful and aesthetic. They inspire me and make me curious.

There are those scientists who can't be any other than creative. Most of the scientists I work with do work that can be based on recall, which can take you a long time of your life to remember all those facts you have learned and those names, labels, and equations. Those scientists can teach, they can function and assemble many things, they can appear creative, but I don't call that creative. It's not *new*. It's logic and practical application of what is already known.

Artists might think that all scientists are alike; they are not. I think it's a belief of many artists that scientists are not artists. And let's not mix the technician into this. Technicians remember a lot of processes, they can teach and produce, they can do new things, they are creative—but that is not creativity, and they are not scientists.

Peggy O'Kelly

I grew up in Oakland California, in a very chaotic household. Mom was a trained schoolteacher. Dad was a doctor. Art and creativity were not respected. In their eyes, that was not the way to make it in the world.

In high school, I fell in love with philosophy and writing, wanted to be a writer and did well. I grew up with a math mind and thought I had zero creativity. I was into sports and considered myself unskilled in the arts because I could not draw.

In college, I went into nursing, pre-med. Dad—who was a surgeon—said, "If you want to be a doctor, you have to give your entire life to it." This was not my goal or vision. So I went back into accounting and finances and finished with a double major. I built my own business after my divorce, when I had to provide for two daughters. I am successful in what I do and devoted to leading an enterprise in a way that does not harm but honors the earth.

The Source of Creativity

The source of creativity flows from the earth. Where else can it come from? Spirit and the Earth. Mother Nature has put everything together in such a beautiful way! She gives us this food, these products we need, and she is so generous.

I look at nature, or my chickens or the eggs, look at those color combinations, and then I use them for the packaging of my own products. They are amazing, and then people admire them and say, "Ah, that is so beautiful." I learn from Mother Earth daily. It's magnificent and fills me with joy and gratitude.

And then I wonder about the customers who praise my color choices. I wonder if they look at trees and give the same response. It's just there in front of us, and its beauty is the source of my color coordination. Look for example at this olive tree and think about its history. It has provided so much for so long: the oil for food and light, the trees for building, the leaves for natural remedies. It is such a sacred tree—how could you not be in love with it?

What is the source of creativity and new ideas for my business? It's everywhere. Inspiration comes easily to me. For example, during my journey to Morocco, where I got supplies for my products—rose oil and olive oil and spices—I was inspired by this old culture. We work together now. They deliver and grow what I need. Yes, I think that's creative business practice. I go on vacation and meet a farmer and make a business contact. Naturally, I am alert, always thinking and paying attention. That brings good ideas. They seem to grow out of the moment as I encounter new situations and people. I think that those inspirations have a divine source. It touches me as it happens. That's how I like to develop my business and my life in general. This alertness is part of my path on this earth. It's part of my natural curiosity. My dad was a very curious person too, very well-read. He influenced me. Other people and their paths inspire me, or incredible art inspires me. When I travel, I go to museums. I seek beauty and new ways of doing things.

CHRISSIE ORR

The creative spark comes from somewhere else and is right here in front of me. Maybe this little drop of water, or a mark on the floor, or a shadow moving, and it hits me. I say, "Look at that!" and catch it in that second—and that's when the spark turns into a fire.

I think I was always a creative person from a young age. And I was always exploring all kinds of new and daring ways. I could never spell or count; I was creative even with my own way of spelling.

As a teenager, I made up stories and performed them. At one time, I was very keen on becoming a dancer; that was when I was in primary school. I was not really good at sitting still. Luckily, I had a teacher who realized that I was much better at practical projects, more like the experiential learning model, so she let me pick a project and just run with it. I expressed myself through drawing and writing. This teacher was a major source of encouragement and ideas during my young years.

I grew up in Scotland, and was born in a small town called Motherwell near Glasgow. It is still a mining town. I lived there until I was five or six. It was my art teacher who inspired me to put together my portfolio. He recognized my talents, and so did my parents. My father encouraged me as a reader. My mother was a very creative person in the home. She made all our clothes, and she was a great gardener. Even though my parents would not have called themselves artists, they were very creative people and always supported my curiosity. Their creativity was expressed in the way they lived their lives.

My father was an amateur photographer. We had a darkroom in the house. I spent my most wonderful time with him in the darkroom, helping him develop pictures, magically. When he passed away and I looked at these photographs, I saw how skilled he was.

After high school, the art teacher encouraged me to apply for college, but I said, "Look, I am a scientist." He said, "Put in your portfolio anyway!" So it went to all the art colleges in Scotland, which were Aberdeen, Dundee, Glasgow, and Edinburgh. But I thought I would study botany. So I left a door open, made this deal with myself: If I would be accepted in art school in Edinburgh, I would go. And it was a really difficult college to get into. At that time, the cost of college related to your family's income: If there was no wealth, you could go to college for free. In fact, you would even get a stipend! But it was really tight. You had to work really hard to get admitted. And, to cut a long story short, I did get accepted in the college of art in Edinburgh. I remember going there the first day and I still wondered, "Did I make the right choice? Can I really do that?"

It was a four-year course, and I was awarded the Andrew Brown Scholarship. I basically got a free ride: a travel scholarship. I had a fabulous time. The task was that you had to basically create an exhibition.

To be a creative person, you need to be incredibly aware: who you are and where you are in relationship to this universe—and beyond. So to keep open to it, you are not only vulnerable to its beauty but also to its horrors. At times, that is overwhelming. There is so much mystery to explore—there's where the suffering happens.

What are my sources of creativity?

The creative spark is always there, ready to catch fire, and I never know when it's going to hit me. Sometimes it disappears. It's in the trembling leaf of the grass, in a sound, light and shadow, an encounter with someone, a story they tell me, the words they speak. You have to have your senses honed all the time, keeping your vision totally open. Live with your perceptions alert.

THEODORA CAPALDO

What is the source of creativity? That's the hardest question on your list because—what do we really know? Sometimes I don't know in the whole universe where it comes from, but I know that it is part of the whole scheme and is necessary to continue so it can sustain us. There's no way to imagine a world without creativity! A world without music? I am a madwoman for music. I could not exist without it. I am Italian, so a choice between music and pasta would be torturous.

So I do know why we have creativity and that we need it to sustain humanity, but I don't know where it comes from.

Here's my quote of the year that I carry in my weekly binder:

Against the ruin of the world, there's only one defense,
the creative act!"
—Kenneth Rexroth.

So where does creativity come from? Thinking as the psychologist I am, I confront Eros and Thanatos. One is propelled toward birth and creativity, the other toward death and destruction. That lets me believe that it comes from the core, the deep conflict of our existence. Destruction can be fertile if it's not just violence for the sake of violence. Nature's destruction is always in service of creation and allows something else to emerge and be nurtured through decay. So creativity might be the driving force and the product.

I think that falling passionately in love lights all of your genes on fire and kindles creativity. So you are lit up, you are on Go!—enthused and creative and energized, all of that wonderful stuff. It's a high. The wisdom of growing older turns those flames into embers. That's fuel for creativity; those embers are fuel for your deepest self, your body, heart, and soul.

Creativity comes from all levels of being human. The bottom range brings depth and compassion; the passionate and happy range is just delicious and nurturing.

As I am reminded of the intensity that this all stirs in me, I am most in touch with my marveling at how amazing life is. This is when I am truly motivated and have the energy to make something new or fresh happen in a proactive way, not in a reactive way. I am fortunate to be born under the sign of the archer, allowing me to see and aim ahead while both my feet are firmly planted beneath me. Creativity is this same vision. It is proactive, looking firmly at what is and at the same time at what can be out there beyond the here and now.

Chapter Six. Darkness and Shadow

Our capacity for dysfunction, for destruction, for malice, for evil is unparalleled among the creatures of the earth. We do have choices, we can choose how to use our creativity and for what purposes.
—Matthew Fox

*When your heart breaks
The whole Universe
Can flow through.*
—Joanna Macy

Hiroshima

The human craving to create and manifest is neither good nor bad—it's a driving force that moves the whole universe. But it requires choices. On the one hand, there is the creative force that gave birth to Mozart's Requiem and Monet's gardens, and on the other hand, there is the invention of the nuclear bomb and poison gas used in wars and concentration camps.

The creative force urges and manifests non-being into being and thoughts into objects. It needs the artist or scientist to apply the skills and genius to shape the outcome of this vision. Without the courage and skills of the artist or scientist, a creative invention is not available and cannot physically exist.

If we look, for instance, at the terrorist attack of 9/11 in New York from this view, it would seem to be a highly creative approach planned and successfully executed like a piece of art, a performance of Shakespearean grandeur.

And so we ask ourselves: If creativity is neither good nor bad, what was the vision that created the 9/11 attack, or the explosions of the nuclear bomb? Did this vision include the destroyed city, the burnt skin of the victims, scattered children's shoes, the heat that melted stone and pavement and shrank human bodies to the size of dogs? Are there situations in which the application of such an enormous horror seems justifiable to the creators?

Whenever I had the opportunity to discuss this question with someone who worked at Los Alamos National Laboratory, I heard very reasonable arguments for the invention and use of the bomb: "Because of its horror, it brought us peace for half a century," or "If I reject working on the bomb, I might not have a steady job and my kids can't go to college," or "It ended the war," or "It provides work and income for thousands," or "It makes America extremely powerful," or "If we didn't stockpile the Big Ones, we would have used many smaller ones against Japan." Or simply: "We built it and we will use it because we can."

Creativity can turn into an addiction and obsession. There's power that comes with the exquisite experience of new discoveries. And this power is extremely seductive. It can stimulate a love-dance between the creator and the object of discovery that ignores the horrific damage to human life.

I believe this is one of the most consequential questions, one that demands our judgment: Is there a moral limit to the use of creative killing machines? Even Leonardo da Vinci used his divine creativity to construct weapons. Are there moral principles governing the handling of creativity and its products?

In 1989, I lived for some time in Japan and visited the site where the first nuclear bomb was dropped on living people. It was dropped at noontime, when the children were on their way home from school.

The Japanese built a museum/memorial in Hiroshima containing collected remnants of this horrendous attack. I walked through it with sickening heartache and breathless horror. And then I stopped for long time in front of a life-sized head of a Buddha that had been exposed to the extreme heat of the bomb. The right side of the face was beautiful in its serenity and the heavenly smile of this sacred figure, but on the left side, which had been exposed to the blast of fire, the stone was melted and the face distorted, with traces of stone-tears on the cheek. As I stood there, Buddha's head evolved into a symbol and metaphor for what had happened. In this Buddha face, heaven and hell had merged. I imagined what such a heat blast had done to the bodies of children—if it melted stone, it would eat flesh.

Here, in Hiroshima, we step into the zone of absolute No!

Nuclear weapons are not and shall never ever be used to force political decisions.

Confronted with Hiroshima, I felt in my guts and heart that there is a limit to the application of creativity. As we move steadily toward artificial intelligence and its possible power over the human mind, the question of humanity's values and responsibility has increasing importance.

The splendid minds of scientists developed the most destructive weapon of mankind's history, and our humanity could not hold the politicians back from applying it in battle. Creativity seems to be neutral, but people are not. We decide about the use of our creative products.

Beware!

Maybe creative energy is driven by a grand scale of heavenly or hellish motivations, and every step demands conscious choices. We are free to use our abilities in various ways, but we will carry along the consequences of those choices, as a burden or as a blessing.

Spring Equinox

Birdsongs unfurl like tattered
Ribbons from west to east
Towards the rising light.
The morning winds
Weave whispers through
Barren aspens and broken stems
Of last year's sunflowers.

Blotches of snow hide
under the lilac bush
Where purple clusters of
Blossoms are sleeping
Inside hard-shelled buds
Smaller than the size
Of a baby's fingernail.

Equinox weighs spring
and winter equally.
In one hand, ashes of the last fires,
And in the other, the humble buds
Of lilac waiting to rupture
And scatter their purple
Scent into the songs of meadowlarks.

My soul, too
Flies with two wings.
One soars
The dark spheres of grief.
The other
Tumbles into the place
Of trembling joy.

This poem doesn't mention
The gloom of winter
Nor does it scratch
Into the tender scars that
frost leaves on the skin
of the earth. I must now
speak the missing tale.

When Simon Laks played Bach
In Auschwitz
The music's splendor cracked the
frozen stupor of the inmates
and pain boiled over unbearably.
In that cauldron:
Beauty is torture

Clay, Fire, and Sake

When traveling in Japan in 1989, I was invited to work in a pottery studio where the traditional climbing wood-fired kiln, Anagana, was lit once a year to fire and produce the most astonishing ware. The kiln ascends like a huge caterpillar, its head pointing downhill, and the lowest point is the place where the flames are dancing and the fire is kept alive through all the dark hours of a whole night. The technique of Anagana is an ancient tradition which came from China to Japan during the fifth century.

The Sensei, Ono San, a master potter, loaded his collected works of a whole year onto the shelves of the walk-in kiln, feeding it from a side entrance. He carried his pieces with slow and gentle movements as if they were alive. Then he closed that opening with bricks after all his work was placed carefully on the shelves. And then he began the long process of firing by placing a bundle of dry twigs every four minutes in the firing pit at the mouth or bottom of the kiln to create a steadily growing heat. Before he lit the fire, he serenely positioned several small ceramic cups near the opening and filled them regularly with sake "for the potter and his helpers and for the gods and goddesses of clay," so that they might bless his precious work and the arduous process of firing in this old and traditional way.

A group of his friends had gathered, sitting on tree trunks or metal folding chairs in a half circle, telling stories and drinking sake and taking their turns to place the bundles of sprigs in the firing pit every four minutes. I could not understand their language and the jokes triggering their laughter, but I felt the sacredness and deep reverence for this ritual of shaping earth into clay objects and surrendering them into the transformative glow.

Creativity worked here with the power of earth, fire, air, water, and human invention in a joint process, forged through heat. Deep darkness of the night surrounded the mystery that was happening inside the kiln as the trrrill! trrrill! of a night bird filled the dark spaces between the trees.

The process of wood-firing in a climbing kiln has a stunning effect on the ceramic ware. The pieces characteristically have two different appearances on the opposing sides, related to their position in the kiln behind the fire. The side turned toward the fire is darker than the other because the heat and the wood ashes are more intense than on the opposite side where the heat is lower. The fire and the wood ashes within it work on the pieces like invisible alchemists. This process gives a specific character to each piece. Because of the enormous effort and time involved, this firing is celebrated only once a year. The shape of the climbing kiln inspires tales of birth and the anticipation of mythic creatures and proceedings carried over from ancient times in this magical culture. Pottery in Japan stirs a deep longing for beauty and perfection.

The night progressed as the heat slowly increased, as in the archetypal cauldron where lore suggests that lead is being transformed into gold—if one knows the right formulas and follows the sacred procedures with devotion and humility. The potter and his friends sat through the process all night long, warmed by the glowing kiln, until the light of dawn crept through the trees.

The kiln needed several days to cool enough for the sensei to open the entry gate just a crack. More waiting, more patience. When we finally unloaded the precious pieces, there was the feeling of arrival at a pilgrim's destination.

The power of the mighty element of fire was used here not in destructive fury, but in masterfully controlled ways. Steady heat worked as agent for transformation as darkness shrouded the process. Fire appeared as friend and helper. And I was permitted to see into the soul of artists who created beauty with devotion and humility, as they followed the ritual path of their trade and culture.

Darkness and Shadow: The Interviews

> There is this grief,
> This unbelievable sadness,
> That overcomes us at random times.
> —*Esther Marion*

ESTHER MARION

Is there a dark and destructive side to creativity? Sure, artists are familiar with this aspect, and people always want to know about it.

I am thinking about Francis Bacon, whose art pulled so much out of him. As in flamenco or butoh dance, there's an edge to jump off. It needs courage to live on this edge. But it's the place where creativity blooms.

Janis Joplin, Judy Holliday—all those powerful women—their creativity and courage sparked their talent, but it also pulled them down into despair and devoured them.

I believe there is no boundary between the dark forces of ordinary life and the dark mystery of creativity. The dark can be so seductive and surprising, and it is rich and full of treasures. But I think the draw into what we call the dark side comes from excess, from desiring or having to bear experience that overpowers the artist who hungers for the extreme, the artist who invites too much of the tragic into his life and is tempted by the mystery of it.

Flamenco is a life and art form that can handle and express the full range of these excesses. Flamenco gives those forces expression in a given structure. And by plunging into and facing them full on, it offers catharsis; it offers the experience of spirit, of duende, at the darkest moments! These then are the treasures from the dark side of creativity! Through a creative life, we can participate in this darkness with the chance to evolve and not be destroyed.

Michael Broome

Yes, there is a dark and destructive side to creativity.

I went to Houston recently, where we went to a chapel with all those Rothko pictures, eleven canvasses, all of them big black things. Beautiful pictures. He did not really paint anything after that before he killed himself. It feels very dark, like an obsession. Seeing those pictures will take us down into our deepest dark place. Yes, creativity can take a person who is suffering into their deepest agony. And it can end with suicide. But you cannot condemn this darkness. For some artists, it's their response to life. If they don't capture it through art, it might manifest in reality on the street. Artists are not angels. Darkness might find containment in the art of a creative person.

Tony Juniper

I think I have not found a dark side yet. Yes, there are dark sides to the work I do, but it does not come out in a sinister way.

In the world at large, yes, creativity has all kind of dark sides, like technology. Some of it is obvious, like the invention of bombs. In the 1940s, in World War II, everybody tried to invent these killing machines as fast as possible, and it was the Americans who were ahead. It existed and so they used it, and now it is a constant threat to human existence.

Less extreme but very destructive are some of the downsides of pesticides, or the way we have made peoples' lives more comfortable with the help of carbon products' burning but at the same time we are threatening the atmosphere and poisoning the environment.

The purpose of my work is to create a situation in which human beings can thrive and have a future. But we keep this incredibly destructive system intact instead of stopping it. We see species becoming extinct, CO_2 going unchecked into the atmosphere, and the oceans growing point by point more acidic. We are continuously closing down some of our options for change.

That's where I work and put my ideas into action. I keep up my energy and hope by doing my work. I am an optimist and was so from childhood. I have to be hopeful if I want to continue doing this kind of work. The view that it is too late will become more credible. And what that means, and how people talk about these topics—that's going to be crucial. It needs this sense of optimism, because optimism is as plausible as pessimism. So there remains the question of how you inspire the one to prevail over the other. And actually, one of the conclusions I have come to during the last years is that pessimism, if it is too prevalent, becomes a self-fulfilling prophecy. It saps hope; it saps the sense of things that you can change the situation, and that's darkness.

Economic growth is not going to stop. China too wants to have its goods and luxuries. There is a danger that people who are on my side of the argument play the outlook as too dark. They paint the sense of ruin and catastrophe too hard. Then you ask, How do we get off the road to ruin? The answers are much less clear than the problems.

We did have to go through that dark phase to say, "Yes, there is a massive problem here," and most people seem to agree that it's the case. It goes up and down depending on how much people care. And in the moment we are a bit in a trough.

CAROLE WATANABE

My good friend, a homeopathic doctor, once asked me, "What is your dominant feeling?" and I immediately made this movement, meaning "going toward the light," and he asked, "And what about darkness?"

I replied, "That's for me like a murky pond filled with green slime. That's where the sickness is. The dark side for me—that's the icky yuck! I don't want to go there."

He said, "Are you sure? What are you afraid of?"

And I said, "I see my dark side—it's like going downstairs and always finding unopened suitcases. If I open them, something is going to escape that I don't want to."

"And you know," he said, "whenever I am sick, I open a few more suitcases."

So I got encouraged to explore my dark side, because that's where creativity and wisdom hide. I usually have visual experiences of it. Once I saw it as a huge black panther lying right on top of me. I embraced it, put my arms around it, and we started breathing in the same rhythm, and it was so very empowering. He has become for me the symbol of my dark side now. He is my power. I am glad that I finally made friends with him.

I think for an artist it's easy to go crazy. That's darkness. You put your soul in a painting and hang it on the wall, and people might say that they don't like that, it's ugly—and you can go crazy over that judgment. One has to learn not to listen to either the negative or the positive—to protect the creative spirit. That's a hard but important thing to learn. The creative spirit is vulnerable.

CATHY ATEN

I had to face and honor shadow. I have spent so much time in that realm. I am not afraid anymore. Who I am, with the richness

I feel today, is based on the recognition of the shadow and darkness. In a piece of art, to me, the shadow is just as important as the actual piece. I believe that the shadow speaks and enforces the object, without me having to explain what the piece is about. The work of the artist Anselm Kiefer is inspirational to me. The quality of dark and light in his work is powerful—I look for that. I find it in this landscape of New Mexico and in this town, with all those shadows on crooked adobe walls.

Shadows in my own life come with illness. My body constantly reminds me of mortality. This morning I spiraled down—I have to watch that. I cannot follow it, but recognize it as shadow. I need to switch it into the opposite. I got down on the floor and stretched, so that I could be present with you here for this interview. When I fall into darkness, I need to do something physical about it.

For example, my younger brother and I had to deal with financial things, but both of us shut down, made each other feel wrong, feeling righteous ourselves. That was two years ago. We masked that for two years, not talking about the shadow of this conflict. But I needed my brother on board. I knew I would need help in the future, so I called him up and connected, against my resistance. And it worked. It's about facing monsters; they seem so big and strong and insurmountable. But every time I open the door, just a little bit, those monsters shrink. I am an action person, and that includes handling my mind. When I wake up and my mind is tense, I meditate and soften. We are all so armored—it takes a long time to have a soft heart.

Darkness in my life, yes. I had an alcoholic father. Was married and got divorced; that was darkness. I was raped and went through the whole process of putting the guy into jail. That was darkness—I was twenty years young. It needed much courage.

There is this theme that comes up in my life. It seems that I have it in me to be a voice for people who don't dare to speak. I have the ability: During the trial, I faced my rapist. I was being carried by the wisdom that I was doing this for the other 99 percent who did not dare to speak up. I overcame my fear and discomfort. I had to stand up for justice, and I did. I followed a calling.

AARON STERN

I do know from my own experience that darkness arises in the creative process. How it shows up?

I think it manifests when you sit there and write, and then you just can't sit anymore. Something interferes—all the forces seem to want to stop the creative act from happening. The conversion of that negative force happens through patience and perseverance. This is not a very dramatic description but mundane and operational. When that happens, it's eating my energy. I just can't go on anymore. And whatever those dark forces are that cause the angst, they are resisting the creative process.

There's something I will play for you on the piano that will explain it clearer. When Lenny [Leonard Bernstein] died, I wrote a piece for him. In it, I remember the despair and the darkness and the loss. When I think of all of those memories I can't go on anymore, doubting that I can continue without him being alive. Where will I get my courage now?

All of that sits in the shadow of fear, of doubt, of not being able. The fear of not being worthy: "Who am I to sit down and do this?" That's how darkness shows up in my life. I remember what Lenny said to me, how he questioned himself on his deathbed, asking, "Have I done anything that has meaning and made a difference?" He had the romantic vision of taking opera to the next point, elevating American music. It was all mental fire and full of ideas.

Back to your question about darkness. I am reminded of the thunder and lightning storms of my youth. That darkness was very frightening. Our own darkness might hide in the shadow, and if it stays there and festers, it could become debilitating. And it could also be projected into the world, as anger and destructiveness. I believe that the shadow parts inside us always try to make themselves known. And if we have the courage to harvest that and bring our attention to it and find an expression for it, we are actually making the world more whole, we are integrating something that is pushed aside, disregarded and scapegoated.

In this Academy for the Love of Learning, that's what we do all the time—we integrate it. That is part of our work, embracing the dark and overcoming resistance.

ANYA ACHTENBERG

Is there a dark side in creativity? Of course! What comes to mind is the movie The Red Shoes.

If you are one of those expressive people, you know that what you deeply desire to do, like create justice and liberty and chances for everybody, is impossible. It's a vision, but it's too hard to live and create. And there are a million voices telling you it's wrong, but that's not your business. One can get overwhelmed and hopeless, because as an artist, you are battling too much with the darkness of life. You can get exhausted because you are so deeply connected with the difficulties of this world and with the suffering of human beings. You get really tired. You get really frightened and so full of grief. And then you have to pull yourself out of it and tell yourself that you need humor and keep some balance.

My own darkness? I merge with every character in my writing. They are like me—or not at all. That in itself is a darkness. The darkness is what stops me, holds me back. That's the pain during the process of creating. Artists are sensitive people, but there's great joy too. There's light behind the darkness—and that keeps us going.

ELIAS RIVERA

I used to read Dostoevsky with passion, and Kierkegaard, Nietzsche, and Eugene O'Neill—you can't get darker. I don't know how to separate that. Those authors are my mentors who took me to dark and wonderful places. They have a certain kind of honesty which I admire so much.

Darkness is the self that expresses itself. You have to be very watchful to dive into that murky well. You need something to express what you experience—maybe the artist in you creating art can take you to different places.

There are certainly dark places to visit. At this time, we see so much ugliness in this world, and the artist observes it and holds it inside in hope of transformation.

We observe such mean-spirited people around, like the Illuminati and Guildenburg—it's disgusting. So disgusting! It never seems to stop. That's darkness challenging us.

I am very mindful of the existence of that dark world. We need to counter that darkness with gifts from the heart. For example, there's a great DVD around that's called "Thriving." The producer devoted his entire life to finding out about this darkness. He looked at all the issues we have right now, and he found solutions everywhere. That's creative light countering darkness.

Life naturally wants to be creatively active. Why are we constantly blocked? Why is there so much pain and suffering? Hawkins is another example of light. He is such a beautiful and creative man, and he discovered those small companies everywhere all over the world. They are called "Seeds of Hope."

I heard him at the Lensic Theater in Santa Fe, and I watched the DVD, again and again. That's where I go to rejuvenate my soul. I seek nourishment. I get inspired by visionary people and by knowledge. I am seeking truth and big minds, and they are around right now.

When I paint, I leave this all behind and I go where the soul expresses itself.

YAEL WEISS

Contemplating about darkness, I am immediately thinking of Robert Schumann. His music was incredibly dark—he had to be with it and allow the experience to be able to communicate it. Identifying with certain things in Schumann's music can be very unsettling. Sometimes it's not difficult to get to a place where things get out of control a bit. It's necessary to do that—and also keep perspective over that and so to be able to create a piece of art from that place of despair.

My own darkness? I felt much attraction to his music in its darkness. It depends on my age in life. When I was younger, in my late teens and early 20s, it really pulled me in, but now I appreciate balance in a new way. Our responsibility as artists is to find some order in chaos. And we use our art for that. Yes, there is a dark side to what we do, and our artistic expression helps us to understand it without getting lost in it.

UWE WALTER-NAKAJIMA

I have met and lived with many artists who were quite crazy. They are so tense and driven—they must create or they would lose their minds and explode. Creativity is a force that crushes them. It's a nervous energy, restlessness. At the end, I was tired of this life as artist, as an avant-garde. I needed a focus and structure.

I was in a butoh dance group. I felt that the nervous energy bordered on insanity. That was darkness. Butoh is about darkness.

I wanted to overcome that, and so I sat in a zen temple for twenty-four hours in silence. Insights and visions come up with a force that one does not even want to know about. Darkness. One has to go through it to be free of its chaos and its terror. But after facing that, it's a liberation, and one's art unfolds more freely—it grows wings. Sitting in meditation, I looked at my own darkness and faced the fear. That helped me to overcome and integrate it.

When I meditated and studied Noh theater, I felt often as though I was in a tunnel, but I saw the light and knew that this light was my place where I wanted to go. I practiced intensely, for hours every day. Noh theater and chanting—that's all meditation.

And that's where I found out that I had this power to influence people through art.

The field of technology can also be called art. That's where darkness hides and thrives. I think technology is dangerous. If it develops and becomes independent, we might not be able to control it. Look at the mess in Fukushima! On the other hand, I think it's our fate to study and find out and invent new things. We need transparency in the field of science. Too many researches are hidden—there's no transparency. That's leaving us in darkness.

Tim Gosnell

When I worked at the lab (Los Alamos National Laboratory), I read some history, trying to get a better perspective on it, for example the development of the atomic bomb and the end of World War II. Some experts think it was not really necessary to drop the bomb on people—and others do. I don't know if there is ever a truth to be found on that subject. It's hard to ignore that burning question when contemplating morality around those events. The question that occupied me was, "What is the morality of all these weapons around here?" That was very hard for me to answer in a satisfactory way—it was not a black-and-white thing for me.

And at the same time, these things are pretty terrible devices if they can evaporate a whole city. The best I can do is to argue on both sides of the story. Maybe the bombs were necessary, but I would not want to defend that in court. So I mostly set it aside for things I can do something about. Most of the things I did up there in LANL had nothing to do with the bomb. I did not really have to confront that; I was lucky in this area. I thought about these things a lot. I was not really part of it. I was not really troubled by it, and I left the lab for reasons other than that kind of question. I worked on the Star Wars project when I started there, though I had my doubts about that program. It's possible that there were some compromises there. Yes, I was able to work at LANL without losing much sleep over it.

Is creativity seductive? This is one of your questions that really got me spinning off. I believe the natural world will know how to take care of itself, but I don't think we humans really have the talent to survive. I think that a good example of that inability right now is the climate change situation. To me, that is an existential threat. But it is politicized by politicians who can't think straight to save their lives. I just don't see humanity having the necessary insight to realize the power of nature when she is doing her thing. At the end, we will not have much to say about that.

JERRY WENNSTROM

For me, shadow was experienced very personally. I was entangled in my family shadow. I have recreated my father's life entirely, right down to his psychological wounding. When I realized that, I experienced a catharsis. My liberation was being able to go to my father and simply love him. It was a total gift to be freed of that history and darkness—it was my epiphany. The shadow in creativity? I think we make too much out of our art as creative act. It's like playing Russian roulette so that we can have something happening. When an inspiration emerges, we grab it and hang on and go with it, fly with it. Sometimes you need the gods to scream your sin. That's when darkness becomes visible and audible. So maybe the atomic bomb makes us aware of the dangers of creativity.

And sometimes a riot brings attention to what needs healing. We have choices as to how we use it—even the creativity that went into the bomb and the timing of its explosion. What we do with the product—take a Jackson Pollock or an Andy Warhol—the essential spirit of the creation has nothing to do with what is done with it. The creation is separate from its use. Look at Christianity, how religion has been misused for wars and destruction. That was not Christ's message.

I am still a bozo like anybody else, but I feel that my shadow has become conscious. Now, I watch what I do as an ego—I am conscious about that. I make mistakes, but my mistakes can't hurt me in the same way as in the past. When my shadow kicks in, I stop and realize the error and I watch it go away. I just stop. I know also when my humanity kicks in. I do everything in my power not to let that little bastard (me) interfere with the beauty of the possibilities inside and outside. I have given myself to the mystery and to the gods, and I have given myself into their hands and it's up to them to interfere when I blow it. And to keep it okay. "Okay, God, if I'm not meant to be here, take me away." Clarity is in the surrender; when I blow it, I know it. It's when we don't want to cop to it, try to make it sound good, look good, justify it—that's the stuff that keeps the water muddy. That's darkness, that's where the work is and the challenge.

VIJALI HAMILTON

I think it's important to be honest about our dark side. I went through a depression years ago. I did depression pieces—some are in my book. Some of my art is just pointing out the situations in the world that are off balance. I personally like to concentrate on what is right in our society and not what's wrong. That's my basic substance and philosophy. Art can point out darkness and has done so for several decades. That is part of the truth art is revealing. Yes, people have experienced darkness and need time and energy to heal the wounds. Art reconciles. You have to meet people where they are and hold up the positive elements of life.

AMANDA MCPHAIL AND WESLEY WEST

Wesley: I came from darkness. There was a lot in my life. Yes, my brother was born when my father was away in the war. He came home and wanted to love this new son of his, but because he had been away, my brother didn't understand who this man was. So my father didn't want to have anything to do with him. My brother behaved like a stranger with him. When I was then born one year later, my father decided to stick with me and delegate my brother to my mother. My father didn't talk to him, only beat him. But I was my father's preferred son, and that influenced my whole life. I had to be like my father. So therefore my character, my extroversion, was forced on me, not naturally grown. And it wasn't until I met Amanda that I became my own person. Now, I am finally that. I had always tried to be something that I wasn't.

So as a small child, I realized that if I abused my brother, I would get approval for that. So I learned to hate rather than love. That's why when my father died and I was eight years old, I left home. Because I knew, even at eight, that they were waiting to get back at me, my mother and brother. I remember my brother laughing and me crying when my father died.

I was not really supported in my family around creativity. It was a very separate thing for me because when my father died, I carried on trying to be him. He was very imaginative, bordering on the insane. He would see a movie like Jekyll and Hyde and then put on an evening gown and go out in the fog in London and frighten people. He was a nut case, but he was wonderful to be with. He is where all my creative spirit came from. He was not really a creative person—he was very sick most of his life. He was a hairdresser from a Jewish family. Drawing was my playground; it got me out of challenging situations, even in the Navy. My drawings helped save my life. I could always translate the events around me into a drawing, and that kept me sane.

Sara Warber

Creativity carries darkness when you become obsessed to the point of self-neglect or neglect of environment. When you don't eat and take care of yourself, everything falls into a mess. Before I became a physician, I was a designer for theater, and when I was working toward a show, things around me fell apart. It was a productive obsession, and there is a price for that. My interest now is to be creative and still be balanced.

Darkness creeps into creativity if medicine is used solely for personal aggrandizement rather than as a gift to the world or as expression of joy and delight. Joy appears in its purest form at the aha! moment, when something new is being born. I feel it in my body, even in the early stages of expression. If I am creating something in the realm of art, I can get so lost in it. I love that—that's totally joyful!

Ruth Bamford

I observe there is jealousy about artists and scientists from less-creative people. That creates darkness and estrangement. I think that people who've never had anything dark and bad happen to them have less depth. They have not experienced mortality and might not be touched by the bigger questions. But if you have imagination, you risk a lot more in life. Imagination is a terrifying capacity. I have never been in a war myself but can vividly imagine the consequences. I think I could never recover from that. It would suck me in and I would dwell in deep dark layers. I suffer because I cannot deny that this beautiful universe has that darkness in it.

Imagine, as an example, the development of the satellite clearing system. It could potentially be very destructive when used in the wrong way, because it could knock out other people's communication and survival tools. I made a promise to myself that I would not work on something that has such a potential of misuse. I want to be able to say to my kids, "Look, I show you what your mother is working on." I believe that scientist have to be very watchful about their inventions and imagination.

Peggy O'Kelly

Yes, there is darkness in creativity, and I believe we usually don't honor and recognize the dark side, in life or in creativity. I wonder if darkness is part of a creative person as well as of our society. Look at the destruction of the nuclear bomb or of the earth. We have highly creative technologies but seem unaware and unconcerned how dark the applications are. It's eating us up. Take, for example, the iPhones. When I was in New York, I noticed in the subway that all the people, from every level of economic strata, had something in their hands, and as I was looking over their shoulders, I saw that they were playing games. Nobody allows their minds to just be and observe life around them. Look how quickly this took over our habits, to shut off our own thought process for the sake of this little machine and its entertainment. This is darkness: We have become seduced into separation.

CHRISSIE ORR

Yes, creativity has a dark side, like everything. Otherwise, it would not have a form. Think about a drawing: Without the shadow, the object would be flat. So you are creating something by use of its opposite with the help of the shadow. Without the dark side, there is no form.

That's the darkness that hit me in my beginning artistic career when meeting the guy who collected my work. He had no idea about art. Without that encounter, I would not have seen the truth of the art world. As a consequence, I went to a dark place of despair. It shattered my ideas and ideals. I felt unstable and rattled; my comfort was broken.

For me now, the question is: Why am I doing this work. Why do I work with community through art?

Is it just a way to get feedback? As an artist, you need feedback and response. So is it just for my own ego that I do this work? I truly question myself about that. That puts a dark and kind of weird side to it. I hope not! Or maybe there is nothing wrong about that either. Maybe one needs that kind of ego to get going and exposing oneself to the world so vulnerably. I have to show up in community, and I have also to take a back seat. I might come with my own ideas but have to let them go in the moving process. These are important questions for me. Is ego helpful or hindering in the work? Yes, I have doubt and I get attacked by gremlins; they get me all the time. That battleground is a form of inner darkness.

Look at Richard Serra's work. He triggered people's irritation by cutting off their way of walking in the park. He used irritation as part of his creativity. His work was finally removed because people protested.

A lot of contemporary art today feels for me like playing a game, to fit in or not to fit in. It does not feel authentic to me but rather superficial. There is a lot of game-playing.

THEODORA CAPALDO

Darkness? It's a bit like the Miracle-Gro of creativity, because sometimes as you go into darkness, it is in some basic ways challenging to explore how you feel and what you see. What kills my creativity? Is there darkness in creative endeavors? I see darkness in the cruelty that is creating suffering for animals, and that darkness motivates me daily to my work and it triggers creative responses.

If I think of a death or a lost relationship, that's suffering, and being the artist and activist I am, I go inside and try to work through that deep, dark level of emotional challenge so that something new can emerge and will be given birth to.

We are constantly confronted with the old questions, "Is there evil in the world? And how do we recognize it and why does it exist?" We have choices. Whom does it serve? If I look at ISIS destroying thousands-of-years-old Buddha statues and temples, that's as devastating to me as the death of people. That's a deep loss of the sacred.

Nature's destructiveness is different; it makes sense. In nature, things fall apart and make space for the new to emerge. A dead tree feeds the young ones as they grow out of its bark.

Feeling unloved either squashes me or infuses me with passion. The degree of cruelty and degradation on our planet eats my life energy and makes me want to retreat. I have to fight that—it's not who I am. When I get to a certain point where I feel like it's hopeless, it makes my inner lights go out. Everything gets dull. I just want to recoil. I have to be very, very careful about how much of that I allow in. I know it's there—I don't deny it but cannot always dare to come face to face with it, as that's too painful. And if I come face to face too frequently with that pain and suffering, it reduces my energy and my passion to do something about it, so I protect myself. I think I share that with a lot of people now as we see such cruelties and disregard all the time. I suffer to see the Earth suffering. I am her lover; I am the lover of animals and trees. To be a lover hurts. Love is not the easy route; it hurts more to love.

Chapter Seven. Resistance, Procrastination, and Suffering

So what if creativity happens not in spite of procrastination but because of it?
—Adam Grant

For resistance, properly integrated, is one of the great cornerstones of the creative process.
—Victoria Nelson

The creative process is akin to nature and has cycles that are similar to the seasons
—Linda Schierse Leonard

Strangling the Flow: Writer's Block, Boredom, and Sacrifice

Procrastination and blockage seem to plague most writers. I will share with you here my encounter and struggle with this dragon, and how we became friends.

My personal journey through blockage lasted a year or two—and it still shows up from time to time, with changing symptoms. Writer's block had become somehow a steady companion that bothered me like sharp rocks in my boots. I found out that "just do it!" does not work. Creating art is a love story, and art is a delicate lover that will not yield to force.

Each day again, this lumbering labor of the beginning. Each night again, Jacob wrestling with the angel, yelling, "I won't let you go if you don't bless me." This slow and tedious awakening toward the activity of writing is like a smoldering fire that stings the eyes; smoke lingers but no heat—yet.

I am committed to this exploration. I am writing a book on creativity, and so I interviewed twenty artists and scientists in my search to understand this mysterious force. I am fiercely attached to this work, and will, like Jacob, hold on to the heels of the angel with clenched fists until I'll be blessed and gifted with understanding and completion. From where I kneel, I see the feet and toes of the angel, and the light at the end of the ladder is calling for action.

But there's resistance and a dawdling hesitation before the actual step into artistic expression. Yes, inspiration and ideas are knocking at the door in the form of insights and stories, but I feel held back and restricted by the fear that the transition from vision to object, from thought to physical reality, will distort and suffocate the life of the original idea even before it has had a chance to breathe.

How does the artist deal with the discrepancy between the idea and the reality of her or his work, knowing that the gap can be deadly for the unborn creation? I wonder why we block and avoid what we otherwise love with passion: the process of writing, the delight of creating art? Why are we in artistic flow at some times and so awkward and clumsy at others?

What I am doing here seems self-indulgent. I dissect the experience of blockage and shower it with much attention. But I am a psychotherapist and curious by nature about the enigmatic roots of creativity and the painful resistance to its demands. What is the real source of the blockage? I am driven by the hope that it will soften and disappear like a disease after I diagnose and fight it skillfully. If it has a name, we can tame it, I believe. And if others are burdened with the same disorder, we can overcome it—can't we? Or at the least, knowing we do not suffer alone will reduce shame and secrecy.

I find excuses and wiggle around the actual sorrow and fury. But finally, I have to admit to myself that I am stuck, strangled by writer's block. Here, it is finally named! This disease is new and frightening to me. The name appears like that of a ghost who lived in the basement of my house and suddenly roams and rustles and clanks against the railing.

How does it make itself known? The most difficult time to initiate creative work for me is in the morning—the daily beginning and its slow, hesitant crawl toward inspiration and passion, when our resistance to action and creation leaves us feeling lame, sluggish, and sticky. It stifles newly emerging ideas and hides behind justifications and passive-aggressive piles of "real" needs and seemingly important necessities that have to be done today, like changing the car's oil, the gross receipts taxes, and the shopping list. Just naming them is a killer of enthusiasm. Suddenly the world is full of things un-done! That's the dangerous territory, the roadblocks where what we do not want to do keeps us from doing what we love to do, and overshadows that love. It's the indication that we have to watch out so procrastination does not become a habit, an unwanted visitor living in our creative house without our agreement. It holds us in a perplexing grip that strangles our creativity and makes us feel inferior. The beginnings of a new project might seem wonderful and promising, like a new romance unfolding. But then we may drag our feet because we realize there's hard work ahead as we seek to create what will take us into the unknown, and we don't know if we are up to it.

> *It's not the writing part that's hard;*
> *what's hard is the sitting down to write.*
> —Steven Pressfield

And then, in rare times, the inner longing for creation wins in this struggle and stirs us to heap new logs on the fire, heavy, moist, waiting for a wind or strong breath to bring heat, waiting for tending. Patience is a requirement for the artist who is triggered by creative ideas but stuck in resistance. Hang in there!

Usually, when I dare the first ordinary, simple steps toward action—for example, sitting down and moving my hands into activity, like molding the smooth clay in my studio, digging in my garden to prepare the spring bed, cleaning the paintbrush, or letting my fingers tap along the keyboard—when I am handling the tools of creative work, the energy begins to flow and creativity stirs and kicks like a fetus in the womb. Each time again, it waits for this new beginning like waking from winter's sleep or pushing a wheelbarrow and grinding the rust off its screeching wheels.

And then, encouraged by action, something melts and moves. It says "Yes" and yields to the emerging heat of the fire, gets out of the way. Something new wants to be born and shaped into an object that had not existed before: a poem, a clay pot, a picture. And this not-yet-born being is the third force in the creative love-hate triangle, a triangle that is being formed by artist, inspiration and the object of creativity. This not-yet-existing object craves manifestation. It urges us to act, and takes on leadership in the process; it uses the artist to give birth to itself. And this is the crucial moment when the writer needs to step into the flow to overcome the blockage and let creativity ignite the process. This is the moment when Jacob grabs the angel's heels and yells, "I will not let you go except you bless me!"

An artist argues and fights with God. The creative mind is a wilderness, animated by beasts and nightmares as well as fairies and angels. The artist needs courage to create and give birth to vision. Picasso's Guernica is an example. This monumental picture about the horrors of war is an unforgettable encounter for me. Picasso gave shape and image to the demons of destruction. The mother in the painting is an archetype of anguish—she holds her destroyed child in her arms, she drops her head backward in wrenching pain—and she is etched into my mind and heart for a lifetime. Art is a key to the mystery of beauty and horror. And maybe this intensity of involvement and expression is a reason for the block, a hesitation against the urge to look deeply and to be killed by the revelation.

Resistance, Procrastination, and Suffering

For beauty is nothing but the beginning of terror which we are barely able to endure, and it amazes us so because it serenely disdains to destroy us. Every angel is terrible.
—Rainer Maria Rilke

Creativity is always stirring to be transformed into something physically "real" that can be touched and grasped with our senses. It is a force that rattles and shakes the work out of its slumber. At every breath, something longs to be manifested into existence: A tiny current of sound quivers in the air and wakes up a song. A word or sentence in a book or poem ignites the mind of the reader into a story. A quivering willow branch in the wind invites a dance. We are the blank page and we are the moving hand that writes. We are the womb with child and we are the child wanting to be born. Creative forces move eagerly into such space if we are willing to give attention, if we are ready to behold this sanctuary so these forces can settle in to change us and themselves. And thus, we step across the threshold where resistance yields and—finally—melts in the fire of creativity. This is happening here and right now where I sit and breathe and enjoy the act of writing.

Where the spirit does not work with the hand, there is no art.
—Leonardo da Vinci

And so, I suggest some proven helpers that assist me in overcoming resistance. First, I read. I ingest Annie Dillard or Marilynne Robinson or David Whyte or other beloved writers. Their words grab me and bring my attention to the churning in my own mind. These writers lift ordinary life out of neutral territory and make it sparkle. Or I might just sit and meditate, or I listen to music and dance for myself. I drift and dream as I watch the movement of trees in the wind outside my window. I let thoughts bumble around and allow them to idle. Or I make an appointment with my writing coach—which forces me to show up and produce, and it softens me into humility as I ask for help. Thus, I actively detour resistance, doing it a day at a time, growing through curiosity into a possible friendship with it.

Creativity is eager to ignite sparks into fire. Some places are more inviting for that process than others. I like to go on retreats to work on a writing project, or take my tent and seek the solitude of the wilderness. But the cracking and removal of the block can happen anywhere. Recently I sat in contemplation with closed eyes for an hour. In deep exploration, I watched my avoidance of the toil of writing, and I judged myself for the lack of discipline in my work. When I opened my eyes, a sudden snowstorm had turned the outside world into a magical landscape. I stayed motionless and recognized that the stillness of not-doing had allowed this shocking beauty to penetrate me, and so the block had silenced me and become a blessing. I had found the way home to my inspired self by choosing such conscious tranquility. The ensuing stillness dissolved any resistance and filled me with joy and gratitude. I was easily motivated to just simply take my pen and write about the power of surrender to this moment of life. Just giving attention to what was in front of me had turned into a harmonizing force for creative work.

Whatever the artist creates and completes is self-gratifying, self-indulging, and fills the heart with deep delight and satisfaction, especially on the heels of a successful struggle through resistance.

Ah, flow!

The completion of my first book was such a moment of utter joy and contentment! In my publisher's office, I sat in a big red chair, holding my new book pressed against my bosom. I felt that something was really done; something was not demanding more attention and discipline—it was complete and lived its own life now. My book was like a child walking out into the world, daring its own decisions, attracting fame or failure. It was a pebble thrown into a pond, casting little waves along the edges, creating movement and sprinkling lively reflections onto the water. We artists need to feed on those moments; they make the hard work attractive and provide us with the motivation and energy to live through blockage.

I think when the artist ruminates too much about his or her "gift," the object of art becomes a mission, a task with a purpose. On the contrary, if art is just created for its own purpose, it will be full of divine joy and spirit. In the claws of writer's block, I imagine that we are being tested by the Muses: "Do you really mean it?" "Can you lean into the wind of creativity without falling or being blown away?" Resistance has a purpose. Oh, mystery!

Sometimes when I am blocked and down in my energy, I sit at the edge of the river of life and watch myself watching, distant to the river and a stranger to myself, separate, alone, without meaning. Then I judge that just sitting and not-doing is a waste of time and a "sin" in the sense of uselessness. The block feels physically numbing. It lets colors fade and weakens imagination. I have moved past eighty now and wonder if these blockades are part of my aging process. I usually face problems head-on, so I don't recognize myself as lazy and held back. Who is this me, this strange person who is blocked and lame?

I fear that as I am growing older, I will sit more frequently at the shore away from the crests of the waves, get less involved, feel less delight. I fear that Jacob's angel will leave without giving his blessing, and that resistance might win. Do I have, I ask myself, the right to live if I am not actively participating in creation? This block seems to be incarcerated inside my mind. I don't understand it. I want to demystify it and break its neck. I feel anger and disgust about the limitation of writer's block, and want to ram my teeth into it and chew it until blood seeps through its skin and soaks the earth where I stand.

But I crave creativity as a path to the river of life. When flowing, it invites and motivates me to step into the current. Active creativity and conscious silence are for me the most effective ways to overcome the creative block. I am beginning to consider that passive, quiet contemplation has value and meaning, even when it seems to show up as a block. The block slows me down and makes palpable the swinging rhythm of the heartbeat. It mirrors the rhythm of inhale and exhale and the natural flow of the changing seasons. The substance of time grinds in my head and slows me down. I am conscious of its flow.

"I am not a procrastinator"—so I believed. I remember how I wrote my childhood memoir with great devotion, discipline, and passion. But today, I feel different. I admit that this dreadful and lazy resistance walks shoulder to shoulder with me, like a rebellious sister whom I didn't know in the past. The sister is sluggish and does not want to be disciplined and structured. She ambles around. I feel pressured to make friends with her and learn to honor her way of acting through non-acting. She is homeless, seeking shelter. She demands asylum, acceptance, and embrace. She claims her place in my exploration of creativity, and she adds a bitter spice to it.

And so one day, I realized that a book on creativity would be incomplete without experiencing writer's block and the yearning of an empty womb! How could I ignore the experience of nothingness and boredom? How could I succeed without touching failure?

How could I dismiss honoring the fact that I am just a vessel to hold the creative spring water? How could I discount the boring emptiness of lost inspiration and not see it as a gift? A challenge. A purpose. This blockage is not a mistake. In the context of my exploration of creativity, it's the expression of spirit, brushing me calmly like the wings of a bird, whispering into my ear what it is not. Creativity is not ego and eagerness; it's not something to be forced; it's not a construction of logic, and it does not bend itself into my will. But it yields to my desire to catch meaning inside the void. Rumi says, "Keep quiet like the flowers, so that the night bird might sing." It's the quiet, the waiting, the listening with hesitation that appears as a block, but the truth is hidden in this dark silence and the night bird sings into that emptiness. That's how I heard the nightingale sing inside the velvety black void of night some years ago in the French Montagne Noir. The silence in between the sequences of song gave shape to the melodies. As I observe my own blockage, I become familiar with my deepest self and with the song inside that silent inner space. Nothingness is a container for all possibilities.

And so I learned to say "Yes" to emptiness and resistance.

Yes, my block hinders inspiration. Yes, the block turns in circles and curls the flow against itself. But I also see that this block makes me conscious of the promising emptiness in the heart of the Creative Divine. My pet beliefs and theories about writing fall away. There is stillness now, no struggle, just a new and vague yielding into what is. I feel a promise of revelation that makes my heart sing. Emptiness is full of life that yields, according to the shape of the vessel that holds it. I am emerging from the frustration of blockage, eager to become such a vessel. Emptiness is the ultimate richness that allows the not-yet-known to step out of its dark folds. This no-thingness is the cradle of creativity.

And very slowly, I begin to sense that this no-thingness reveals secrets I have not yet considered. Being friends with emptiness might open locked doors for me. Somehow, through patient attention, I have learned to honor it. So here is one of the stories of how I discovered the blessings of laziness and learned to accept procrastination.

We have a cat named Yoda, a thirteen-pound Maine Coon, and she has a strong presence in our life. Her fur is light gray with white socks and a bushy-haired white chest. She has a fluffy tail and long silky hair that almost trails along the ground when she walks like a queen. Her amber-colored eyes keep deep contact, and I imagine that she is from another planet, dropped into our home as a gift from angels. This gentle cat introduced a new ritual into the flow of our days. At six o'clock in the morning, she utters discreet sounds in front of our bedroom door, like a soft whistle. My husband usually gets up to brew the first delicious cup of coffee, and that's the sign for Yoda to walk into the room and take her seat between our pillows. When the coffee is ready, we sit up and lean against the headboard, our cat between us. And so we indulge in being utterly lazy and laid back and watch the squirrels and chipmunks outside and the deer at the pond while snowflakes gently fall on the garden furniture and the sun climbs above Rowe Mesa east of Santa Fe to announce the new day.

We talk and we scratch our cat's belly and behind her ears and we tell our dreams and thoughts about whatever and we read and we discuss some opinions in the New York Times. Our cat purrs and snores, and we know that this is a morning when we wish to live forever, and we are lazy and do nothing for an hour or more, and this doing-nothing feels like one of the really good things in our lives. We procrastinate the activities of the approaching day that are waiting to be tackled, and we don't feel blocked but totally in flow with the rhythms of natural cycles and well-being.

And so I ask myself, What if procrastination and resistance teach us to change and explore our relationship with time, which means the relationship with our own lives and their place in the universe? What if it assists us in the patient shaping of the creative process as a path to deep joy, held in balance between inaction and the engaged endeavor of the artist? From this point of view, who would insist that action is better than stillness?

On the one hand, when I am productive, as I am right now, writing, I am standing with my two feet in that river of creation. I watch what swims by and what happens under the surface. I am engaged with the work and with life all around me. I take notes and formulate my observations into language, moment by moment.

The more accepting attention I give to resistance, the more it softens and yields. Whatever swims by might not carry great importance, but its movement merges with that river and sparks my imagination. And now that I can finally write about this process, it is ripe to offer me its gifts. I suffered through it with disgust. But I have given it more than a year of exploration and time to find my way out of stuck-ness. What I learned enriches all parts of my life. The shaping of this process into an essay and the sharing of it with you enhances my transformation. I experience with cautious excitement how I awake into a new point of view. For an extended time now, I have been contemplating the writing of this essay, and I feel a wonderful and sustained writer's bond to it. That means I think about the topic incessantly. I am alert. Flashes of understanding hit me from various angles. New insights nestle on my shoulder like small birds. They whisper and stir, promoting an awakened relationship to blockage and to myself as I am enduring and healing it.

Wow! This has become an ode to writer's block.

The angel has blessed me.

And that's how even my cat taught me to embrace a new way of viewing not-doing and resting with vigilance in the Now. Writer's block is just a form of meaningful procrastination, allowing creativity to be tinged with laziness and to hang out in a space of timeless relaxation, moving slowly, awakening to the work of the day through unhurried unfolding, like the New Mexico sunflowers in our field in summer when they turn their yellow and black faces toward the morning sun, ready to greet the unfolding day. Ah! Flow!

Everybody suffers. It comes with the territory. It has not to do with creativity. It's just part of being human.
—Jerry Wennstrom

Resistance. Procrastination, and Suffering: The Interviews

ESTHER MARION

Yes, suffering is part of creativity, maybe even a source of it. It makes your art deeper. Suffering inspires the art form of flamenco. My dancing is a craft, and I use the skills that help express and transform suffering. That skill allows the dancer to scream or stomp and explode and let out the pain. It's a channel. Through it, suffering takes on an artistic shape and form. It transcends pain.

But boredom? No! I don't feel bored. I write a lot. I rehearse my dreams. And then it can happen that the flow might just stop and stay stagnant, but that's not boredom; it has purpose. It's like a vacuum, so I slow down and wait, allow it to be there, this nothingness. I allow time for this internal process of emptiness, I am patient and trust that it does its own work inside. And then, after some time, it wants to come out, it needs community. It turns around, naturally, like a seed pushing out of the ground or like a bear in the cave waking up after hibernation. There's new movement of energy and new ways of being and performing.

Resistance? Yes, when I was a teenager, I didn't know how to feed my soul. I resisted my calling as a dancer. I was so young and developed bad eating habits—was tortured by that. That was a difficult phase and caused much pain for me. It was a dark time and I suffered. My life presented itself in resistance to my passion. But then I heard this voice, this deep flamenco voice, as I walked by a music store in Zurich. It hit me like a lightning bolt. I walked in and bought the record and carried it home, and as I was sitting in my kitchen listening to that LP, I stumbled through an open door of song into a new, totally captivating culture, inspired by this voice.

So I studied flamenco in Spain for some limited time, limited by financial restrictions. And then I crossed the ocean to come to America, in the same month that my then-unknown husband crossed the other ocean, and we met here on this continent—that was fate. Not so many people meet a mate with whom they can unfold and create a life like ours for such a long time of more than twenty-five years now. And today, I watch my grown son. He is passionate about developing his music, and it gives me great joy to see my daughter so involved with theater and dance, mentored by her father.

What a beautiful way to focus and inspire your children! We live the creative life. There's something very powerful about loving and living and creating together. Yes, I believe our life is a piece of art. We bring a basket full of skills together, ancient and new ones, old and new world come together in our family. Inside our community, there's support and inspiration, not resistance or boredom.

MICHAEL BROOME

Suffering? Resistance? I think that all art comes out of some kind of mild to extreme frustration. Many artists work through their pain by having a deep dialogue with their art. Some of the greatest artists have gone through agony. If you are broken, it seems that more light comes through the cracks. Nobody escapes those cracks. I have not met anyone who does not have a crack somewhere, whether light comes through or not. Even my Buddhist teacher has a crack too. It's part of who we are as humans. It does not need any outside trauma; it comes from inside, is a condition of our mind. It is our unsatisfactory bend that we have to transcend. Everybody has that in his or her life, and we can approach it through art or meditation. That is our challenge. Some people react with anger or feel lonely or cover it through addictions. Being broken open motivates art and its expression in our society.

Sacrifice comes from the Latin word *sacrificium*, making holy. That is interesting—making holy. Yes, the usual artist sacrifices his comfort and luxury for the sake of his art. Winning the lottery is an illusion. Perhaps we all sacrifice to make our lives holy. I know painters who focus only on their art to make it holy, but the rest of their life is chaos. Here, at Ocamora Retreat Center, all of the work is a work of art. This whole place is infused by art—that's how I live. How we move here and how we place things—that's holy-making.

Art can be work too. If it has not worked out for you and you have to push, that can be really hard work. Nothing is just totally sacred; everything has its moments of frustration, struggle, and pain—and that's all worthwhile.

TONY JUNIPER

I think I have sacrificed and suffered in this environmental work. The sacrifice is mainly in the form of time. I put all my time into this work, and that's a sacrifice for my family. My wife could confirm that.

There is suffering because there's all this stress involved in being in almost-constant battle mode. As an environmental activist, one is constantly at war actually. But you get used to both of those sacrifices. The intensity is big. I am fifty-three this year and still going. A few years ago, I was burned out and thought I would release this; I couldn't do this any more. That's like an engine, revving over at high speed and ready to blow a gasket. That's where I am at now, without the engine actually exploding but going very fast and close to the red zone. Very unpleasant.

It is quite a lonely place to work like that. I am the one who is doing the thinking. And then I am sharing the thinking and might get a pushback reaction. But one of the reasons that I stopped my big job at Friends of the Earth is that I had the responsibility of running a big organization where you have to accommodate everyone else's point of view as well as your own. So you are in the position that you see all the points of view—and then you can't do it because you have to bring all those other people along with you. And that is really quite stressful. Stepping out of that situation—I am now very much on my own—is the price for the release of all that other complexity and responsibility that comes with that role.

I have now become used to being that self-sufficient as I am battling on with high intensity, but I definitely have become very careful with how much I am taking on. Spirituality does not mean a lot for me. I think I call myself a neopagan, more leaning toward Stonehenge than Westminster Abbey.

CAROLE WATANABE

I see creativity as a privilege—not a sacrifice but a gift that I was lucky to receive, and I am forever grateful for that. I am in my studio ten or twelve hours a day, painting and talking to other painters who create there, getting inspired there.

The painting on my business card is my watering can in Collioure in France. When I was painting it, I started to cry. So I sat in my rocking chair and asked myself why. And it was some time later that I realized: It was my self-image. I am the watering can, and my job is to inspire others. It's a blessing to me. I have been graced to be able to do that; it never feels like a sacrifice.

If I feel bored, I usually change media. It comes when I have done the object for too long a time, when I have explored a theme so thoroughly that it's penetrated. It has come to an end and I feel it. It is drained. If my boredom is related to painting, I give myself a task, like only painting in shades of white or only in two colors. And I lean deeply into it until that is exhausted. Or I do mosaic for a while or take a class, something that sparks me awake.

Cathy Aten

Resistance and procrastination gives us time to catch up, forces us to be inactive. So let's be tolerant with ourselves, gentle and forgiving. To let go of the cultural identity which pressures toward action is not an easy choice. It means being naked, vulnerable, lost. I was hard on myself, but I am wiser now. There's intelligence in procrastination. There's intelligence in the pause between the actions.

People think that being an artist is a really glamorous thing, but it's not. We deal with monsters and angels. And there's the monster of resistance, expressed as procrastination. I discuss this with artists: Why don't we always desire to stay in this nurturing, exciting place of creativity? There's something scary about it. It is The Void. It means it is full of everything, an emptiness full. That is the birthing place of creativity.

Sacrifice? I once gave a talk and said, to my surprise, that I am not interested in being around people that have not been shattered! What does that mean? I realized that there's something that happens when people are shattered. It's not just having a difficult time. Rather, shattering is like changing the molecules; the whole identity that you have sculpted so carefully is blasted apart. I know I have a choice: to crawl in the closet and pull the wool over my eyes or face and live life. I made my choice. There's a lot of inside shattering that happens when one is disabled by illness. The response to that choice builds richness in a person. I do believe there is a depth that you can never reach unless you have been shattered.

Creativity is inseparable from the acts of daily life, and M.S. is a big challenge for me. You call it illness, and it sounds as if something is wrong with me, but I do not really believe that. I think that if God would come and say I am gonna give you a really hard job that will transform you and its going to be really hard work, I don't think I would want a smaller lesson than the one I carry.

I think my ego is big. I was a big faker and poser. This comes from my family, where I needed to survive and charm people, be a faker in social situations. I felt into other people and gave them what they needed. I walked around as an 80 percent false person.

She, this faker, is part of me, but not the whole deal. The whole Cathy was challenged and revealed when I got the diagnosis of M.S. I was always very athletic, using my body in strong ways. Then, on a hike in 2000, suddenly my legs gave out beneath me. It's a progressive disability, and mine is an insidious encroachment of disability, slow but ongoing.

In the beginning, it was easy to hide, but when weakness got worse, I had to hang onto walls, and it became very visible. There came a time when I realized that I could fall and break something and it was not going to be okay, because I live alone, and nobody would take care of me. When I was talking to someone about using a walker, she suggested seeing the walker as support instead of showing disability. I've now gotten to see it as support.

I cannot hide anymore. I use a walker and a wheelchair. I realize that everybody I know has something going on that is really challenging—everyone. Suffering is part of being human. Mine happens to be very visible; I cannot hide out. I had to become transparent and vulnerable. When I tell the truth of what's going on with me, it gives others the permission to tell their stories and be vulnerable. When the doctor told me that I had M.S., he was aghast. I had to care for him. I am a survivor. Some people think I am in denial because I seem so happy.

AARON STERN

There's a great song by Leonard Cohen, an anthem: There's a crack in everything, that's where the light comes in. Yes! Oh my God. I experience suffering every day during the creation of this place, the academy, every day! Given that my quest was to create a live-in place for music and studies, I suffer when I see something go awry, when a detail is not happening correctly, when human relationships fall apart and break down, when there is aggression—there are so many examples I could give you. It's a heartbreak for me. I had to get over these "how am I going to do this?" I feel completely alone in it because, really, I founded this academy and created it. I worked on this project since 1980. And at that time, I was the dean of a conservatory, had two groups I taught, and I went to China on a cultural mission. In 1980, the Cultural Revolution was just ending and there was no capitalism yet. There were only bicycles, no cars. When I was in the Ming tombs, I had this flash to know what I would be doing for the rest of my life. I knew that I was to create this place, the Academy for the Love of Learning. It was a mystical experience, one great opening. And I got completely lost in my vision.

And the nitty-gritty? Does it happen that I am bored or blocked? Yes, sometimes I am bored or blocked. I used to say that being bored is the same as being angry. What comes to mind is Stravinsky's Symphony of Psalms, which begins with psalms of inspiration and movement, full of vitality and presence, very celebratory in the first movement. But the second movement is, "God has forsaken me! I am lost and alone. I have lost my faith and I don't know what to do." It is some of the most powerful music. I call it Waiting Music, waiting for God to come back. And that's what I do when the boredom happens. I have to trust, find faith and patience, and wait—there's nothing else I can do. It's a deeply suffering time with crazy thoughts. Overwhelming!

Yes, there is a huge sacrifice for the work I am meant to do. I sacrificed love to create this place, because this was a greater love, a greater passion. I sacrificed sleep. I sacrificed, in a way, being an active musician because this had a deeper value for me. I found that bringing music to life is more important to me. I had to sacrifice part of my heart when sacrificing being a musician. I could make the case that it was not just in it for me and that's not what I most valued. It was a choice. I faced my new challenge and was very restless about it. I also sacrificed comfort and ease as I lived on the edge of my challenge. I honored my soul's urge to learn. This was the greater trial and my truth. I had to follow this life's path, and I sacrificed an easier ride.

ANYA ACHTENBERG

I was very young when I decided to become a writer. Remembering this, because of your question about sacrifice, is very helpful for me. I wrote poems at a very young age, and when I got into school, I got crushed. That helped me understand that writing was subversive, under the desk. When I was about eleven, I wrote a story about a black man coming into a small town, trying to rent a room and being insulted and thrown out. After he left, there was a robbery, and he was accused and hung. I wrote this piece and got negative feedback. But after I left this school and went to a different one, they suggested that I have it published, after they did some ideological editing. I learned in this case that there were restrictions on what you can write about in school and what not.

When I read something that was rich and fascinating, even if I didn't understand it fully, it woke me up. I remember reading

Conrad's *Lord Jim* and Jung, and getting the truth that reading a text and reading the world are very similar.

Then things got circumvented, and I left high school at about sixteen. I was a smart kid in a poor neighborhood, so I went to Brooklyn College and got a scholarship. In the late '60s, the open admission policy brought in a lot of kids of color.

I decided to become a psychologist, and studied psychology and a lot of comparative literature. And a lot of art history. I was homeless for much of my time in college. I was displaced, didn't have a place to stay, so I sat in coffee shops all night. Couldn't go home. I got a job taking care of a child, cooked and cared for that child. Even though I began at sixteen, it took me five years to finish school. Graduated in January of 1970, when I was twenty-one.

It got worse, but I kept writing. I had many notebooks and started doing some readings. These were very difficult times, as I was out on the street a lot. It was a form of suffering. In 1973, there was a nationwide depression, especially in New York in specific neighborhoods. It wasn't just that I was lazy. The general idea was that if you were female and had a college education, you became a secretary. But I couldn't even type. We were trapped into an academic training.

Life got more and more difficult, and I got more and more connected to people whose lives were difficult. Some were in and out of prison. I was politically radicalized by Vietnam and by questions of race and civil rights. I was around those kind of people and I kept writing, which kept me sane. I had been in a cocoon, not a safe one but in a box, away from language and away from real communication. I used language as an observer, and very often I could not speak. So what I was writing was like in a test tube. I was writing in an extremity, psychologically and in my outer life. So the language was very intense and idiosyncratic. I dared to express my thoughts, but a lot of people didn't know what I was even talking about. That was actually very important for me. I was in a process of experimentation with language. I think it gives you a vision of the world that is hard to take. There are societies for those for whom creativity and beauty is part of life—it's understood as worship. Think of Bali, where beauty is naturally in their daily lives.

Yes, I think that suffering is part and source of creativity in much powerful and effective art. We live in a world that has so much suffering in it, and the artist suffers as she creates her work.

Suffering means that you are in some way out of place. You don't belong. It shows in your art. It certainly shows in the art of Van Gogh, as an example. He had more energy than what he could contain.

And for myself, suffering is part of my life and art. I suffer the unanswerable and unexplained mysteries. It's like someone gives you a most amazing gem. You have to do something with it, show it to others. Look at the ancient Greek tragedies, the plays; they are so very moving. How do you contain such intensity? How do we contain what we perceive in our daily life—floods and hurricanes and wars? I am so overwhelmed by the world: Some of it is so magnificent, other experiences so grievously sad. But we have to walk around in clothing, earn money, pay bills.

Am I sometimes blocked or bored? Not really. Right now, I spend a lot of energy and time in survival mode. I take care and edit for other people and don't direct my own energy into the fierceness that I have for others. Survival has become an essential issue which holds me back. I don't want to teach English as a foreign language. I want to write. On the other hand, I need to finally find a secure income. I also want to travel, as I am fascinated by foreign places and cultures. I have to battle the idea of myself as deprived of life.

When I was a young kid, I was literally held in captivity. So today, I have to go dancing and hear music. Most of us creative people have our own battles and struggle to do the creative things. When I have and take the time not to worry and just create and celebrate, I do fabulously. I dance!

Elias Rivera

There's something nurturing about suffering. Suffering is deeply part of the human experience. The arts invite you to this journey to help you discover if you are an artist and what is your specific gift.

I never realized the extent of the responsibility I took on when entering this world of art. It became richer and richer for me. I realized I had a responsibility to it, to my talent. I take it as far as I can. When I am painting, it takes every bit of my energy. I took a portrait of two dear friends. They realized how much energy it takes to be so involved. I gave one of them a mirror so that they could watch my process, so not to get bored but stay engaged and interested.

I think it was through art that I realized there was a dark quality to life. It's more recently that I have been diving into those dark corners. I am concerned about mankind. I have choices to make, and sometimes that means sacrifice. In the whole equation, I want to be responsible to my calling. What lasts in my life is my art, and that's what I am supposed to be doing. I was not given a talent like that without responsibility. If I don't use my gifts, I would be missing out. The expression of it holds the outer possibility to be closer to the source.

The journey has been so nurturing for me, and I realized what my talent gave to people. I feel so much gratitude for the journey, because I love beauty. As I have gotten to know my sense of responsibility to life and to the expression of it, I feel much hope.

Yael Weiss

Suffering is part of creativity—we all know suffering at times. Most people try to understand and alleviate it and find some way of healing. Music tries both ways: to explain suffering and to seek to heal it by bringing forth its power. Some composers and some of the music I play touch me deeply. My first love is Schumann. I always felt very close to him. He tried to commit suicide, and throughout his life, he went through phases of suffering and darkness. He sought in his music to express those experiences. Other composers, like Beethoven, tried to integrate it through beautiful balance and organization. So the suffering provided creative energy for him, and his mind found a structure for it so that it was possible to bear it and find that it made sense.

I definitely think that suffering is part of creativity. If one holds it and does not push it away, one has more material to work with. Luckily, there is so much to do to perform a piece of music and to communicate it to the audience. There's a lot of skill involved and straightforward hard work. That keeps me grounded. As an example, I need to find the right fingers to perform a specific piece, or study the metronomic indications—that's work to do. Or for example, a bit of historical research is necessary around a piece of music, a lot of interpretive work. It's very good; I need that. I also need to practice a piece many times. If I feel that something creates resistance or is overwhelming me, these practical demands help me to overcome that resistance.

UWE WALTER-NAKAJIMA

That's where it started: I was ten years old and wanted to go to a higher school, so I had to be gifted and became part of the in-group. I became creative for survival. They accepted me as the class clown. I was shy but struggled my way through. I became a performer to protect myself and to be accepted.

My mother was very fearful, and I wanted to be free of that. I tried to find a kind of freedom in my weaknesses, so I joined a theater group—I was into Jung, Reich, and bio-energetics. We worked with mentally ill people. Then I studied therapy, where I found out that failing is okay, that one can be strong in acceptance of that. When I fail, my armor of resistance breaks, and I have experienced that!

I was very serious, worked on the tightrope, then trained actors to study their text on the tightrope. Was very successful in theater and TV, but I thought we were too young for success and needed first to explore and practice more. So I studied with Grotowky, who was a model of what I thought an artist should be. I rejected engagement into the army and had to go to jail for that—going to jail was suffering. Suffering in my life comes from society, not from art.

What I am striving for now is to overcome the fear of death in my mind. I try to face death. I don't want to be afraid or escape but to truly accept death as part of life. I want to be true to myself. It's not easy to talk about death, and we usually avoid talking. We resist facing what it means to be mortal.

My vision of a good Noh actor or shakuhachi flute player is that he or she is able to stand at the edge of an imploding supernova and plunge into black matter. I would like to get into that state of mind and abandon fear. This is the task I gave to myself now, maybe the final one. I want to live that without fear.

My music is going to change. When I play for people, I lose fear. I have to do more practice on that, more practice facing fear. This is in the character of the Japanese arts, to work on your inner state of being. I admire those monks who live in monasteries in Japan. When they feel that they are dying, they go out and dig their own grave. They then sit inside, don't eat or drink, just breathe and dry out.

When I played for a lot of famous people, the German ambassador or princesses and statesmen, high-ranking people, I experienced a lot of pretense in them. I wonder why is there such an urge to be in power and recognized. I believe there is a fear of death as a driving force and an urge to define their essence through importance and fame. I think there is real freedom in becoming finally a part of this earth and allow our personal finality to be part of our history.

TIM GOSNELL

Suffering, for me, comes from the fear of failure. That's a real battle I fight. You might work for a year on a specific experiment and then comes the day of truth. "This is it, guys," either success or failure. Here's a serous shift toward something new, or being stuck.

Science is not just a reasoned, intellectual thing, but in order to use the brain well, emotions are involved in the process. It is an emotional thing to be doing science; it is not a neutral activity, cold and inhuman. That makes me think that the artistic and scientific activities are not so different. How a genius works—that's a mystery to me. It is said that Einstein just was very persistent. He had this ability to focus intensely for extremely long periods of time. He also preferred to work alone. There were other physicists who were deemed to be even more talented, but Einstein was this almost-mythical figure.

Nonetheless, most of us all work in obscurity for most of our life. Maybe that agrees with the notion of "suffering." I have this notion of writing an autobiography of an average scientist, because most of what we know of the lives of scientists is written about those superstars. There is this whole different experience of those who never rose to those heights.

Resistance and blocks occur when you are trying to do something and don't get anywhere. You have to adjust your focus to what you can do. I am in some sense most proud about some of the problems I tried to solve when it did not work out. For example, I tried to make a motion picture camera take single pictures. It could not be done at that time, because it was too hard, even if it was a great idea.

For me, resistance comes from the fear of failure and fear of success, when you get intimidated by the brilliance of all the people around you. It takes some courage to step into unknown territory as a researcher. On the other hand, there's this friend of mine who is absolutely fearless—nothing slows this guy down. I have to work at it, as my anxiety is a blockage.

I am nervous about using this word sacrifice; it has such different connotations. The things that got me into physics and hold my attention now are well beyond the worker days. There is not a lot in science that's interesting all the time; it's mostly hard work, and to spend a life with it takes some persistence that I did not have. It also speaks to the difference between art and science: There's still tons of stuff that I want to explore and learn about. I want to understand more about how the universe is set. I am as thirsty now as I was as a kid around that stuff. But the fine arts that I pursued when young—that's done. But the hunger for a view into the function of the universe is still there.

JERRY WENNSTROM

Everybody suffers. It comes with the territory, has not to do with creativity; it's just part of being human. Creativity might come out of that but not predominantly. Art comes out of that if we are willing to participate fully in life and in the suffering.

Those twelve years I spent without home and belongings—yes, that was suffering, but once free, I could not get back into the box. Suffering happened for me when the next miracle did not come in time. It always did, but with its own timing. I survived from miracle to miracle. I could not have lived through this strange journey I was on if it wasn't a self-maintaining system somehow, if it didn't carry my life. All I know is that the initial leap really set it in motion. There was no going back, no return to comfort! When I jumped into that life of homelessness at the edge of society, there was no backing out of that.

You jump and gravity is bringing you somewhere, and it's not back to where you left. That's the truth of the moment.

People with a career put up with tyranny and lies in their work, and if they don't deal with it, it stays around and we hand it on to our own kids. That's how the box happens and how we get into it. I needed to cut the patterns and go for the truth, and I believe that the gods will meet your poverty halfway. I am a wild card. Marilyn, my wife, knows about the territory. If the truth is the truth, it's not mine; it's the moment's truth. Stay alert for that!

Is there a softer way to do that, one with less suffering? No. Your way is not going to be soft. If you strategize softness, it's going to be hard. For me, it's the radical way. I always lived already outside society; it was not such a stretch. It was my level of trust that carried me.

It seems that no matter what I do, my path has always been about growing deeper into emptiness. A strange journey I have been on—it's often difficult to describe what it is about.

A friend said to me, "What you did, leaving your career and society, almost everybody is fantasizing about that." I left and walked into total freedom. Most people dream about that at some time in their lives: the wish to give away everything and walk into the unknown.

There's some part of the psyche that knows about the birds in the field being taken care of. I was coming at it as if nobody really gets it, but my guess is that everybody does. In such freedom, death is the ultimate limitation. Life is to die again and again. We cannot even let go of our ideas about ourselves—we cling to them and defend them.

How are we supposed to let go of everything in the moment of death? It's going to require great creativity and inspiration. I think we should deal with death as early as possible, so as to live fully in life. If we are running from death, we will never be free. The only way to deal with that bogeyman is to look him in the face.

VIJALI HAMILTON

I feel that suffering and challenges are gifts from the universe because they push us to open new parts of our selves and learn to survive. They make us who we are today; like my harsh childhood, it's part of who I am today. They are gifts, when you look back at them. If they had not happened, you would not have developed in that certain way. They force you to take another road and grow. Being beaten every day as a child was just life for me. At that time, I did not compare myself with other people.

I missed my mother and father, and it was hard to understand that I was not with them; other children were. My father visited me once a year during my childhood. Later, he took me out to

California and put me in a boarding school, visiting once a month. Then he gave me the greatest gift of my life: He introduced me to oriental philosophy. I went to the temple in Hollywood. I became very interested and started meditating regularly. When I went back to the girls school, I found a little place in the garden where I meditated. By the time I was fourteen, I decided to become a nun, and I was there for ten years until I was twenty-five. The convent was in Santa Barbara.

I am very grateful for that experience. But as I grew up, it became very negative. The girls treated me badly, sensing that I wasn't really nun material.

I was so ready to leave, and I was wise enough to do just that. I left and went to Canada and got a job. I was not trained for normal work. Then I got a job illustrating a book for the National Research Council. I interviewed different scientists about their work and did visual representations of what their work was about. I had learned to draw in the convent and used all my free time to practice my art. They saw that I was talented, so I took some online courses to learn. I wanted to go to college and study art, so I asked the swami if I could go, and he said no.

When I had the job in Canada, I worked during the day and attended college at night. I went to the best art college, in Montreal, and the following years, I went full-time to college. Then I married, and divorced after seven years. I married with the condition that I would finish my degree in art, but that became impossible, and my husband disagreed with that. But I finally finished and got my graduate degree from Goddard.

I was so shy, a loner, and it was a breakthrough to step out into the world. Sometimes I wonder why I was called to do this kind of work, as I am shy. Somebody who is not shy but dynamic might do a better job than I, but that's just how my calling goes. [She laughs with glee.]

Blockage? I never feel blocked. My path just unfolds and guides me along. I meet people and they guide me to others.

That happened in Siberia during my journey around the globe. I had only a few things: my sweater and raincoat, a tent, and boots. At the end, after I had sculpted the piece, we had this wonderful ceremony. It was televised and many people participated. I loved it because we brought different religions and cultures together.

We created a piece and all the participants celebrated! We also loved the presence of the media because these people finally could express their needs and stories. They had the feeling that nobody knew about their hardships and circumstances, but now the world listened to them and their voice was heard. They were starving. One woman sold her marriage ring for food. I stayed in someone's house and sometimes we had just one potato that we shared among the three of us for a meal. I gave them $100, and they were so enthusiastic that they framed it and hung it at their wall.

I was so elated that their voice was heard. In the ceremony, I had everybody talk and express themselves. Poets came, writers came, artists came—and all of them were heard. It made me very happy.

Such a simple life as mine could seem like a sacrifice, but it's not; it's very, very rich.

Amanda McPhail and Wesley West

Wes: I was born in London; my father died when I was eight years old. I left home at that early age and lived with my aunt, and then I joined the Royal Navy at age thirteen. I left the Navy at the age of twenty-two, did various jobs for about a year, then joined the banking system as a trainee manager. I didn't like that, left it, and then, five years later, at the age of twenty-six, went to art school. The first part of my life was painful in many ways, but after art school, I stepped into the beginning of my official creative life, and I haven't looked back since. My life up to my present age of sixty-four has just been completely fun. Enjoyable!

Is living the life of an artist a sacrifice? I think it's the opposite—it has been a bonus to our lives. Art has always added to our life instead of taken away. In my life, I had a pre-art-school life and an after-art-school life, and I did a lot of traveling during the first one. I was not trained then. I did not really see and explore, was very simplistic in my perception. But when I went to art school, they opened my eyes, they trained me in new perspective. And that was the most important effect that art school had on me.

They taught me how to see! And from that seeing came all of my visual creative life! I swear, I can teach people how to draw, but the main thing is to teach them how to see. Drawing is about continual looking and checking and looking again.

Amanda: I disagree actually! You only move your eyes when you draw, not your head. It's a seeing thing to be an artist and a teacher.

I remember when I first went to art school. My eyes were exhausted. I looked and looked. I remember just looking! And it was beautiful or angry or shocking.

Creativity for me is deeply frustrating! I see work and think: I want to be able to do that! And I can't! In your head, you know exactly what you would want to create, and it won't happen—that's deeply frustrating. You need a great confidence in your work and yourself to get through such a block. But I could not see myself to live without that struggle.

Sara Warber

When I was young I thought you needed to suffer for art, you need to have had dramatic experiences from which you might be able to create. As young person, I lived a privileged life, so I thought I had missed something by not suffering. I was always a very emotional person. But during my early 20s and into the 30s, I was learning how to live. I went from a life where everything was provided for to having to find ways to put food on the table and a roof over my head. I made some poor choices of husbands along the way. I am sure my parents were very distressed, worse for them than it was for me. There was pain and humiliation. Life was hard. It was my school-of-life period. There was lots of suffering. I don't dwell on that now and don't want to think about it. I got out of college and into the real world, learning to make ends meet. I went into medical school. I learned a lot, and today I have a very deep empathy with my patients when they suffer, because I know what that is. I can use this knowing when I help them and we create a way to deal. The human condition includes the experience of suffering, but it is not the only foundation of creativity—joy is equal in it. Anything that has some juice in it is a great opportunity for creativity.

I am sometimes blocked when too absorbed in my own struggles. Resistance appears when I am writing and combinations of fears attack me, like, "It will take too long" or "I don't really know anything, " a typical gremlin attack. But that happens only in my work as a physician, not when involved in art or craft projects when making something with my hands. My fear is that I will make a mistake. The world of science and research is so competitive. I need to get over that fear; that's resistance.

When I am choosing to be alone during the process of creating, I sacrifice companionship. I retreat and miss the fun of relating. There's always a form of resistance in all kind of disguises. That's part of the territory. Creativity does not come easily into your space; it wants to be courted.

RUTH BAMFORD

I think most people are not creative. Most want to stay within their comfort zone. It creates huge anxiety to stretch beyond the known. It means facing chaos. I just want to be free. A lot of people cannot face existence without being in control.

When I was in my teens, I think, one of my teachers discovered that I was dyslexic because my spelling was consistently incorrect and my reading was so slow. It was seen as lazy and not understood then. But anything I heard about dyslexia I found to be fitting for my situation and complications. I was actually diagnosed when meeting scientists who researched this topic.

I am dyslexic and think in my own unique ways. I flow where others might be blocked. I am intelligent and believe that my visionary and conceptual capacities are related to my dyslexia. So I embrace it and do not battle its effect. I have been talking to other intelligent dyslexics who have managed professional occupations, and found that we all have the same quick leaps of understanding, a comprehension of the whole of a situation as opposed to its detailed parts. But what is obvious to us was not seen by others. I gave a talk on the neurology of this issue, and I called it humorously: "What's wrong with my brain?" I went through a brain stem test to get a free picture of my brain because I wanted to use it as my screen-saver.

It was discovered that the dyslexic brain is physically distinctly different. You can diagnose dyslexia from the shape of the brain stem. We dyslexics use the imaginative and intuitive side of the brain, like my children do. We translate what we hear into a picture. Creativity as a mechanism is different for a dyslexic person. I see pictures in my head and translate hem into words. I manipulate objects with my imagination. Even in math, I can see the equations without writing them down. It takes me longer to work out a solution in lexic language than in dyslexic.

Blockages? Yes, I feel blocked by the male attitudes around me here at the institute in Oxford, where a woman scientist has to struggle constantly for acceptance and input. I do research in space science and have developed a great concept to protect objects in space. Science is not just the equations—it's the concepts. And that's based on imagination.

When I was about sixteen, I had a choice of pursuing fine art or science. I only stopped doing art because there was no university offering both—I had to choose. I still make a lot of drawings about my projects, and I do photography. I love that. It's very artful photography, like the edge of an object with snow along the surface, rather abstract. I see the world a lot like that, lines in specific angles, light and shadows. The light in Oxford in spring is gorgeous. So you see details and contrasts that are very artful and esthetic. I enjoy that a lot!

Bob Bingham in Rutherford helped me to recognize the way I was thinking when I developed my research concept. Two things just came together—I could feel it—like in a three-dimensional movie; the only thing missing was the smells. But all the sensations and pressures and thoughts were in my head, and I was aware of that. Even right now, I am translating it into linear words. I am remembering the moment when I formulated my thoughts for Bob. I have a sense of how much light was in the room. I recall the entire sensory experience, not in micro-detail but the full feeling.

PEGGY O'KELLY

Suffering is definitely part of my life as businesswoman. There are the reactions of people who don't understand my changes and growth, who know me from former times, before I had this much deep focus on spirit and respect for nature. I do not want to do anything that could harm the Earth—that is extremely important to me, and some people wonder why. They judge me, and that creates suffering because I am not supported. I feel like an outsider and alone.

Yes, I think that in the creative process, one is very alone. It's scary and lonesome to walk such a path of integrity when in business. But I am still driven to move forward in authenticity. I told my daughters, "If you want to manifest your visions, you have to walk with fear at your side and risk something. Move forward; trust and continue. Otherwise, your dream will never happen."

Yes, sometimes I feel bored, and that's very uncomfortable. This happens when I am running in too many directions and get scattered. I am rarely stuck and stay there. I move fast, or I even run, but I will not stay frozen in doubt. I nurture myself and watch how I eat, spend my time, light candles, appreciate my environment.

What kills creativity is time pressure and administrative demands. I fill up my days with those business demands and then I have no time to reflect and just be. I need to create specific islands of time to think and imagine and appreciate. Like today, when I got the new products from Morocco, I had to wait to unpack them and be alert and relaxed with them. These are products from the land and sea, like olive and essential oils and salts—they need respect and gratitude.

I don't have a lot of fear or blocks. I am not attached in a serious way, and I am willing to fight for the planet in whatever way is needed. I am waiting for my number to be called.

Chrissie Orr

Resistance shows itself to me as exhaustion and feeling overwhelmed—I want just to retreat and deal only with myself, needing distance from the world.

Yes, I feel exhausted sometimes. Oh yes! Then I wonder where the Muses have gone. I am not good at recharging my batteries. I get tired from a lot of computer work and too much mental work. What really helps me is walking on my own. I take my camera and my journal with me. I get energized by work in my garden. I recharge when I am getting excited about a new work or when I move my body and create.

No, I don't go much to see contemporary art shows. I would rather look at people's gardens—that is art, living art, for me. But I love the old museums in big cities or our folk art museum. I'm more an outside person; I get recharged by nature.

There are many specific artists who inspire and nurture me. Anselm Kiefer's work is so powerful—those gigantic paintings with lots of tar and dirt in them. That rattled me. I love Botticelli, I love medieval work, going into old churches in Mexico, watching the colors and the light. I love many, many artists and art events. When I saw Monet's water lilies for the first time or saw some of the old Renaissance paintings, it cracked my heart open. And I feel so inspired by Jean Tinguely and Niki de Saint Phalle. They don't take themselves too seriously. I rarely feel bored—there's too much interesting stuff to explore.

You don't need to suffer to be creative. But you need to take risks, and that might produce suffering and anxiety. If I didn't suffer, would that reduce my ability to create? Maybe it's like giving birth; the suffering has such a fantastic result that you take it on willingly.

How I express and experience resistance? By not keeping my eyes open, being too much in my head, suffocating in too much administration, getting too caught up in theory, losing contact with my body, cutting myself off from the flow, forgetting my feet on the ground. I need to get back to that feeling place where I tap into my essence, be watchful and listen inside. That's how I overcome resistance. It always works.

THEODORA CAPALDO

Yes, I do sometimes feel all of those: boredom, resistance, blockage, and at this point and age, I have learned to just wait it out because I have enough trust that this too shall pass. I wait. It's a short chapter of my time, and it will resolve itself in a week or month or even a year, for God's sake! Especially when I can't find anything in the external world that seems the root of it. Nothing to account for it, it just grabs me and holds on. I might call friends and talk about it. It has its own timing and will leave when it is ripe to go. Uncomfortable, but I always learn something new.

Chapter Eight. Community or Solitude

I like the community of family and the community of scientists, because I love the challenge of the other's mind in exchange with mine.
—Ruth Bamford

The Artist and the Audience

During my Vision Quest in summer of 2014, I was sitting alone at the edge of the deep, red Canyon de Chelly, in northern Arizona. Four days of fasting and solitude had opened all my senses and alerted me to feed on the beauty of the outrageously wild and mysterious red rock formations. Puffy clouds sailed in the sky. A heavy silence hovered above the desert. I imagined that I was the only human being left on the planet. If that was the case, I asked myself, would I still write? Would I still write just for myself? Would I write hoping to direct my stories, thoughts, and ruminations toward an imaginary future when desert dwellers might find and decipher my messages?

Would any cave-dweller carve or paint pictures on rock walls if there was not a community to witness, marvel, react, and have ceremonies around the products of the artist's imagination? Art cannot exist and come to vibrancy without the community in which it was created: this place, this culture, this historical moment. Even a prisoner creating art in his lonesome cell is influenced by the setting, the horror and hope of his prison community. Olivier Messiaen composed his Quartet for the End of Time in a POW camp.

Art cannot fully come to life without the others' eyes to see it, their ears to hear it, their hands to touch it, or their tongue to taste it. Art's final products have their own life, and they long for publicity and acknowledgment. The lonesome artist in his or her studio or behind the computer screen is yearning for the other as mirror and response. The artists' creations are bridges between lives. They lead toward a deeper understanding of the self and the members of the community as well as the great mystery of this universe.

Being part of an art exhibition is like opening the door to your inner life for everybody to notice. I remember my first show of clay work at the gallery of the Institute of American Indian Arts in Santa Fe. On the day of the opening, an enthusiastic viewer picked the Maya mask that I had created, the first piece in a series to come. He held it in his hands, turned it left and right, looked at its profile for a long time, and then walked to the cashier, paid for it, and left with a radiant smile on his face. I had observed this interaction and asked myself with excitement, what had happened here? My language of form, color, and medium was understood by a stranger? Somebody recognized its meaning. Somebody cherished this piece like I did? So "I am an artist," I thought! This moment of outreach and response was the threshold I crossed when I began to connect my creations with an audience. I felt the delight of recognition, as if I was initiated into a new tribe, the artist's tribe.

As creators, we feel the joy of a child that has built a high tower out of blocks and is surprised that it holds up and doesn't crumble. The kid will run to mom and grab her hand, pulling her toward the structure. "Look, here, I did that!" There is so much delight in building something, or composing and writing, or dancing or cooking. It brings satisfaction for the artist to reach out with the creative object to an unknown audience and to receive a response. Whatever we create, we mirror with our work how we see the world and ourselves in it. To be acknowledged by the community is delightful feedback and an invigorating confirmation of our existence.

I once saw a client in my practice, a painter who created beautiful works of art. She was shy and did not dare approach a gallery to ask that her paintings be shown; instead, she stored them in her basement and felt sad, as if she had abandoned her children. She finally realized that art needs to leave the solitary place where we grow our artistic works and move out into the world, so that the creator and the receiver foster each other and come to life in a mutually inspiring encounter.

On the other hand, in today's art market, there are bankers in Japan and China who hoard precious artwork bought at auction as an investment, speculating that it will gain value over time. These works are locked into bank vaults and don't see the light of the day; they are caged and unable to shine in relationship with the viewer. Not allowed to live a life above ground, they are just objects for financial trade and tricks. This is imprisoned art—its energy and creative vibrancy are strangled. It is misuse of art, or even abuse.

I doubt that any creative work could sustain its radiance without being loved and perceived, without being embraced with attention and integrated into our ordinary life. Everything and everybody longs to be seen in their truthful and unique way of existence. Art comes to life through the creator as well as through attention from the audience. When we create, we long to touch the other's mind and heart and inspire their imagination. This way, we unfold together toward a more beautiful and conscious life. Art needs community as much as community needs art.

I think that we are all geared toward others' approval and feedback, hungry for recognition
—Tim Gosnell

The Magic of Music

Summer's heat hangs like a heavy curtain above the roofs of San Gimignano in Tuscany. I cross the piazza and walk through the portal of the Basilica di Santa Maria Assunta to enter the cool and quiet space inside. My eyes adjust to the muted light. Stained glass windows spread veils of color between the columns. I sit down and allow the cool air to settle on my sweaty skin. A fly buzzes, carving erratic sound patterns into the silence.

Famous frescoes fill the interior walls. "Painted by Bartolo di Fredi," says my guidebook, "during the early Renaissance, some of the oldest in Italy." As I wander along past the images, I enter into a long-gone time that is still flourishing today through the vivid depiction in those frescoes. There are biblical scenes inhabited by lively human beings who move and point and sit, busily occupied with their glorious Mediterranean lives. Their gestures are so lively that I imagine the warm blood pulsing in their bodies. I reach out to them and they seem eager to encounter me and step out of the painting, eager to walk onto the Piazza del Duomo outside and mingle with the folks—the gelato sellers and the children in summer dress, the frisky dogs chasing each other and terrifying the nervous doves.

I am delighting in the cool space inside the basilica and walk slowly. In front of me, in the fresco, I see three men involved in passionate conversation. They point to a full-bodied woman as she leans over tomatoes and garlic, fingering the spices with one hand and holding an infant at her wide hip. On a porch, a family gathers around the supper table laden with steaming sausages and broccoli, and wine in goblets. On the opposing wall, Noah is depicted drunk and sprawling backward, his legs spread wide and without shame. And there is the ailing man Job, surrounded by loved ones, wrangling with the grip of his angry God.

I feel shy as I stand close and observe these people in their intimate life and see the tears shimmer on their cheeks. Job's sorrow is caught in this fresco, and I think of how he has been dying in this church for centuries. The artist's hand has transfixed him into this scene. The tears of his loved ones will never dry. These frescoes depict heartache and loss like a mirror of human grief, theirs and ours.

I stop at the fresco of a red-faced woman in an adjacent house, spread on crumpled sheets, giving birth to a baby. She too has been caught in this painting for centuries now. She has portrayed women's labor pain, hope, and fear for six hundred years; out of her womb, life will continue to emerge as long as this church stands. The power of art enshrines such a moment. Art crystallizes our knowing into form and holds it—allowing it to become fluid again in our own hearts. I lean my head against the cool stone and feel how the lives of people depicted in these frescoes flow through me, with the pace of an ancient glacier that carves into the landscape of my soul.

Suddenly, sweet music wafts through an open door. A harp concerto fills the sanctuary with waves of sound and measured rhythms. I step through a stone arch into the bright sun to find the source of the music. A man sits with his back toward me, leaning against wrought iron bars near the side entrance. He is embracing the instrument between his strong brown arms and legs. His hairy hands dance along the strings, caressing them as if stroking a lover and making her sing in ecstasy. I see the veins and muscles of a man who does heavy work. His fingers are stubby, and the skin reflects the colors of the Tuscan earth: ochre and reddish-brown with highlights of gold and yellow. This man seems to have stepped out of the frescos inside the church and onto this piazza. He plucks sound out of his harp with an intimacy that makes me feel like an intruder. Casting a spell onto the small Piazza Luigi Pecori, he weaves his music into the spaces between the listeners and the nichos and windows of the classic Italian houses that surround this place.

I sit down on the cobblestones and rest my back against a cool stone wall. Beside me are other quiet travelers delighting in the magic of the moment. The harp player spins us into a web of community beyond place and time. Children move closer to him in a circle, attracted like the birds to St. Francis. One wavy-haired boy, too small to walk, sits on the ground. In his light blue shorts, he inches his behind toward the man until his tiny hand rubs the wood of the harp. Another little boy stretches his chubby arms to catch the music between the palms of his hands. A rugged black dog lifts his leg at a cornerstone and then strolls over to sit beside the musician like a guardian. A dreamy late summer sun hovers over this place. Tourists entering the piazza turn their heads to find the origin of the melodies. They interrupt their talk or close their guidebooks, and then they look around, as if embarrassed, caught observing the intimate embrace of a man and his beloved music. He pours his tunes into our memory, which will behold man and harp for times to come. It flows in between the houses and into the Basilica di Santa Maria Assunta and around the gorgeous frescos. This moment is perfect.

As I relax against the mossy wall, time and history are transcended; the figures inside the cathedral step out of their ancient paintings and join us in this marvelous space of beauty created by sound. The harpist with the dark, strong hands gently carves memories made of sound. I will never forget the Piazza Luigi Pecori filled with tunes of Bach, Monteverdi, and Corelli. The music is a gift, offered with great humility. From the artist's hands, it radiates in small circles toward the quiet and transfixed audience, where it fills the open spaces in our hearts. Bonded by this music, we have become a community of listeners, gathered inside sound.

Life at the Edge

At the edge of my life, most things are round and smooth.
At my age and at the edge of this life, I face the truth that
I could stumble at any moment and fall off the edge into space.
At the edge of my life, there are doors that lead to unknown
   territory,
To everything or nothing, to endings or new beginnings.
At that edge, I am aware how familiar this earthly place
Has become, during a long life of living along edges.

COMMUNITY OR SOLITUDE

At the edge of this day, there's a delicious moment when the light
Of the day surrenders to dusk, and that's also the time when
The bats begin to circle my pond and dip their chests into the
  water during their flight, leaving dimples on the surface.
They sail with high speed and absolute trust, that they'll find
Their way without eyes, simply directed by inner sound.
At the edge of my trust, I wonder if I am too naïve, believing
That everything that hovers on edges is guarded.

If I slide over the edge, I trust some great and graceful hand
Will catch me and all my questions will find answers one day,
Or they will continue to rattle me and force me to fly blindly
Into the world, like the bats around my pond at dusk.

At the edge of today's summer heat, a thunderstorm hovered
And hesitated, and then it brought us this delicious cool air,
  punctuated by
A harsh rain, a gift for grasses, and critters,
hummingbird, and squirrels and for the four women who sit in
  circle on this porch.

At the edge of my friendship with these women,
With whom I come together and write, there's a bond that can
  withstand
Conflict, oddness and mistakes. At the edge of this creative
  writing circle
We are startled by our flaws and limitations.

We risk and we stumble, we fall or succeed in awkward and
  graceful ways.
We practice being authentic by allowing space for each other's
  otherness.
We love and we hurt each other, and sometimes, like today,
The love and the hurt
Leave the same
Sharp sting.

Community or Solitude: The Interviews

ESTHER MARION

It's a good life to be in community and partnership. My family is part of my creativity and art. We are Cultural Creatives. We live in some ways at the edge of society. Money and status do not mean much to us, but we are in the core of this society; we are movers and shakers. We trust and risk and get involved.

I am very blessed. I feel guided by the Muses, but they demand discipline and devotion, urging me to stay skilled at what I do. Perfection has power. Discipline is good. I hope I can teach that to my kids. Without discipline, there is no art. My husband and I are both involved in this process of active creation and we are learning from each other. We choose not to watch TV but to be creative ourselves. We are fulfilling a certain vision of our lives as a family. We create in a little network of people, and we support each other in this colorful circle of friends. We have conflicts, yes, but we resolve them, and we create beautiful things together—not only in our separate studios but wherever we connect and mingle and perform.

I want to live where creative things happen, like taking my daughter and her friends to the Oregon County Fair, where's so much originality and community—it's utter delight. I see it as an act of love to take young people to those places that initiate the spark and fire of creativity in them. I arrange for us to participate in events that might have a long-lasting effect on these young beings.

The members of our extended family live all over the world and share their stories. That influence sparks growth and learning. The places where we live hold part of my sense of family. I have learned to embrace both of my homes, the Southwest and the Northwest. Sometimes that's hard because I am such a sun person and feel deeply challenged by the rain and darkness in Seattle in winter. On the other hand, that's the time when my inner life is richest. So I go inside during the dark season.

In the high desert of the Southwest, I feel so at home. I want my daughter to get a feel for this magical land, want to create a book with photographs and walk the canyons with her. It is very rewarding to know and visit places that are familiar and close to one's heart. And I always leave something with the land, a gift or personal piece. When I left Santa Fe to go north, I buried my silver snake necklace in the Sangre de Cristo Mountains. I leave those gifts all over the world. Like acupuncture points, they connect with each other like a network of love energy.

We are global citizens and hear stories told by amazing people from everywhere. I feel encouraged by empowered women. Those who inspire me are part of my community. Great musicians and dancers, especially in flamenco, have inspired me all my life, such as guitarist Paco de Lucia, singer Camarón de la Isla, La Galleguita, dancers Juana Amaya or Yerbabuena, Manuela Carrasco. Then the masters of the inner world such as C.G. Jung, C.P. Estés, Robert Moss. And the movers and shakers, activists and also powerful voices such as Bernice Johnson Reagon, Miriam Makeba, Mercedes Sosa, Rigoberta Menchú, Jean Houston. They are my community.

But I will also mention here a trailblazing dance team: Alvin Ailey and Judith Jamison, who have created the most powerful and celebrated dance company in the world. In ethnic music and dance, I have been touched by the greatest performers from many traditions, but especially in flamenco. And there's my own family, my parents and my children and husband, who are a constant source of encouragement.

MICHAEL BROOME

An artist works solitary or in community. I create in solitude though I do look at other people's work and get inspired. There's a kind of society of creatives, but I don't quite fit into groups. Recently I went to the Acoma Indian dances and met the Native American potters. I sat with this old man and we talked about pottery. Because I know about pottery, we could talk to each other and became very close. I think it was our art that brought us together, like a key that opened us toward each other—otherwise, it would be difficult. So I know I am part of a community, and I have a language with them, a connection that allows me to meet certain people at a much more mature level. Our art and craft connect us.

I have not really cared what people think and know about me. One of the things to know when living a creative life: You have got to make your own decisions! You've got to shape your own destiny. So it's helpful if you don't care what others think and believe. If you're going to be an artist, you have to be—to say it straight—almost selfish because you can't be worrying about others' opinions. What you are interested in is finding out who you are.

I don't sell very easily. I make it difficult to buy a piece. I don't need to; it's not my livelihood. That would be dangerous. It distorts the picture. If you get paid, you might make things that you did not want to make originally. My friend the ceramic artist used to do all sorts of pottery. And one of them—he called it a pebble pot—sold like crazy; it literally walked out of the shop. And then he was in a squeeze, and he realized that if he didn't make pebble pots, he didn't make money. He was caught by his own product and its accomplishment. He didn't really want to make them anymore, but they sold so successfully. That's a sad story. It's not easy to find a balance between satisfying your own visions and those of your audience.

TONY JUNIPER

I am very sociable. I love community and prefer working with other people. I interact with a load of people in many different organizations rather than having to be responsible for just one thing. I realize the creativity that comes from working in five or six different places at once. So I am working with my own narrative, I am lecturing, working with the Prince of Wales, with a university team, and with half a dozen major corporations, with a bunch of CEOs, and governmental groups, with different communications groups. I always have teams of people who inspire and realize my ideas. But I am not responsible for all of them and don't have to negotiate a line of politics with them.

And all those different perspectives, like a mining company, a food company, a consumer goods company, a technical academic unit, the university perspective, the Friends of the Earth, and the Greenpeace perspective—they are all looking at the same thing with different mindsets, and I have the luxury of all those different inputs. That's something unique that I have to offer, and it is quite valuable. But it needs to be kept under control. Otherwise, it turns into a monster. I try to understand those different points of view instead of getting frustrated about them. Some of the writing I am doing is to understand where people are at now, rather than telling them that they are wrong. But the stress can lead you to say "You are wrong," and all that does is make people resistant to what you have to say. Consequently, frustration needs to be kept in control.

So I tell myself that if this does not work out, this situation—that 9 billion people are destroying the Earth. I want at least to be on the right side of the argument, in terms of my own perspective on this, rather than giving up and doing what people do, like sitting at a beach, not caring, and ignoring the world in distress. I must confess that I am drawing on the wisdom of many other people to be able to make the connections that create the bigger picture. I tried with the book *What Has Nature Ever Done for Us?* to synthesize and bundle all that into one big story. There are a lot of isolated facts and figures that have to be combined into a bigger idea of the relationships, in this case between people and the natural world.

CAROLE WATANABE

Do I consider the recipient or buyer of my art—and consider the community? Of course, because I have my eye on making a living as an artist. I call the woman who runs my gallery in Collioure, France, and ask her: "What sold well last season? And what do I need to replenish?" And she might say, "Oh, I need small such and such, or a bunch of these kind of paintings" or so. And then I do some of it, even if it's not what I am interested in right now. But I am practical and listen to what needs to be done. But I also keep doing what I want to do artistically, because that's where real art happens. And that's what—in the end—sells best, because me heart is in it. I work in community and love that. I always think that I want to go out there on the land by myself and paint, but the reality is that it always evolves into a community. I am happiest painting with other people. We inspire each other tremendously.

CATHY ATEN

Being an artist all my life has led to a very precarious existence. I am not a team player; I live and survive solo as an artist. I am comfortable and familiar with insecurity, with my life's circumstances not being predictable. I am not afraid because I have already faced a lot of darkness in my life and know how to survive. I am fifty-eight years old now and still trying to figure me out.

I believe that we are probably in some kind of "agreement" with the major events and turns in our lives, the things that shatter us and help our souls to grow. Multiple sclerosis really transformed me. I am thinking of sacrifice, a word which comes from the Latin *sacrificium* and means making holy.

People think that being an artist is a really glamorous thing, but it's not; we deal with our monsters and angels. And then there's the monster of resistance, expressed as procrastination. I discuss this with artists: Why do we resist our artistic work? Why don't we always desire to stay in this nurturing, exciting place of creativity? But there's something scary about it. It is The Void. That means it is full of everything, an emptiness full. That is the birthing place of creativity. I charge my batteries by allowing a lot of silence; I am not tolerant of superficial encounters. Silence and nature are providing source-energy for me. So do talks with people, books, music. I have the luxury of spending a lot of time by myself. I indulge in silence and solitude. Many people never experience or choose this luxury.

AARON STERN

Creativity is paramount in my life, and my relationships to others serve my creative inspiration. But when those relationships interfere, I leave them for my work—I end them for my work; I sacrifice them. I have to move with my calling so that I don't betray the muses. I have always followed a deep intuition. When you do so, you leave people and companions behind. But then, all the forces of the universe come in and support you; in that way you are not alone. Making that choice again and again, we might be alone. But if we don't live an authentic life, we begin to die already while we are still alive.

I care not a lot about the audience. I am much more interested in the work and the question: Do I mean this note or not? Is this music actually in congruence with or informed by the original feeling and discovery? My community is with my work. The work itself is my main question and concern. All the rest is secondary for me.

ANYA ACHTENBERG

The reader of my books—do I think about my readers as I write? I try not to think about them. When I really trust, my work reaches people.

I come from a home where I was smacked around. I grew up not being supported or seen. Culture, language, economics are a challenge in my life. I could be easily dismissed and devoured by feedback. If I am reading critiques about what and how my writing is supposed to be, it's like drinking rat poison. Community can hurt. Community can be bloody.

On the other hand, I am so much with people. I teach and do workshops. I work with youth at risk and others who live a crazy life. I am utterly present and drink them in; they live inside me. I love them and ache with them. I too grew up in chaos and insecurity. I have compassion.

I trust myself. Not in a lot of practical ways like resting enough or cleaning my house and such things, but give me that room full of kids who are lost, and I will be on the ground with them—I understand them. And that is art; that's living a life as art. I feed them, and me, with art.

That makes me trust what I know about life and how I live it. Writing is going it alone. The same with my trips to Cuba—I go alone, and I am so welcome there. I have my community there, and it makes me very happy and alive.

I need to have community. I love to share art with others, laugh and talk with others, exchange ideas. But writing—you can lock me in a cellar. It might be better if I came out and let others react to my writing. But I write alone, because I am not alone when I am writing. I have visitors around me: ancestors, spirits, guides.

I never had a relationship that was truly supportive for my life and art. Sometimes I am just sad, and then I feel loneliness and abandonment, and suffer this cold Minnesota winter. I believe that some things inside me are not as healthy as my creativity. In my creativity, I am a lioness.

Elias Rivera

Do I think about the viewer when I work? Yes, but only when I work on a commission. Otherwise, I totally follow my own inner guidance. When I paint, I am transported to a different place.

When I was young, we had a lively community with inspiring and supportive people around us. Community is important for me. Here in Santa Fe, we are all surrounded by friends and artists. This town is a place of inspiration and community. We care for each other.

And what about the business of art? Sue, my wife, is incredible, a trouper. If I had her not on my side, I would be dead. She is incredible. She loves me a lot. Aside from that, she is a very smart and no-nonsense person. And she is a big pain in the rear too.

My parents only supported me when they thought I could go into commercial art and make money. We lived a very social life. We had the most wonderful Latin music and food. We danced. My mother was from a family of twelve, from Puerto Rico—that's community. We had wonderful parties. But my mother had no concept of art, no reference for that in her background. My father was a carpenter. His biggest curse was that he fell in love with my mother.

He was such a sweet, sweet man with a big, big heart. He looked like Charlie Chaplin, was really short. He was encouraging, and he always said to me, "Keep up your art."

Yael Weiss

The audience is both for me: It means everything and it means nothing. Because, for example, if I play a concert somewhere, I am asked what repertoire I want to play. In my choices, I consider who is going to listen to me, in the same way as you write and consider the reader. And that also includes the place: Where do I play? If I play in a place where people hardly hear any classical music, I am not going to schedule a program of lengthy and more complicated music. However, I will include something adventurous. In that sense, it is important to consider the audience.

One of the main reasons performers are nervous when they perform is that they feel their separateness from the audience. They feel that they will be judged; they think the audience is going to critique them. Many times, younger performers get incredibly nervous when they walk on stage. I try to help them to realize that the audience wants them to be successful. Younger people sometimes don't see that people are there to share an actual experience—that without the listener, the piece cannot actually exist. If nobody is listening to it, it will be meaningless. The triangle of composer, audience, and performer is needed to create the musical experience. When I am performing, I feel how the audience is participating; I sense whether they are interested and attentive. My lifelong experience guides me. The more attentive the audience is, the more connected we are in the triangle. So the audience is a key element to the performance.

At the same time, it is generally not a good idea to be focused on the listener or on a particular individual or be concerned about them. In that sense, I see the audience as not so important. The glory of the music itself is the focus.

UWE WALTER-NAKAJIMA

I like to be by myself. I have so many ideas and create often in solitude, like when I am composing music or writing my stories. I walk alone in the mountains, but I also get inspired by people. I am a group person, I believe. I long for the others, for people of similar philosophy, people who are not afraid to open their hearts and create something real on the spot. I look for comrade musicians and performers. Maybe I will find some here as I perform and travel in America.

When I was young, we toured with a circus tent, and in winter we lived in a farmhouse. Twelve people living, working, and performing together—that was real community. There were many tensions, and it was not easy. There was much hidden jealousy. When I think back, I believe that it was not only the sound of the shakuhachi that moved me to go to Japan—it was also an urge to take on responsibility. I wanted to become a real adult, a man.

When I came to Japan, many of the Japanese artists were married. That was not an easy life. The men created art and the women worked in jobs and looked after the kids—this was difficult. Giving birth to a child is the ultimate creativity, I think. Many of the artists are not married because they are eager to give birth to their art.

I fell in love with a Japanese lady and wanted to get married. For that to happen, I had to prove that I could take care of a family, so I gave up music and took a job in a company to earn a regular income. I really wanted kids and to have a family. I worked in the company in order to convince her father that I was a reliable person. Today, I am glad about all of that. I married and we raised three boys. I did a lot of hard work for the family. During rehearsal, I fell off the tightrope, which caused a fissure in my vertebra, and I burned myself during a fire dance. But you see my kids are healthy and strong. They grew up in a natural environment, with the philosophy of self-reliance: If you are hungry, bake bread; if you are cold, chop wood, all that. You can study the arts or science or so. If you have a dream, act on it.

It's so fun to be with my kids, to talk to them and have a whole family gathering! One of them is on a pilgrimage to Santa Maria de Compostela. He wants to get away from his strong parents to find himself. I think that's great. Another studies astrophysics.

I believe that art based on the realities of life is healthy art. Having the feet on the ground, getting inspiration from that ground—that's art emerging from the life you live, from the joy of harvesting! I mean real fruit. It's a great joy to harvest red rice. I expressed this experience in a song. And it is also a great joy to be with a child and chant or sing a lullaby; this is the art of living with delight, with music. An active family is its own community.

TIM GOSNELL

Yes, the receiver of your creation has to be considered, because scientists have customers, donors, funding agencies, and you have to be attentive to their needs, ideas, and interests. There are people who don't have to worry about that, the superstars of science. I was lucky; I had an 89 percent success rate for the financing of projects. I can write really well and can present my ideas in out-of-the-box language that fills them with excitement. That's the inspirational fun part, when you are preparing a proposal. Then comes the hard work, when they give you the money and you have to make it succeed.

I am not so interested in the personal achievement part of science—I am a team worker. The community that builds around science means something to me. My goal now, as I am growing older, is about living well and letting go of great ambitions, waking up every morning and looking forward to joining my colleagues in research and invention. I want to enjoy spending time with my friends, my wife, cooking. I want to be doing so many things now which I did not do when young because I was so busy getting an education. I was making $10,000 a year until I was twenty-nine years old. I left graduate school with three hundred bucks in my account.

My purpose, if I have to design one, is to be as free as I can be. I don't have an ambition to be a philanthropist or to fix the world. I want to deposit my creative abilities in a container that doesn't push back so much as the working world does in our institutions. Scientists are people of community; the work is too specialized to be done as solo pursuit.

JERRY WENNSTROM

I prefer solitude during creative work. I feel I can communicate more clearly with the gods and allow the spirit of the time to come through when I am alone. There is always some level of self-consciousness that comes into play when the eyes of the world are upon us. When I am alone, I can disappear from myself. I can take seemingly "crazy" risks and feel clear about the rightness of an inspiration, which allows some deeper meaning to coalesce and reveal itself to me. I can also feel out how the world might respond to a creation without actually having anyone there responding or reacting. Then, when a piece is ready to enter the world, I can feel free of it and free from others' reactions, good or bad. At best, I become Nothing and no longer exist. There is also a whole lot of grunt work involved, and whether I fail or succeed, I have no one to look to but myself.

And when I work in a team, I generally find myself taking care of people and not taking what is being done really seriously. There are two fronts I am tracking when I work with others. Perhaps there is a bit of, "Let not the left hand know what the right hand is doing" involved. At one level, I give as much as I can to tending the needs of others while at the same time I attempt to listen to the deeper whispers of the gods. Sometimes the scream of the world drowns out those whispers and the creation suffers or is simply reduced to a non-event. And it is all creations I speak of here, whether it is a creative conversation or a work of art. It is all the same— it all requires tapping into some level of inspiration.

However grandiose this may sound, I think as an artist, I have always set out to change the world through art. I believe art has always done that, and as an artist, I didn't want to settle for anything less. I guess it remains to be seen if my life's work actually changes the world or not. It all may turn out to be a big illusion on my part.

VIJALI HAMILTON

I didn't create community with my art projects until I started the World Wheel work. In my environmental art, yes, there are many people involved, and that is part of the purpose for this work: to create community based on a peace project. Before that, I was alone in my studio.

Before the work out there around the globe, I was a shy loner. It was a breakthrough when I stepped out into the world. I wonder why I was called to do this kind of work. Somebody who is not shy but dynamic might do a better job, but that's just how my calling goes, that makes me laugh with glee.

A donor gave me a piece of land out there in the Galisteo Basin south of Santa Fe in the desert. We built a hogan there for sacred ceremonies, for art and retreat. We meet every Sunday in a meditation circle for prayers for peace. Those things happen all the time in my life: There's always support in the right moment, generous support.

You see, I love stone. Stone is the most basic matter. And to penetrate into that is like an opening of spirit. That's my basic philosophy: the integration of the world, the darkness, and the spirit. I travel around the world and build peace sculptures out of the stone I find on community land, and then I involve the whole village in the project. The doing of art creates natural bonds. To do this work in community is deeply meaningful. The effect goes beyond the usage of language—it is soul work.

Amanda McPhail and Wesley West

Amanda: The nature of my ceramic work lends itself more to individual and solitary work, but I like to teach others; that's a special talent and interest I have. That's what attracts me to groups, the teaching part. If I have a new idea, I get a pile of paper and I draw and draw and use up every idea until it sparks. For every finished drawing, there are at least forty or fifty that went into the bin. In my technique of hand-drawn pictures on ceramic, you can't do it slowly; it has to be flowing and quick and it needs freedom of expression. When I did book illustrations, that was different because I was constrained to what the publisher and author wanted.

Wes: I have most of my life been working in teams. And if you've got the right group of people together, it all goes much more easily because there are always gaps in skills and in the path from your mind to your hands, and that shows up if there's only one of you. A group can correct that easily.

I like working with others, and, I tell you, I like working with young people; they have a younger mind. And they are strong and can carry things around. I remember Roger Law, who ran a big art organization. He said that within two weeks, the young students had learned everything he knew, and in three weeks, they were beating him. They were like sponges, always asking questions. The power of the group inspired and propelled everybody.

SARA WARBER

Solitary or community? I say yes to both, but primarily I work solitary, holding the space for that really creative aha! moment. Theater work is always community work, and I loved that very much—that was a wonderful time in my life.

Also, work in research is always done in community. It involves others, and I enjoy the interchange and how we build on each other's ideas. Talking about projects with colleagues generates energy and ideas, and then I can go back into that solitary place. I swing back and forth—both styles generate rewarding outcomes.

RUTH BAMFORD

My first community is my family. It's the smallest unit but most important for me, and then my colleagues in the field of science. Bob and Max think like I do—we understand each other. I want to be understood—that's a typical southern English trait: We call a spade a spade. I am a rule breaker. If you are a scientist, that's what you do. That's your work, to question the already-existing. Never accept anything because an authority says so. I like the community of scientists because I like talking with people and exchanging ideas. It's much more productive to be sharing with others than mulling over one's personal ideas in a solitary way.

And yes, I think about the recipient of my work, especially my children, who are twelve and ten. My daughter has her own alert perceptions and can very quickly follow what I am saying. So I know that her mind works in the same way as mine. What I appreciate in her is that she will not be alone with what I throw at her. She is very creative and often thinks differently than others. She calls our house rabbit a cabbit, because the rabbit thinks he is a cat. Our son loves to have fun with whatever he does. He is my audience, and he is having fun when we work on something together, play and spin thoughts and toss mind games.

I like the community of family and the community of scientists, because I love the challenge of the other's mind in exchange with mine.

Peggy O'Kelly

I work and function best as an individual—I have not done a lot in teams. I place myself between the two. I do well in teams, but I need to be the leader, the decision- maker.

My energy drops if I am alone for too long, but I also need silence and solitude. There are needs in both directions, solitary and community. My audience is my customers; they are my commitment and my focus. It's serious. I am devoted to them, and they respond to me in similar ways. That's a form of community, and it works well for both parties.

Chrissie Orr

This was the beginning of my artistic path when I used the creative process and my creativity in a different and more connected way—away from the art college and the gallery and the art market. It was the way the arts should work, I thought. It was more than creating an object of art. I was actually using that spirit of creativity as they did in tribal societies—that's what art is about. It needs to have a function inside the community to tell the story, to hold the story, to hold the culture. It's taken me many years to do that, and it's still what I am doing today. This weaves like a thread through my whole life: art in community.

It's taken many different forms, and I tried to give it up, but I stuck with it and basically gave up any kind of solitary work in the studio. And today, it has shifted so that my work straddles a bit of both sides—because I feel now that you really need that, you need that reflection time in the quiet. I can't do the community work all the time like when I was younger and got going all the time. That had a sense of urgency and drove us to be activists. I learned a lot on my feet. But it took several years for me to look back and reflect on that activist work.

We were in community to build relationships through the arts and the creative process. In the school for the deaf here in Santa Fe, I remember, it happened very fast because there was physical closeness. The children came and explored my face, touched to get to know the body and the person. They made connection—it was an incredible experience for me. Their handicap allowed intimacy. It opened me up to another level of relationship.

You have to be pretty centered in yourself to be able to work with other people in a really authentic way. Otherwise, you get thrown out of balance; it is challenging. I have always worked on myself, and I am not perfect. I have a lot more to do.

It rips me open to hear people's stories as I work with them. And I think this being ripped open is necessary when you work with community. This collaboration opens me up to know things I would not have come up with all by myself, or by being in communities where I would normally not be involved—it's a challenge. And that challenge is what I am looking for. I want to be able to create. It's like a blank canvas or wall in front of you. "What do you put up there? How do you get started?" You can just wildly put some color on it to start, just to get rid of the white, and then you see what emerges. That's how I work in community: They put their mark on the white canvas, and however those marks inspire, we glean out a way for the process.

Yes, I do individual work too. I draw a lot; I write a lot; I am an avid journal keeper. I have shelves and shelves full of them. But the work that is out there in the world, the work I am recognized for, is the work created in community. It's social justice practice. We work in all media. But much of it is mural work. I have my skill base, but I am always willing to learn and might drag somebody in who uses different media. The choice of media comes from the community. I might have an idea and then I realize that's not the best way to go. We find out together what's the best expression to tell the story of that specific community.

THEODORA CAPALDO

Am I a team worker or do it all by myself?
All by myself! But I am also a team worker.

This is how it works for me: As a first move, I need to do my own solitary work and shut everything else off. Then I am at my best. After that, I can go back and forth with a team for input and changes. Remember, I am an only child; I don't have childhood experiences of negotiating with groups or siblings.

I learn from animals and children; they trigger creativity and joy. They are a major part of my community. So here's the answer, simple and even coming close to truth: watching animals. They have a capacity for joy and live it in community. That is pretty stunning. The joy of being patted, of chasing the ball, of running around in circles, tail is happy, ears are flapping in the wind, and then coming over for a hug or kiss. I think human beings have a similar need and capacity for joy and play, and fewer places in a civilized world to express it. I think the creative act becomes a joyful place. But if I start running around in my office to express the joy, the board of directors would be concerned. Animals and children can express their joy in unselfconscious ways. We grown-ups have constraints and rules around why and how we can express joy.

And so I think that the creative act is a socially accepted way of manifesting our aliveness and joy and need for community. Creativity is wild—paint and words may fly all over the place. That can be frightening. When expressed on a page, it seems safe because there is the restriction of the boundaries. I often take animals as teachers; I watch them! My dog Keebo wants to live and be joyful and finds many ways to express his aliveness without any hesitation.

Chapter Nine. Money and Creativity

*I don't have a talent to deal with money. It's my Achilles heel.
I know many artists are in my place.*
—Elias Rivera

The Maker and the Taker

This tapestry is a celebration of color and texture, applied by an artist of wild and unlimited imagination. Hundreds of different objects are lovingly arranged and stitched to the background fabric: metal, lace, jewelry, feathers, leather—simple objects of daily use as they take on new associations. I am delighted and also aware that there is something erotic and seductive in the flirtation between the perceiver of art and the object of the art. I am aroused as I am standing in front of this colorful tapestry in Le Grand Renc'Art Gallery in Sorèze in southern France.

This is one of those "dangerous" moments when I get caught in the brilliant net of art, hypnotized by its beauty and charm. My body feels heat; the palms of my hands tingle. I lift my shoulders. I want to reach out and move toward the piece, embrace it with all my senses as it triggers the first inkling of falling in love with the piece and the maker. I feel physically attracted, and I am glowing with delight. And there is naked desire: I want it!

Oh, but there's also a grown-up and rational person inside me who walks over to the piece and looks at the price: Can I afford it? This encounter with art-desire triggers my creative self: "Yes, I can." But frugality resists, arguing, "I am not a spender. I like my life—and my walls—unburdened from responsibility for precious things." But art is not "things," I tell myself; it's alive, has soul and a personality. Art is a breath of spirit turned into a physical object. Desire hits me in my heart and stomach. My craving melts rationality, and I regress into a greedy child caught in wanting. This child inside insists, "I want that piece. I lust for it; it was made for me."

How is money related to art? How is my own relationship with money related when I create or desire art? I am semi-retired and have limited means but enough to indulge from time to time in a spontaneous gift of art to myself. After this first sparkling encounter, a fire has been kindled inside.

I go home and find all kind of information about the artist on the internet. Her name is Christine Fayon. From what I read and see, I like her joyful attitude about creativity, her creatively chaotic studio. The picture of her as she is embracing her aging mother is "like me and my daughter," I think. Becoming familiar with the artist increases my longing for the piece she created. I realize that knowledge of the artist intensifies my enchantment with her art.

I fall into an inner discussion. My rational mind resists and needs to be consoled. Art seems to be luxury; it's the thing one gets when other necessities are taken care of, like a new water heater or winter coat. It's embarrassing to admit, but that's how I manage my desires: I need to justify the indulgence of spending on luxury. Art is necessary luxury. It is soul-sustaining luxury.

Next day, I am back in the gallery. I scurry around and weigh all the pros and cons. I remember my own art and recall the experience of being its maker as well as being the receiver experiencing the buyer's delight and joy. I never planned to earn the major part of my living as an artist. I despise the anxiety of waiting for the approval of a viewer, being hurt when rejected and ecstatic when a piece is sold. There's something "obscene" when a love affair like art-making has to be urgently promoted and used for necessities, like paying the mortgage. I am aware that this is an entitled point of view, but it's so often the harsh reality for artists. I allow myself to make art for the pure fun and excitement of it, and I celebrate every artist who is able to combine the need for income with the passion for creation. My experience confirms the belief that money and income and art are in constant battle and bewilderment. I do not understand it because, as a counselor, I also offer my work as an expression of creativity and love, but I am not hesitant to charge money for my effort and time. If this sounds confused, it mirrors what I feel.

After returning twice to the gallery to connect even more deeply with the tapestry, I use a trick to convince myself that I can afford the object of my desire. Some time ago, I had received a substantial check from a gallery in Santa Fe for a ceramic relief that was sold there. I was delighted, and I cashed the unexpected check in hundred-dollar bills, put the money in an envelope, and stuck it in my safe with the intention of using it for a special occasion. I wrote on the little package: "For a special occasion."

Now this special occasion has shown up in my life, and I say yes! I will gladly invest the income from my art into the art of another creator—that elicits great joy and meaning! Money spent on art connects two artists across continents. It weaves a sisterhood of creators and spreads delight in even measure to the maker and the taker.

The tapestry is now part of my home, placed on a white adobe wall. A skylight allows the bright New Mexico sun to splash over it and bring its colors to vibrant life. I often turn my head as I walk by, showered with delight.

All things considered, in most matters of art, it is more nourishing to be a maker than a viewer.
—David Bayles, Ted Orland, *Art & Fear*

The money and the arts are two different worlds.
—Chrissie Orr

Money and Creativity: The Interviews

ESTHER MARION

When I was a teenager, I studied flamenco in Spain. I would have loved to stay in that country, but when I was young, I was very shy and modest. I should have asked for more support from my father to pay for my education, but I was too humble. I lacked the courage to speak up and be firm about that. But, I was also proud and wanted to prove that I could make it on my own.

Today, flamenco is for me a source of money in some small but steady ways. It's very satisfying and joyful for me to dance and sing for people; they have a delightful evening, and I get my pay and go to buy food for the family. That's down-to-earth living, with a balance between giving and receiving—that way art feeds real life.

I work in the healing arts—I am a massage therapist. I put my hands on people and help them to feel well. That is devotional work. To serve like that is for me a state of mind and I call that creative work.

I know that the area of our work defines us. But I am not so involved in the question how the world sees me. Opinions of people don't dampen my devotion to the art of dance or healing; there's so much satisfaction and joy in those activities.

I believe in the power of place. Where I am live now, in Seattle, in the northwest U.S., my art form is solitary and not a lively part of this culture. I am here because my children and my husband have better chances; as a family you have to yield to the needs of the whole. You can make that work. When my children are grown, I would like to travel again, from community to community, work and create, like we did that in Australia for a whole year. I am deeply interested in community in all its forms and in different places around the globe.

In Seattle, we live near our friends, like an extended family. Most of them are artists and for all of us it's not easy to make a living, but we love our lives and the inspiration that comes through artistic activities. Our children are held by this community and very much supported in their exploration of creativity. I feel so proud and fulfilled by the way we honor the sacredness of the performing and healing arts and live them in our daily life. I feel blessed and don't worry too much about survival, because the arts I practice fill me with prayer and purpose. My husband worries more than I about practical and monetary issues. I think that any new challenge that we have to face will also bring new skills and blessings. I am much more concerned about our Earth right now than about finances. I wake up and feel pain about the Mother, our Earth. It hits me in the middle of the night, with heavy worries and sadness about this globe. In our family, there's ongoing communication about that. We are walking around with open ears and eyes, and we are alarmed, we suffer with our earth and often our art expresses those concerns.

MICHAEL BROOME

Money has never been a big issue for me. I was born in England, in Norfolk. We lived in Leicestershire after the war. I went to school in Leicester and later to Leicester College of Art. I left school very early, when I was fourteen. My father was an engineer, and he translated my painting skills into my becoming a draftsman. But the job I got at the end was to be an apprentice to a watchmaker, where I learned real hands-on skills. I served as a watchmaker for five years after school, until I decided to go to college. And since a friend of mine was a photographer, I thought this was a good choice. So I went to night school and met this instructor who said to me "You've really got talent. You should go to college to learn and hone your skills."

So that's what I did. I quit my job and went to college. I had his recommendation, and that helped me get in. This teacher not only got me into college, he also got me a full grant, which was very important, since I come from a poor family. I thought, wow!

you can even get paid for doing what you love to do and learning at the same time! I really enjoyed that. I graduated, I think it was in 1966, and became a professional photographer in London for about ten years, doing freelance work for magazines. That was a very lucrative thing at that time, as it was a very open field with lots of new magazines and not many photographers.

Working in that field, I met a lot of modern artists. I liked the atmosphere of the art world; loved the exploration of it all. And then we had this group coming over from America, called the Symposium of Destructive Arts. It was a trend in the arts at that time: trying to be anti-art. You see, art is about making objects, and members of this group despised the idea of the final object that then would be exploited in the art market, would be sold and re-sold, like in the stock market. This group wanted to make art that never got that far, that destructed itself before it turned into an object of the market place. And one of these people coming over was Yoko Ono, as she was part of this movement.

I have always been interested in art and the people who make it. And it provided a good living for me. I slipped into the whole modern culture and I am familiar with all the arguments and discussions about abstract art.

During a trip to America I went to Santa Barbara and met my old friend Patty, who said, "Look, I am tired of living here on the West Coast. I want to move. I want to get out of the city and do something new." She had lived on a Greek island before. "I want to start a retreat center on a beautiful piece of land. Do you want to do it with me?"

I said, "I don't know about that, but I will just come with you and live at the bottom of the garden and find out if I want to get involved." That's when we came here, to Ocamora, in New Mexico, and founded this retreat place. It was 1980.

I had a colorful travel history. I'd left London in 1971, then lived in Wales, and for some time with Karen in Vence, in France. It was time to settle. So, that's my story. In 1981 Patty and I came and settled here, and the rest is history. She bought this land and I got involved; I own half of it. In the course of this development, I sold one house back to her, I needed something that made money, but a retreat center does not. I needed some real money so that I could buy an investment that did. So, I own now some office buildings in Las Vegas New Mexico, an hour from here, they bring regular income.

Do I place my work into galleries for sale?

No! I hate galleries. They take too much money and are a disgrace to the artist's world. During the impressionists' time, they took only twenty percent, but now they take fifty. The effort of making or selling is different; I don't want to be part of that. And I don't have to. My katsinas sold very well last year. I continued to make them because they are most interesting as a large group, where they have more impact. People have used them to have conversation with spirit, as they see them as what they are: little deities.

I don't sell my art very easily. I make it difficult to buy a piece, because I don't need to—it's not my livelihood. I am independent. Making art to have a livelihood would be dangerous; it distorts the picture and the artist. If you get paid, you might make things that you did not want to originally. My friend the potter used to do all sorts of pottery. And then he invented what he called a pebble pot, and they sold like crazy. These pots walked out of his shop, and that got him in a squeeze: he realized that if he didn't make them, he didn't make much money. He was caught by his own product. He didn't really want to make the pebble pots any more, but they sold so well and brought him a good income. He was locked into his success. That's a sad story. But it happens a lot when art meets commerce.

Entrepreneurship and creativity are soul-mates. Learning to establish financial security is extremely important for us creators.
—Carole Watanabe

Tony Juniper

It's not lucrative being an activist and environmentalist. The reward comes from the doing of serious work and at the same time getting paid something. What's the allocation between earning an income and making the difference I want to make on this globe? I have been in the amazing position during the last five years, when I stopped having a salaried job, that I have been able to do just that: make a difference. I have been extremely fortunate in working with Cambridge University and some of the companies I have attracted. I am doing exactly what I am meant to do, and I am getting paid as well. Since I receive income from that, I can be generous, and I can do a variety of other things that don't pay much at all. Some of the conservation groups are charities, and they struggle financially.

There's quite a creative challenge in being able to match what needs to be done with the practical sense of survival. It's a tightrope-walk keeping this going. Unlike some people in this area of work, I did not come from a privileged background. I have actually quite a unique position between some of the high-profile environmentalists in the U.K. Many of them come from the elite and from aristocracy, and that's not me. But I would not want to do anything else even if it's well paid. I love my work.

Carole Watanabe

When I got out of art school—the California College of the Arts in Oakland and San Francisco—I left the city to live in a wildlife preserve. There was some hesitation in my parents about my attending art school because we did not have much money and art school is very expensive. We were not able to afford that. But then, Mrs. Roselle, our neighbor and a dress buyer, died about that time and left her house and car and all her amazing outfits to my sister and me. I said to my dad, "That's for my sister and me, and it's not your money. I will use it to go to art school." And so I did.

Then I got a scholarship to get my master's degree. By then, I had discovered this nature preserve in California. We were in a pilot program, fifteen students picked from our school to do this program in the wilderness involving us in art and ecology as a course of study. It was suggested that all the incoming students would be taken out into the wilderness, getting to know each other before we went to college together. It was a great idea that emerged out of a small college with about four hundred students.

I fell in love with the wild life and wanted to live there. I got married to a painter, and we moved there right after school. I did not get my master's, said no because I would rather be out there in the wilderness. I was a weaver at that time, so I taught the women in that valley how to spin yarn and dye it with plant dyes. A lot of apprentices came from a nearby festival. They had heard about us and would just show up.

I was in my garden in the nude, planting, and there was this woman coming up the hill in her little Volkswagen with all she owned tied on top of it, and said, "You told me I could learn how to weave if I came to you to visit, so here I am." She was one of my first apprentices. Then more people would come, just show up at my place, so I trained a lot of people and they ended up buying land around us, and now there is a community of weavers there. My first husband still lives in that community.

I had a two-year-old son. I grew tired of growing everything myself, making my own yogurt, baking all my bread. It was survival out there. This was about 1968, and I was the bona fide hippie out in the wilderness, where we were building our own house and growing our own food.

After six years in the wilderness, I left, wanting to move into the city and develop my art career. I moved to San Francisco, where I had already established connections to sellers for my weavings. I was weaving these beautiful pillows and shawls, large, for couches, and they were being sold at design houses. They introduced me to different design centers. One was called the Ice

House at that time, owned by Henry Adams. He was building a huge, brand new design center. Henry's wife, Claire Ellen, was a weaver and knew my work and me. I told her that I wanted to open the first tapestry gallery, because there was not such a thing at that time anywhere in the United States that offered tapestry on a big scale, for corporations.

They built a big glass atrium with a huge glass roof, which had balconies all around with glass elevators. They had all those empty walls, and Claire Ellen suggested, "We could use your skills to create huge tapestries for those big brick walls for the showroom." I had been looking for gallery space, and it was very expensive. But I was an artist with a young child and had no money to invest. So they created this wonderful contract with me by which I would pay a percentage of what I sold, and if I didn't make income, I would not have to pay any rent. But I was also doing a service for their building through my art. It was perfect, and everyone was satisfied.

I rented a big five-thousand-square-foot place in a design house near there and hired people to work for me. This was a new thing, tapestry weaving, and I also created smaller pieces, maybe ten to fifteen of those, in my showroom. And then I had these monumental works, 10x20x12 feet. I created them in my garage. And I also sold the pieces made by friends from art school.

During market week in San Francisco, I could not believe it—there were people ordering ten and twenty pieces for their showrooms in New York! I was saying that I needed six to eight weeks for delivery. On the second day, I panicked, thinking, "Oh my god, no way I could deliver all that."

After hiring a bunch of weavers, I realized that I really had to do business here. I could not disappoint all those buyers waiting for the pieces. I think I got close to $100,000 worth of orders for tapestry during that week. It was just phenomenal, after living close to starving for six years out in the woods. My dad came and helped me build a workshop in my garage, a studio space, and I hired other weavers and learned this kind of "dive-and-swim" way of working.

I think I am a survivor. Things work out for me.

I had a really solid mother who was an accountant. She was brilliant and taught me about money. My dad was a machinist and an inventor who had a regular job. My mom was very frugal. She would store money away and buy little houses. As a child, I remember that I helped paint many houses and get them ready for winter. When my mom died at the age of seventy, she owned eleven houses in San Diego.

She was very practical and advised me, saying, "As an artist, you will not have a paycheck. You have to save money and invest in real estate. That will be the only way, when you are older, to have any money to live on. Prepare yourself from the get-go."

I followed her advice, and if I needed any down payment, she would lend me the money and I would pay her back. When I left my wildlife preserve, I bought a little house in San Francisco. My son and I would live there when I got my business going in the design center. At that time, there was a Western Women's Bank. They loved giving me a loan because I was this young woman who started a new business. So I bought a house, and recently gave it to my son, just as my mother would have done. I thank my mother for teaching me like that. She always encouraged me to do what I wanted. I grew up with her ongoing support. She believed in me: "I am sure you will pull this off," she said. And I always did.

CATHY ATEN

Being an artist all my life has led to a very precarious existence. I am not a team player. I live and have survived solo as an artist—that's not very secure. But I am very comfortable with insecurity, with my life's circumstances not being predictable.

I am not afraid, because I have faced a lot of darkness in my life. I am a survivor.

I was blessed to have a father who was brilliant. Despite his alcoholism, he had a high-powered job as an industrial designer. He taught me how to use power tools and work in his workshop—he never stopped me. I got a degree as a textile designer, following in his footsteps. I have been an artist as long as I can remember, involved in the art world for more than thirty-two years. I learned that in order to make a living as an artist, you work with the commerce of art, with a gallery, and then you get pressured to do more of what is successful. It's a scary thing not to have a paycheck come every two weeks. Many artists fall into the trap of doing just that: adjusting to what sells. I never could do that. I had to follow where I was called to go. New things and ideas came up, and I wanted to explore. As I learned to get out of the way, I also learned to build trust.

Aaron Stern

When I met Leonard Bernstein, I already had the idea of this visionary school. When I left China and came back to the United States, I had a name for it: the New American School. Meaning, like the Baja School, a wave, a new style of education. And then Bernstein came up with a new name, and that was in 1986. He called me in the middle of the night and said, "I have the name for our thing," as he called it. "It will be the Academy for the Love of Learning." It was my project—he just believed in it, supported it 100 percent, and spent a lot of time with me to make it real.

There were times when I just could not figure out what to do next. I spent much time writing about it and imagining it, dreaming it. There was more dreaming and imagining than real trial and error. As I moved into the articulation and experimentation, I would write him these proposals, articles, and notes, and I would say, "Come on, you are the guy who writes all those beautiful melodies—can't you just write this section for me?" And he said, "I can't; it's coming out of you. I am your beloved editor. You write and I edit." And I still have all these printouts. He did not know how to use a computer, so I printed it out and he would slash and cross out and rip. This was all part of the process to turn a vision into reality.

But then, in 1990, Bernstein died. The academy did not exist then. And so far, it had been just me functioning as the academy. I would go to institutions and create programs and implement examples of what is now the basic work here. I tested it in different places. When he died in 1990, I didn't know what to do. I was lost and confused and went into depression. It was my forty-years-in-the-desert, a horrendous challenge. And I kept experimenting and believing—like when you write a piece of music, you know that you have something in there that will carry the whole piece. You believe it, and you know and feel it. And it's the same thing with this place: I saw it during its gestation and birth, and I knew I had to build it. I had to carry it through. And I gathered people around me who believed in me and knew my heart and my intention and supported me, also financially through donations. But the first support I got for this project was from Lenny Bernstein. And when he died, I was the only person he dedicated some money to, beside his kids. And it was not huge—$100,000—but it meant a lot for this project and for me personally. As long as he was alive, he supported me with $60,000 to $80,000 a year to do my work. We were always totally a team.

ANYA ACHTENBERG

My misery right now is that I spend a lot of my energy and time in survival mode. I work for other people, edit their books, and I don't translate my own energy into the fierceness that I have for others' success. Survival has become an essential issue for me. I don't want to teach English as a foreign language. I want to write. On the other hand, I need a firm income. I also want to travel. I am fascinated by foreign places. I have to battle the idea of myself as deprived by life.

When I was a young kid, I was literally held in captivity. Today, I am compelled to go out dancing and hear music and be with community. Most of us creative people have our own battles as we struggle to do the creative things. When I take the time not to worry, when I create freely, I do fabulously. Otherwise, the money concern sits always in my neck. That eats some of my creativity and life-energy.

Elias Rivera

I have a brownstone in New York and rent it—that brings me some income. I don't manage money well, so I got us into trouble. It's my style. I never had children, so I did not need to plan a serious budget. I feel regret because I got us into a real pickle with this house. We have three buildings: the house, Sue's studio, and my studio, but it's all one debt. I had this project, an immense painting that had four panels. It was forty feet long, and I needed a big workspace for it. So I created this fabulous studio. And as I had hoped, I sold the painting, and it was a major deal for me.

Money, survival—these are topics that really depress me. Depression is the backside of anger. I am angry that I am still in this position of lack. I know that I am a very gifted artist, but I am struggling. I want God to know that I am here to serve spirit. Let me be, God, let me do my thing! I have a passion to give and contribute. I am still learning and searching and wanting to know and express the truth, and the lack of money cuts off my enthusiasm and burdens me. Sue gets very angry with me because I am responsible for the situation we are in. It depresses me. It is what it is. I don't have the talent to deal with money. It's my Achilles heel. I know that many artists are in my place. I need to keep my innate sense of hope. I am basically an optimist, but I also harbor a huge dark side. I need to watch myself. If I am not mindful, I would be self-destructing! I want instead to plug into constructive energy.

This world is so crass. We don't need art that has been cranked out; art has a higher purpose. Yes, I have to make money, but there is something else we artists are serving through our creativity. I never forget the spiritual foundation of art. It's what all the great artists have: It's being in tune with God. For me, the delicious part of my relationship with my art is that I know where it is coming from. And because I know that, I don't play around with that divine source. I have a sense of honoring that and not letting myself be used for lower purposes. My artistic life has always been focused on that. I never, ever, forget the divine source of my talent. I have reverence, and that is for me the most important trait. Without reverence, I could not do art.

That's the artist's struggle: to honor the divine source of creativity and to also live this ordinary life with all its demands and pressures. It's a giant task, and at times I am failing, which makes me sad.

YAEL WEISS

I actually don't think about money very much. As a musician, I don't need much—my piano and the piano bench. But I do have a little kid, so income is important. When I play a concert, it motivates me to know that I support myself and my family.

For me, money and music are not really related. Even as a kid, I never had to pay for piano lessons. I realize that's unusual, but in Israel, there's a program for gifted children. One can audition there and if accepted, study in the America-Israel Cultural Foundation. They supported my music studies, so my parents never had to pay for my lessons.

And then when I came to this country, I received scholarships. I was incredibly lucky. I started playing in concerts immediately after I graduated. I never made the connection to money, not even recognizing that creativity and money need to work together. I wanted to do the projects and play the repertoire that spoke most to me, and many times, there was just a small audience.

But recently I learned that my activities needed to be profitable. In this world, we are required to function financially. So I created podcasts, to stay connected with a following and to inspire young musicians. People made suggestions to make them more expensive and to create teaching materials for sale. If I find the right way to do it, I will create an online place where people can download those materials, gain knowledge, and feel supported. It's the world of commerce, and I am not yet used to it.

But you see, my students at Indiana University come to me with those questions. At the end of the year, they ask me about income and career choices.

Many music teachers avoid these questions, but I decided it was really important to find venues and means for musicians to make a living with their art. Most graduating musicians from top universities do not make their living through music. They do something with music but not the way they really would want to. They compromise. That is shocking.

Young students come to me and ask: "You are teaching here, and you might give me advice. Can I do this or that. . . ?" They struggle, and my heart goes out to them. We need really to be creative in this economic area, and we need to develop a more entrepreneurial spirit in the world of the arts so we find ways to live with music and not split the practice of music from the means of survival.

UWE WALTER-NAKAJIMA

It killed my creativity when I had a real job in television with a good income. That's so seductive. I made it through two years and survived emotionally by building armor and being less sensitive. It was horrible, not good for me, so I quit.

But I am not worried. I am never worried about survival. That's not part of me. I am blessed, and maybe I don't deserve it. I have no fear. I trust that I will always find ways to have some income! But commerce is not the solution for me. Money has little value, but food has value, firewood has value, a house has value. The real stuff of life has value for me.

TIM GOSNELL

Yes, money has to be considered, because scientists have customers, donors, funding agencies. You have to be attentive to their needs and ideas and interests. There are people who don't have to worry about that; those are the science superstars. I was lucky, had an 89 percent success rate for financing of projects. I can write really well, can present my ideas in out-of-the-box language. That's the inspirational fun part, when you are preparing a proposal. Then comes the hard work, when they give you the money and you have to be committed and make it a success.

JERRY WENNSTROM

What about money as part of my creative life? It just happens when it happens—it does its own thing, and I have learned not to worry. In 1979, I gave away all my possessions and artwork. And today, I trust, and it happens that I just got a $5,000 grant. It's perfectly timed. That's how I deal with money: I don't do it; I let it happen. It's something that I trust. If you do what you love to do and give your talents to life, there's an almost-divine efficiency happening.

I had a benefactor for years who was giving me $34,000 a year. I have gotten grants, but I have never applied for grants. When Parabola distributed the film about my life, I got money. Over the last ten years, I probably have been given close to $100,000. So it's something I don't really worry about. Of course, I don't deny that it is necessary.

How does that work with Marilyn, my wife? Does she share my attitude, or is there a tension between us two? No, there really isn't disagreement. It's interesting. I do well with formlessness, Marylyn is lost if she does not have an external source that directs her energy. So a job is important to her, but I would really feel restricted and restrained in a formal job. So there's no tension because she does what she loves to do. She needs form and structure. If she has too much time, she gets lost.

It sounds very primal of sorts, but it's really what my life is about: being with what is and not getting caught up in the seduction of spending. And it's surprising. Beside the simplicity, we live a very lavish life! We were just invited to a gala dinner, an exquisite eleven-course meal!

And we have traveled to Italy. You know, I am really just a bagman, but life is brilliantly good. It makes me laugh with glee and joy. I have nothing, and I feel an appreciation of things because I don't feel entitled. I don't need lavish living to feel fine. I can do with almost nothing.

To me, what makes me come alive is not the usual sex-and-money-thing but the Mystery. Sometimes, the magic appears in my life with abundance, like getting an unexpected check for $5,000 is magical. If I had to earn that, I would feel like a workhorse.

There is a great quote by Simone de Beauvoir: "I can't imagine a more profitable life than to be completely free and to defeat boredom and find inspiration in the emptiness. . . ."

Vijali Hamilton

I have certain principles, I have never been in debt, have never asked anybody for money because I think you would sell yourself to them. Even having a mortgage, you are in debt, and part of your soul is tied down. I always lived with whatever I have. Then there's not that pressure of finances or debt.

That simplicity is important so you can truly enjoy every moment without that burden—because you have not overextended yourself and so you don't have to worry.

But people are generous with me, let me stay in their cottage, support my vision.

Well, I have never done anything just for money. That's my choice. I do my art following what feels right at every moment. I feel always provided for. If I really offer my life to the universe as being a tool, the universe provides for me; that's the truth.

I actually never worry about money. Never! But I am a practical person. I watch my expenses and keep them always lower than what I have. I enjoy the challenge of how I am going to manage the money that I have, but I don't have anxiety about it. I'm not losing energy over it, even as I am getting older.

I trust and do the best I can.

If there is any renunciation about a spiritual life, it's to renounce worry.

At one point, I gave all my artwork away, and all my tools except the hammer and chisel. I needed a new start to dig deep into the mystery of creation.

I had the powerful and enlightening experience of seeing how we are all connected. After that, I closed my studio and started working outside in the environment. I had a show and gave my artwork away. People came in from the street and were shocked. They said, "Here's something wrong!"

I gave it all away, gave my tools to a friend who needed it. I gave my clothes away too, kept only what I needed and what fit into a small suitcase. I felt overwhelmed with too many details of life and wanted to create new work, so I created space. I longed for the joy of dancing, of stillness in chaos. I wanted to be playful and free and do a number of vital things because I had been so serious and focused. Now I live simple and open myself wide to inspiration.

Amanda McPhail and Wesley West

Wes: Yes, it's crucial to have an income from your creativity. You need to pay for a space and materials. It's so hard for young people today to have an art career. If you really want to live a creative life, it's so very tough.

Amanda: We have always been generous, even if sometimes we haven't had anything. Wes is so generous it's almost ridiculous. I am more careful because we have to pay the bills. And we had a family to raise and feed. Wes often even gives his work away.

I had actually a piece stolen from an exhibition, and I was so excited; it was a great compliment.

Sara Warber

Money is useful. Food and warmth and shelter are very necessary in our society to function and to create artwork. And money buys art and art supplies.

Art doesn't pay here in this country; it's not highly valued. My brother and sister-in-law are devoted and gifted artists, and they truly struggle at the edge of survival, but they don't stop doing their art. When young, I learned to be intensely creative out of need. Art is a response to what's needed.

Creativity is like food or like breathing; it's essential to make life vibrant and worth living. I think that art is seen as non-essential in our country, yet it is vital for our soul. Personal or collective, it's indispensible.

Ruth Bamford

Most people study, get a job, do well—there isn't necessarily any creativity in that. Others have a big view; they can see the patterns in society and in our culture. Creativity is the step into the unknown, the never-before result and outcome.

You are very unlikely to have money as a creative person. The value of many objects of creativity is shaky. Money is not really a motivating factor for creative endeavor. Science is nowadays a field of endeavor that is expected to produce a product that can be sold in three to five years from its invention.

Here's an example: Look at nuclear fusion; it can potentially solve many of humankind's political, economic, and societal problems. But it is put on such poor financial footing that it has taken ages to achieve practical and financial goals. Scientists are kept on tap but not on top. Many scientists are idealists. They believe that no one nation should be allowed the exclusive usage of the results of research because we are one humanity and all of us need to benefit from creative science.

Peggy O'Kelly

Money means to me a constant learning, not a battle but a dance. I have always been at odds with money. As soon as it starts flowing, I feel inspired to turn in a different direction, build something new. That's part of how I operate. I don't want to push the envelope; I want to bring it back and make it work with ease. I want peace around money. I want to relax and not chase it. I can't just let it sit there for security. I need to risk something and develop new possibilities. When I have an idea, I go for it, like this partnership with Morocco to get the natural ingredients for my products. I just made a connection with trade partners there. It's going to happen. I trust my intuition. I risk and change. That's exciting and creative. I am good at doing something with sparse resources to back me up, but it always works out at the end. There are frugal times in between, but I am not afraid.

That's how I can be encouraging to other women. They don't have money but they have good ideas and want to develop them. That's where I get involved and have a lot to give.

I come from a family where people did not know how to deal with money. My dad, a physician, did not care, and my mother did not understand how to manage it. I am still working on my own attitude about money. I want to be more creative around it.

Chrissie Orr

I don't connect money and creativity. A lot of the work I get paid for does not seem so creative to me. But I do a lot of work that I don't receive money for. Here at the Academy for the Love of Learning, that's the paying job that allows me to do and live the rest of my life. I think I always find a way to remain creative. Without that, I would fall apart. The demand to do other people's work is always a challenge for me, especially when working in institutions. I can't always do my own creative projects. That can be a challenge. I yearn to be my own creative self, doing the projects that I feel deeply motivated to do.

I don't know how to answer that question about money and its relationship to creativity. I think sometimes money would stymie me as an artist. If somebody comes and brings this great commission and sets conditions and timing, that can shut me down. The artist needs to be really conscious and watch out—and possibly just say, "No! I don't want to do it," because this outside pressure could take away my urge for creativity. The money and the arts are two different worlds.

Yes, I know the hardships of survival financially. Oh yes. At times when my daughter was little, I would really get anxious about our existence, always be out looking for ways to provide some financial means. Oftentimes, we had no money and were really scrambling. That happened many, many times. But that did not make me doubt my calling and the love of being involved with the arts and community.

I would run workshops just for necessity—and I did enjoy it. An art career is big work. I am an educator, working in and with communities. Art is my tool for education.

THEODORA CAPALDO

For a single woman, I have done well financially. I am good with money. I know how to save and how to spend. I know how to earn it. My stars are in alignment related to money in my life. Since about age twenty-one, I have not had any bad or worrisome moments around money.

That offers the benefit of freedom. It allows me to do the things I want to do. When I built my beautiful pergola, I really wanted copper caps on it, and I could afford to do that. So a major part of my creative or artistic expression has the money behind it to back it up. And it's also my heir, in the sense that I have my estate established and my money will continue to do for me what I have done with my life in terms of my social activism, the work for animals. So the fact that I was able to earn money and create a small estate comforts me. I don't have children or grandchildren and leave a legacy like you with your sons and daughter and grandchildren. There's a way you and your spirit will continue. So for me, it's my estate serving my work for the animals, which has so much meaning for me. That's part of the motivation to be frugal.

I could spend more money but I am saving it to serve my cause. And that brings me great joy.

> Many of the values I deem essential in guiding my journey—passion, imagination, intuition, observation—seem to others useless. Useless
> in the sense that they do not build roads and schools and hospitals.
> Yet they are the bread and water that allow creativity to survive.
> —*Philippe Petit, tightrope walker*

Chapter Ten. Science and Art

Art comes from empathy; science can work without it.
—*Theodora Capaldo*

I think risk-taking creates the best art if you are willing to go through the fire. Science is cooler.
—*Carole Watanabe*

Artists are usually a bit more private.
They don't need to involve the world.
Scientist have to face colleagues and boards and committees.
That makes it more challenging.
—*Sara Warber*

Science and Art: The Interviews

ESTHER MARION

What is the difference between science and art? I find this to be such a difficult question. The universe is a vast and moving space with infinite forms of energy that constantly shape themselves in new ways, and so it seems impossible to define differences. Though art might come from a much more emotional and experiential place within, the passion for the exploration could be very similar. Art is science, and science is art, really. Consider the myriad examples of that! Art, just like science, has infinite systems, existing ones that we learn or the ones we discover from within by finding our own path and message. The systems are deeply meaningful. They hold us together, in science as well as in art. They create the pathways for us to study, follow, and develop with freedom and knowledge, intuition, and refinement.

Michael Broome

On the fundamental level, there is no difference between the creativity of science and of art. A scientist has to be very present and pragmatic to sense a new and unfamiliar discovery. It's the same with artists, who have to be highly focused to make that leap out of the confines given by the material they work with. Both are looking for what has not been seen or perceived yet. That is a similar search. We are working with the force here. We artists call it divine because we don't know where it comes from. For me, there is no other word for it.

Tony Juniper

The difference between artist and scientist? I found a very good explanation the other day: Science is the discipline of finding answers to things that have answers, and art is the mode of exploring answers to things without answer. That summed it up for me. And the two go together, because science is limited; it only gets you so far. And then it leaves you with a blank "and so, what are we going to do now?"

The limits of science are in ethics and values and in risk-taking and uncertainty. And that's where it meets art. How do you address the questions where there is no answer?

Carole Watanabe

My sister is a scientist. I observe her. She always starts from a logical place, and she bends everything into the logical; otherwise, she would not trust the outcome. She insists that the results need to be repeatable. That's exactly the opposite of how I work as an artist.

My inspiration comes out of chaos, and then I fit things together in a way that is pleasing to me. It has nothing to do with logic; I shift things around until it's right. We can bridge that difference sometimes, but it's not easy. I have never been really close to her. We don't see reality in the same light. I don't think she respects what I do as an artist.

I think scientists are making creative leaps too but less frequently than artists. Scientists don't like risk-taking; artists do that all the time. My sister needs to have everything really sure, not in question. I think risk-taking creates the best art if you are willing to go through the fire. Science is cooler.

CATHY ATEN

A great scientist has room for not knowing! Creativity has a lot to do with the combination of knowing and not knowing. That is the creative tension. Think about Picasso's *Guernica*; he was holding the knowing and the not knowing. It represents the essence of him, plus what he himself received as a channel. Knowing and not knowing is like light and shadow, a very fertile ground for art as well as science.

AARON STERN

There is this famous story about Einstein which states that a theory had fallen into his awareness from nowhere. He spent the rest of his life proving the equation. Where did that come from? It did not start as an induction induced into his brain; it came out of thin air, and he had the antennae to catch it.

ANYA ACHTENBERG

The difference between art and science is in the level of remaining abstract. Science lives in the abstract reality. Art brings to life what's real and gives form to what might remain abstract to other people. The artists are so down-to-earth and inside the human, physical, sensual world. I don't know if there is more or less freedom in that. I am in general more stuck inside the artist's world. I am sensual.

Elias Rivera

I don't think there is a difference between the scientist's and the artist's creativity. I am not a scientist, and I could not really judge that. I have a specific orientation. I could have easily been an abstract painter and dealt with different approaches for my art. I took a certain path. I was a peasant. I am so interested in people and their faces. I look at people all the time, in the subway or bus. As a child going to school, I was always watching and sketching people, their faces and movements. My soul was deeply interested in them. I believe that the soul expresses itself in their faces. The eyes are the most expressive part of the body. I had to be a figurative painter. I had to. You take a physicist and an artist and both dive into this miracle we call life, and both are very reverent. They express their humanity and concern through different avenues. But in the end, both worlds meet and they are really one. Both scientist and artist are curious and want to find answers and an expression of truth.

Yael Weiss

Scientist and artist are similar in the sense that both are seeking truth. I think both are discovering some kind of truth about our world in their different mediums. And they communicate it through some kind of structure. Art has the luxury of being more flexible about the way and the choice of medium to describe that truth. For me, science, or even just words, are not as precise as music. If I want to say or describe something, I use only music. Science or words can be misunderstood, but music, because it is not as specific as science, is more precise. I can only convey a particular truth with a specific sound or music or harmony. There is no way to do it in that exact way with other means. I have always felt music to be the most truthful means, beyond words, but I know that people often think it's the opposite.

Uwe Walter-Nakajima

I have many scientist friends. My own son studies for his Ph.D.

in astrophysics. We have long discussions when we meet. Depending on the angle from which one looks, art and science are very close. People tend to emphasize the differences, almost like religions, and take a dogmatic stance. I don't see why and don't have this problem. Science and art both help us to understand this world better.

TIM GOSNELL

Yes, practical things are different in the world of science or art.

A successful scientist stands ruthlessly under the fist of the laws of nature. He cannot win that game unless nature is going along with him. Nature is a pretty harsh mistress. You can imagine that nature has fantastic things in store, and she might prove to you that your approach is nonsense. (I mean nature here as the whole universe.)

Artists are not as constrained by a kind of ruthless overlord like the scientist. Most artists work with real world materials. Whatever they create has to be accessible to ordinary senses. Most people are viewing art in relatively simple settings, in rooms or in galleries.

Artists need to make a direct connection to people's experiences with their senses. The scientific world can present itself very differently from that. What you are studying has all kinds of amplifiers between the world of science and the human being—for example, the microscope or telescope. These monstrous machines, like the accelerator at CERN, are amplifiers, and they are multi-billion-dollar kinds of machines. No matter what, scientific exploration needs an interface somewhere, often very sophisticated ones. That's less the case in art.

JERRY WENNSTROM

I believe creativity is creativity, wherever it is applied. That became very clear when I was approached by my publisher and asked to write my book. At the time, I didn't know how to type or use a computer, and I had not written much. What I discovered after struggling with the mechanics of it all was that writing was so much like creating art, even in its structural layout, that I was able to write the book in four months (the time I was given). Creativity requires risk and continual quantum leaps in unexpected directions—all of which are based on intuitive feelings more than plans and ideas. Feeling enlivened by these leaps is the only indication of "success."

VIJALI HAMILTON

There is no difference in the process of creativity between science and art. That inspiration comes from the same place, the "implicate order," as David Bohm would say. Only the skill and physical manifestation of the inspiration is different.

AMANDA MCPHAIL AND WESLEY WEST

Wes: I love scientists. They are wacky. They inspire me. I have a dear friend in Leicester. I always love to go into his office—it's full of mysterious instruments. He invents and builds practical things for his household too—very original things, well functioning. You see that a scientist has built them.

And, about the artist—I believe that the ceramicist is a scientist; pottery is a science. We have to know about glazes and temperatures, have to know what we work with and how it changes during the process of gestation.

Amanda: I have never understood science, but I am in awe of it. It's like magic for me. I was a teacher and was always worn out in the evening because good students make demands on you. At the end of the day, you have nothing left and can't even go into your own studio. I used to teach three days a week. Can one teach creativity? I think, yes! Part of it is attitude: It's the teaching of attitude toward your art, your work.

Wes: Teaching can get a student into the right place, instruct them how to see and look at things. Art has a practical side to it, like science. Both want results; both want things that can be used in daily life.

Sara Warber

Science and art—is there a difference? My first reaction is that creativity in art is so much freer. It's freeing to the soul, less bound to facts and figures. But I ask myself if this is really true or not?

In science, method and discipline impose a lot of restrictions. And so while the mind and soul are excited about creativity and discovery in science, it has to slough through an awful lot of minutia in order to actualize the creative discovery.

On the other hand, in arts, you have discipline and the knowledge of your craft and the application of it, and that made me realize that it too has its boundaries. You might have a lot of ideas but might not be able to actualize them in reality. So science and art might not be so different. The similarity between them is the call for actualization in the world and the challenge that comes with it.

It's in the execution that the creator in us is challenged. In that process, you bump up against the difficulties, but when you work through them, the final product is often better than you envisioned. And that's true for both of them, the scientist and the artist.

As long as you imagine, you don't see the details—it's just like a gestalt, and later, you bring all this together so the final thing unfolds into a bigger frame which you have not seen before. That means the process of creation will enrich the original idea.

So let me be more specific. In science, there is the great idea, and then you collect all the detail. Maybe you have more questions, need others to help and seek, then write a paper. And in the process, you bump up against all the rules of the trade. Finally, you get to the end, and after completion of this long process, you are very happy.

Theater was my special field of creativity when I was young. It's so similar: You have ideas and envision them on stage, and you have to do all the minutiae to make it real. It's a huge human enterprise, and in that process it comes to life. At the end, it's better than you expected,

Science and art: The means and tools are different, but the process in general is very similar, from the first idea to the final outcome. Artists are usually a bit more private and don't need to involve the world. Scientists have to face colleagues and boards and committees. That makes it more challenging.

Ruth Bamford

I invented the deflector shield for space exploration. It is a protective umbrella in space, a force field that will keep humans safe from cosmic rays outside the atmosphere that protects us. This active magnetic shield is a portable protection outside the spacecraft. We are using its own nature and energy against it.

I think it's a perception and belief by many artists that scientists are not artists. That is related to outer circumstances, like it's possible as a scientist to be employed but artists rarely are. Employment provides safety. Look at technicians: They remember a lot of processes, they can teach and produce, they can do new things, they are creative. But that is not creativity in its deepest sense, and they are not scientists or artists.

I'd like to think about those scientists who are the real artists. They can't be any other than creative. They seek the new and unknown. They think outside the box; they dare to offer new visions and realities.

Most of the scientists I work with do work that can be based on recall. I know that it can take you a long time to remember all those facts you have learned, and those names and labels. Technicians can teach, they can function and assemble many things, so they can appear creative, but it's not real creativity.

Artists might think that all scientists are alike. Artists believe that they are different from scientists. It's a mystery. Art and science are challenging each other.

Peggy O'Kelly

Yes, the scientist has more concrete information than the artist. I can put together a product based on the ingredients and how they relate to the earth they come from. I rely on my intuition, but the scientist will test it and tell me if it is truly effective. The scientist will not only listen to intuition but also to analysis.

But the intuition-based decision is a powerful one in our industry of health and beauty products. We look for cellular regeneration. And I always question whether what we do is harmful or healthful for the customer, as well as for Mother Earth who provides us these magnificent products. I intuitively trust what she grows and offers to us. And I look for natural ingredients—I use what grows in nature. And I still have to have it all tested to collect the facts and figures. So I practice art and science. They complement each other in my work and products.

I am aware that in our society and business matters, we often harm the Earth, and frequently we don't process her products in natural ways. So I hire professionals to test the final outcome. My beauty products come from the Earth, but they were touched and tested by human hands and mechanics. I am creative and free, but I also follow the rules and regulations of the industry.

Chrissie Orr

The creativity of artists and scientists is similar. They allow their imaginations to look at the world, but for scientists, it's more rooted in a database and facts. During the artistic practice, you are throwing all the facts out; you approach the creation with new and risky points of view. Science and art seem to inhabit different places, but in the essence, they are close. The essence is the challenge to get out of the world one knows already and see it expand—dare to go into other worlds and allow that to inform you in new ways. It's the daring and curiosity that both have in common.

Theodora Capaldo

Here's what I think: During twenty or more years of animal protective work in science, I have encountered scientists who had creative genius, but there was often a lack of empathic creative I.Q. I am not convinced that some of the scientific advances need this amount of torture of animals. If there was empathy, scientists simply could not do this kind of abuse to them. If they had inherent empathy, they could not inflict suffering to such a degree.

Yes, sometimes the intellectual approach can be extremely creative, but it needs to be aligned with empathic I.Q. Just because you can do it does not mean you have to go for it and sacrifice compassion for the sake of science. It happens so often that we encounter other creatures, cultures, nations, the Earth, and find ourselves unable to feel it as if it is happening to us.

So here's my guess, from my own experience. Knowing what is being perpetrated every day against living animals, true creative acts cannot occur when the objects are suffering as they do. The scientist has to turn down his empathy and suppress his compassion, admit to his deeds and see them in the context of the whole. So I believe scientific and artistic creativity are different. Though art comes from empathy, science can work without it.

CHAPTER ELEVEN. HEALING

*Attention is the most basic form of love:
Through it we bless and are blessed.*
—John Tarrant

*I often wonder how people who don't paint get through their trauma?
I assume they are writing or dancing or playing music.*
—Carole Watanabe

Creative Encounter

My first year of graduate studies in Expressive Arts Therapy at Lesley College in Cambridge, Massachusetts, was 1983. I was assigned a position as a mental health intern at Emanuel Shattuck Hospital in Boston. My focus was on movement therapy, applied as a healing modality with mentally challenged patients. I was inexperienced and felt shy and insecure. So I settled in the activities room on the fifth floor, where most of the clients would gather during the day to be entertained, trained, and socially involved. I observed them with great interest and imagined how movement therapy might be of help and inspiration for specific clients with various needs and handicaps. I also explored their case histories to better understand the roots and origins of their disabling mental distortions and symptoms.

One man caught my attention. He was tied to his chair because he moved continuously. He could not stop reaching out with his arms, gesticulating, pointing, shaking. As I observed him, I entered his mental world. He seemed to me like a visitor from another planet who eagerly spoke in a sign language that he, and only he, understood. This man was almost frantic to make contact but he was mostly ignored because he was mute. His eyes were without life or light, his facial expression dead and gray. I read in his case history that he had been a normal functioning young adult until, at age eighteen, he suddenly stopped talking. There was no explanation of what had triggered his loss of speech.

The man seemed desperate in his reaching, trying and failing, a lonesome stranger, separate from our culture. Shifting into his mindset and needs, I imagined that I had lived on the planet he seemed to come from. I moved slowly across the room toward this stranger and made eye contact. Placing a chair in front of him, I sat quietly. From this place of physical closeness, I began mirroring his gestures, first very slowly, only hinting, then more obviously moving my arms in the same way he did. He lifted his eyelids and watched me, and then, as if a lightning bolt had hit him, his face filled with surprise, with joy, with radiant animation.

His loneliness lifted, and he woke up in front of my eyes. I had become a tribal member from whatever place in the universe his mind and soul had come to ours. He and I recognized a kinship, and that morning we agreed to connect in his culture and story. His frantic and erratic gestures became harmonious and calm. I followed his suggestions with my own movement as he gestured with his arms, hands, fingers, and elbows. My movements mirrored him with devoted attention. In this way, we kept up a real and magical conversation in the middle of a space that was otherwise inhabited by strangers.

In this peculiar dance in which we encountered one another, we connected on a very intimate level; we talked in a sign language that was meaningful to him. When I joined him in this language which he had invented or learned, we reached from one world to another, the strangeness was overcome, and a new path of communication opened from him to me. The man's face beamed with happiness, and my own heart filled with gratitude and deep wonder. It seemed that my leaning and reaching into his world had made it possible for him to be present in ours. A thin bridge of empathy allowed us to meet as peers in this strange human world, where we need each other to be alive and sane. We formed a most mysterious friendship, and I hope that he too still remembers our "otherworldly" encounters. I visited with him twice a week during my five-month internship, until I had to leave. I told the new intern about our "conversations" and hoped that she too would become a member of his tribe.

To work with this man was very humbling. I could not heal him, but by reaching out into his world, I brought him regularly something like a glass of water or wine. To have met and encountered this friend inspired me profoundly. He was a teacher for me, and I hope that my attention and love gave him some nurturing. Through and with him, I experienced creativity as a force that cracks open the prison of habitual thinking and gives us precious insights beyond the limiting edges of our beliefs. Creativity can create a language to bridge human loneliness. It blooms where the unknown is embraced as a doorway into the Great Mystery.

There is a crack in everything.
That's where the light comes in.
—Leonard Cohen

Forgiveness—The Art of Relating

Forgiveness is ultimately creativity in action. It makes space for a new way of being and thinking. Forgiveness is training in freedom beyond wrong-doing and right-doing. As Rumi said: ". . . there is a field, I'll meet you there." It's creativity working on attitude.

For-giveness—what a fascinating word! I for-give; I give already something before I give, as if there were a before-giving and an after-giving. So giving is encircled by good intentions and sits inside a time-space. And maybe that is true, because grudges and non-forgiveness are always, always related to the past, which means to events that are bygone. What and whom do I want to for-give? For whom do I want to let go of grudges, of blaming, of finger-pointing, as I am hanging out in the space that Eckhart Tolle calls "the Pain-Body?" Yes, un-forgiveness hurts, especially the one who carries the grudges.

Forgiveness can be hard work. It means that I give you back the story you created with me, I return to you what stands between our giving and receiving. I desire to be free and unburdened by this old story. I give back to you the negative attachment I knotted into the web of your actions that have hurt and upset me.

When I choose to forgive, I cut the ropes that tie me to you in a way that I seemingly did not choose. But that is not true, because I chose to hang on to that sticky web, I may have even embellished it for more drama. I chose this web of painful entanglement, but I can also let go of the strings, strings that suffocate and hinder my happiness and freedom to unfold and to be real inside this relationship with you.

If I don't forgive you, I am caught in a trap of my own making. But if I release the old story of hurt and blame, I will be free. Forgiveness means that I am free to see you now instead of being constricted by past resentments and perceptions. You have changed, and I have changed, and we cannot step into the same river twice. Not even in the grudges-river—it's muddy and smells of decay. If I choose to offer forgiveness, I receive in return expansion and inspiration.

Forgiveness opens up a space for joy and love and for the dance of relationship on new and not-yet-walked grounds. I forgive so that I can give and receive in this moment without strings attached to the past, and the effect is surprise and laughter.

Forgiveness is a creative act. It opens doors to unknown rooms inside my psyche. It needs the intention as much as the active application. It is a skill and a learned craft; it has style and color, and it feeds on courage. All of these are necessary traits to create art, in this case, the art of living and relating.

Chapter Twelve. Life as Art

Being broken open motivates art and its expression in our society
—Michael Broome

Broken

My fascination with clay masks began in 1987 in New Mexico, where I studied at the Institute of American Indian Arts and explored the rich culture of Native Americans' ritual art: their regalia and masks for their sacred feast days, their powerful communal dances, their music of flute and drums, their high-pitched songs, and their mesmerizing clayware. I am a ceramic artist, and for many years, my main focus was on the creation of archetypal masks related to the gods and goddesses of various cultures around the world. I decorated those masks with colorful feathers and leather-braided tails, with beads and metal jewelry and fur from beaver or raccoon, and the long, strong hair from horses' tails.

This fascination with masks continued during my year of travel in 1990, when I explored the lives and work of the Aborigines of Australia, the Japanese—both old and contemporary—and the Celts of Scotland. Studying those cultures, I found that masks don't hide but rather depict the deeper self of the wearer—they are the faces of Spirit.

In those three countries, I knocked at the doors of artists and found a clay studio where I was invited to build and fire my work, so I was able to create masks that were related to those cultures and their magical stories. The sale of some of the works helped to finance my sabbatical. And so the experience of art-making turned into a source that fed itself, and also me as the traveling Creative.

Being so focused on one theme—the masks—seemed to satisfy my desire to create in that genre. I dove into new territories, explored foreign cultures and their art, and was enchanted and sometimes ecstatic. I made masks all around the world. But when I came back to Santa Fe in 1991, I was eager to improvise with new styles and materials. So I stepped courageously into a very different use of ceramics.

Inspired by the fantastic, erotic, and whimsical sculptures of the French artist Niki de Saint Phalle and the abstract Austrian painter and sculptor Friedensreich Hundertwasser, I began working with mosaic. That change guided me smoothly into a great adventure: I was ready to settle in the southwestern United States, and that meant building a home in the hills south of Santa Fe. This emerging house became my canvas and gallery.

As I experimented, I found that mosaic is happiest on big surfaces where it can expand and stretch, can branch out and dance and lean into free shapes and crawl along curved walls and ceilings. Three walls of my bathroom are "overgrown" with tile reliefs that resemble a garden by Monet: blue water lilies, iris in bloom, white calla lilies with green leaves, and frogs in between pebbles and shells. Outside in my garden, I created a big mosaic wall with trees overhanging sun and moon; a crane on one leg is patiently holding a royal position. Birds of the day and night trail in the sky. This playful wall hides my ordinary propane tank. Along the ground between grass and rocks, a water channel snakes toward a pond filled by roof water, which houses goldfish. A fountain between red sandstones portrays the goddess of rivers. As she spits water out her mouth, she spreads the delightful sound of dripping rain, precious in a desert landscape. When I sit on my porch and drink the obligatory morning tea, I feel as if I am resting in a Roman garden.

As I became more and more familiar with the medium of tile and mosaic, and as I dared to make wild creative choices, I promised to myself that I would not hold back in my expression. This was my house, and I could play in and around it however the Muses guided me or turned me on. So I created larger and smaller relief pieces to be installed as whole pictures, and I cut tiles into shards or smashed them with a hammer, using their uneven and bizarre shapes as fillers. More and more, I loved the brokenness and "un-orderly" spirit of the material. I was astounded how the broken-ness took on new life when smaller individual pieces became spontaneously integrated into a larger arrangement. I found that these seemingly chaotic material offered more options and playfulness than the already-shaped and planned pieces. Both together allowed unlimited combinations.

As I developed this new style, I saw how it matched the landscape of the high desert of the Southwest. This land is wild, surprising, powerfully untamed. The irregularity of mosaic lends itself well to those characteristics. The usually bold colors of the tiles match the rough walls and surfaces of adobe mud houses. And it happens this morning, as I am sitting here writing, that a surprising parallel emerges: What I do creatively with ceramic mosaic work is such a powerful metaphor for my work as a psychotherapist. Clients come into therapy with a longing for wholeness. They seek treatment for what is broken and shattered in their life and psyche. And when we work together, we sort out the "good pieces" as we give attention to the brokenness. We find the right place in the whole soul picture and place those shards with sharp edges into a new context, and there, they gain fresh meaning and beauty. The brokenness of the psyche finds healing through loving attention and creative acceptance. The fresh placement of flaws into a new context supports and celebrates the uniqueness of this human being. So healing work is mosaic art: Broken traits find a new association in the story of your life.

I am passionate about the joy and playfulness of work with mosaics, just as I am passionate and awed about the readiness of clients to face their wounds and to transform them into a piece of art. As a psychotherapist, I experience and support this transformation, and that allows me a unique place of healing participation in our human condition. I am awed to see how art, again, mirrors our soul.

Artwork is Soul work, and work on the Soul is Art.

The person who completes writing a book is different than the person who started it.

> *The deepest experience of the creator is feminine*
> *For it is the experience of receiving and bearing.*
> —Rainer Maria Rilke

> *When you have a child, you sign up for a love that can carve a canyon into your heart.*
> —Ellen Bass

Life's Longing for Itself: Birth

Finally! The first contractions indicate that the baby is ripe. Meg, Madeleine, and I are present to accompany my daughter, Esther, during this most creative sacred journey—to give birth to a human being. Esther's body remembers. She gave birth ten years ago to her son, Jonah, and now she is pregnant again and due with her second baby, a girl.

It is early morning. We amble around, drink tea, and tell stories throughout all those first drawn-out hours of labor. Meg is a doula and has assisted many women in this process. It begins slowly. Again and again, contractions tighten Esther's belly, but they soften in the span of three or four deep breaths. We sing a Kahlil Gibran song for the baby, Our children are not our children; they are the sons and daughters of life's longing for itself. We lean over the full cupola of the belly where the baby sleeps, unseen, but just inches away from our fingers. We cover Esther's taut belly with our eight hands, fingers intertwined like a net, laughing, rubbing, and massaging. Madeleine, the musician, grabs her fiddle to play along with the song . . . life's longing for itself.

In us women stirs the knowledge of what can go right and what could go wrong. I am full of joy and also fear; they rub sharply against each other. I have given birth myself, three times, and I know about the vulnerability of the woman's body in this event where the edges of life and death cut close to each other's domain. We move around in the house, resting on hard chairs or leaning into soft pillows. We three birth-helpers yield to the needs of the mother and the rhythms inside her body. Beauty surrounds us. Esther dedicated the long months of pregnancy to the creative art of anticipation, like a pilgrim preparing a journey to the Holy Shrine. She transformed the whole house into a consecrated place to shelter the birth of her daughter. Altars with jewelry and pictures from her ancestors adorn the window sills; crystals, found in the river, reflect the sun's light and break it into pink, green, and blue rays that dot the ceiling. Ah, that's my daughter's way of turning everyday life into art, I think. She knows how to celebrate small or big events, elevating life into a feast.

Purple stems of lilac lean into the sunlit room. Sage smolders in a conch shell and spreads its fragile smoke-veils across a Guatemalan painting of a mother resting between corn stalks, her child inside her belly. Candles flicker on tables and bookshelves. All four of us sprawl on the silk-covered birthing bed in the middle of the room, lusciously adorned with silken pillows and shawls.

A burgundy-red birthing quilt is draped all around the corners of the room. It carries pictures of goddesses and powerful women, like Maya Angelou, Alice Walker, and Doris Lessing, as well as the unnamed woman in Africa. The Hawaiian Goddess Pele tends the fire of a volcano, and Artemis strides through the forest, trailed by her beloved creatures. The Goddess Athena is so tall that we can only see her feet with big toes curled upward.

Every image is hand-painted, copied or stitched by Esther. She wove her love for the growing child inside into the stories and songs of womanhood, thus calling on the Goddesses to bless and assist in the birthing of her baby girl.

In the corner leans a chair, a red flamenco shawl draped over the back. I remember Esther's last performance, about five months ago, in the Bilbao Restaurant in Seattle. She moved her body—with the baby inside—in accord with the gypsy tunes, like an undulating flame stroked by a passing wind. With the drumbeat of her feet, she pounded toward the center of the Earth, and she stretched simultaneously upward until her snaking hands grasped the sky. Her body molded the music and shaped the wind that followed the movement of her hips, raked by the fluttering fringes of her shawl.

At about four o'clock in the afternoon, the contractions are increasing in frequency and strength. Esther's husband, Keni, calls the midwife. I focus solely on my daughter, my field of awareness tight and laser-like.

"We are together in a boat on the ocean," says Meg. "The wind and the tides rock us toward the shore." Meg's skilled hands massage the hard-working body of the mother, relaxing her neck and her feet, the broad feet of a dancer, marked by blue veins like lace on top of white flesh. I feel a wave of love as I remember her as a baby, when she was born out of my flesh thirty-eight years ago. I held her in my arms after she was delivered in the middle of the night in the quiet hospital; the nurse draped her in a downy blue cotton blanket with white polka dots. Her hair was black and stood straight up as if electrified. "We cannot wake the doctor; he's sleeping," said the nurse, and she clumsily stitched the bloody wound that the child had torn in my body.

At about five in the afternoon, our friend Abel knocks at the door. He carries his big Mexican harp and places it in the birthing room. And then he weaves us four women into a web of music as we move from room to room. He plays and sings old songs from Mexico and Brazil, Colombia and Guatemala. *Ahora seremos felices.* His tunes gather in every fold and corner of the house. *Lacrimas negras.*

The midwife checks in at about nine in the evening. She steps through the door and exclaims, "Wow, there are candles and incense and an angel is playing the harp. I think I am in heaven."

She leaves when the contractions lessen in strength. We are concerned. I don't want her to go, but she consoles us that this rhythm between effort and calm phases is normal. "It is the way women have given birth for millennia. There's a break in the work, a night to sleep and gather strength. The woman's body knows how to preserve energy. You all rest now and be patient. Everything is well." The night closes in on us like a dark dome without a door. We all fall asleep where we had settled last, as in the fairy tale of Sleeping Beauty. I am cuddled around my daughter on the big bed. Madeleine is on her other side, her long hair spread on a pillow mingling with my daughter's. Meg curls up on the floor, a soft pillow under her head and a blanket spread over her. Keni rests at the foot of the bed, like a guardian. Abel has fallen asleep in the rocking chair; his arms embrace the harp with his head leaning against the curly knot of its frame.

The stillness in this dome is laced by whispering voices of goddesses and muses as the images on the birthing quilt come to life. The goddess Athena with the enormous feet leans across the bed and over the sleeping women, her big hands hold the weight of the stars. Fragments of ancient songs settle like dust on the sleepers' eyelids. *Seremos felices*. Black ribbons of hope and fear weave into the thickets of our dreams. *Lacrimas negras*. The mother and the child sleep inside the same body, still nurtured by the same blood, the baby's heart beating under the folds of her mother's breasts.

Next morning, when the first light reaches with pale fingers into the birthing room, the smell of coffee wafts through the open door. We awake and remember that the work is not yet done. Keni prepares scrambled eggs and toast and a grand pot of chicken soup, as if we were a construction crew. He's slicing potatoes and carrots, garlic and tomatoes, adding chicken thighs and spices. He moves around in the background like a guardian at a temple, weaving manly strength and protection around the women's mysteries. Ten-year-old Jonah goes to school.

The contractions begin again and rattle Esther's body with increasing urgency. We step outside into the early sunlight and go for a walk, three women encircling the mother. Whenever a contraction strikes, we entwine our arms around her, breathing in tune with her rhythm as she leans her head against our shoulders. Her body is laboring in an ancient rhythm, like the mighty force of an earthquake. Trees swing their branches overhead, the young spring leaves full of bustling excitement. Flowers of spring squeeze through the black furrows in the asphalt along our path. Ravens croak and crickets rub their tiny wings to create a raspy song. I am struck by the pitiless everyday routine that moves life along the edge of either promising beginnings or ultimate endings. Birth or death, walking in ordinary boots along a familiar path, whereas we women stand barefoot on thorns, urging time forward toward this awakening day when all the work will be done.

In the late afternoon, the final labor of birthing rolls in like a hurricane hitting the shore. My daughter sits facing me in front of me on a soft gymnastic ball, her legs open and stretched over my open legs, knees crossing knees as in a lover's embrace. We are the lovers of creation, of the most vital participation in life: the making of another human being out of a woman's body. With every new contraction, she throws herself forward into my arms and holds on with intense grip. I breathe with her and feel the hardening of her ripe belly against mine. We are woven into one being; she bears the pain and I hold her in my arms to soften the sharp and ruthless force that tears the path open for the child.

The baby drills her way out of her mother's body, separating herself from her home made of flesh. The small new being of my daughter's daughter is being pushed and squeezed inside the birth canal to find her way into life outside her mother's womb. The creative forces of the universe rattle and shake the mother with fierce fists. She groans, "Oh no, not again, not so fast, give me a break, let me breathe. . . ." but the next wave of rhythmic convulsions grabs her with unrelenting thrust. She is being used in service of life; she is the gateway through which it enters. The room is filled with showers of groans and ruthless bursts of pain. The mother is wrapped in the folds of a fierce thrust to expel the child. Her face is naked, pearls of sweat dot her forehead; her mouth is open, her chin turned upward as if to escape her face.

My daughter plunges herself forward toward my chest, and I scoop up her pain with my hands and my heart. But still, the birthing mother is alone in her endeavor to separate: Out of one body there will be two. This severance is ruthless, forceful, and without pity, but there is also a euphoric and overpowering joy in this birthing work that has no comparison.

Darkness crowds in through the open door. The midwife is not here yet. We are waiting for her arrival. Urgency and the need for patience keep us tense. My daughter and the baby approach the last and most intense phase of birth, when the child is being pushed out of the mother's body with unrelenting drive. Ecstasy and agony grip each other's throat in this fiery cauldron of creation.

We women settle at the side of the bed, on a soft blanket spread on the floor—hard and supportive. The floor is the Earth; the floor is ground and shelter, the lowest point, from where we can fall upward into the heart of the universe. We three women cradle her; we breathe with her. We calm her to hold the child inside.

The midwife is not here yet.

Madeleine wakes Jonah, the brother of the girl being born, the boy who has been anticipating his future sister. He looks for something to put on. His father says: "It's all right, Jonah. Your sister is almost here, and she'll be naked too, big brother." Holding Madeleine's hand, he stumbles sleepily downstairs and settles into his father's arms.

The whole room is flooded with the pounding river of life pouring into itself. The cosmos holds its breath, the stars stop, the wind slows and lingers. And then the door opens, the midwife drops everything from her hands, kneels down in front of my daughter on the floor, opens her legs and sees the child crowning, still in her birthing sack. She pierces the sack and the baby slithers out like a fish, a flood of water gushing and pushing her, the water from the mother's womb smelling like almond orchards blossoming in Portugal. Oh, mystery. The midwife receives the child in her hands—all that in seconds. "Ohh," the midwife calls out. "Oh, she slithers directly out of her bag. What a wonderful sign of a blessed child. She looks right at me. She is well; she is wide awake." The midwife lifts the baby up to the sky, and then she guides this baby's brother to cut the cord that holds the pulsating flow of blood between mother and daughter, and then she lays the little girl into the crook of her mother's arm, like a bunch of pink flowers or a long loaf of bread.

My grandmother used to cradle a fresh loaf of bread in her arm like that before she would break it, and she made the sign of the cross over it—In the name of the Father, the Son, and Sweet Mother Mary—before she reached toward us children with the pieces of bread that would feed our hungry bellies. Oh, this most familiar gesture, always and all over the world: the baby in her mother's arms, the baby that had exploded out of her mother's womb, the baby that cut an open wound of love into her mother's heart, a heart that had not even imagined how much more she would be able to love and how it would rip open her normal ways of loving and how this joy would enlarge her way of being and set her afire with delight.

"Oh, my daughter, my dear baby, my dear sweet one, my pink miracle, my angel, my baby . . ." sighing and singing, pierced by joy and ecstasy, the mother sinks backward into the arms of us three women, into a cradle of bodies, and into the well of the most intense celebration, flooded by the most riveting orgasm of relief a women can experience.

The room opens up to the starry night outside and stretches into the labyrinth of the universe.

Life as Art

Baruch ata Adonai elohenu melekh ha-olam, shehecheyanu vekiymanu vehigi-anu lazman hazeh, sings Meg. All the prayers of the globe whirr like hummingbirds around this child, spreading its sweetness and reflecting its light. And into the room steps the goddess Sophia, goddess of feminine wisdom, who gave this baby her name and who will spark this girl's love for life, spark her fire to protect this Earth and its Soul. Sophia! Sophia!

The baby cries and tests her own voice, and her little song is the most exquisite music trembling through the night. Her tiny shriveled hands grab the air around her and flap as if taking off in flight. *Ahora seremos felices.*

We shout and weep and hug each other and hold on to whoever is nearest. Breathless with joy, we dance and settle around the mother and baby, and then we jump up again, unable to sit still, spinning this moment and this night and this new baby inside a vortex of happiness.

Everybody thinks you have to paint or so to be creative. It's much bigger than that.
You can live your life as an artist.

The reward of art is not fame or success
but intoxication.
—Cyril Connolly

Life as Art: The Interviews

ESTHER MARION

I am an artist of many things. For example, if we invite people for dinner and we cook, I create a table that nobody forgets. I love to create beauty. That, to me, is art. A good meal is like a ritual, like performance art; such a meal is a communal experience. I cherish that.

But the most fiery and devoted creative expression of life is in my dance. I have a passionate love affair with flamenco. When I practice, I close my door and stay in my privacy. For an hour or two, I don't want to be disturbed. After I clear out the clouds of distraction triggered in my head by day-to-day life, I move into a space of great intimacy with my dance and with the music that inspires it.

My life is rich. It's a good life being in community and in partnership with creativity. It's a good life to live like this, active and involved. My family is part of my creativity and art. We are cultural creatives. We live in some ways at the edge of society, but we are also at the core of it; we are movers and shakers. Money and status does not mean much to us. We trust and risk and act.

That attitude is part of my whole life. After finishing high school in Switzerland, I did not go to college but instead I traveled the world with my lover-friend, trusting and risking, learning by doing. It challenges the traveler to define what really matters, who you are, and what your gifts are. That's an alchemical cauldron in which to be cooked. It's the place where you learn to trust in your guiding star and in yourself. It's good to live and trust like that when you are in your youth.

Clarissa Pinkola Estés says, "You have to be able to sleep on a concrete floor." You need to be young for that and not be held back by fear that there's no comfort and security. If you face that before you are grown and settled, you know how basic you can get. I worked to pay for my dance studies, and sometimes I went to bed hungry; that was all part of it, so I didn't get too pussycat when circumstances were rough. That was the empowering influence of my first lover, Mark, who was ten years older than I. He was an influential teacher for me. I learned to survive and trust in myself. With him, I explored other cultures. I became versatile and flexible. I became a global citizen, and that influences my art today.

Creativity is life's substance spread like a web, and I am constantly weaving on it. There's inspiration and there are skills. I am continually working on my skills to develop them. To keep in touch with those resources, I write and I practice yoga. I think that creativity is personal and communal; it ties people and art forms together. And then there are my dreams—they are a powerful source of creativity. It's the window through which creative inspiration flows into my life. I receive and then I interpret and dance the dream.

In my daily life, besides work and children, I have only a short time to practice. But after about an hour or two, I am newly energized. My massage work is part of my art; it's a healing art. I read a lot, but I don't study much in books—I learn directly from my practice, from life. It's kinesthetic learning with my feet on the ground. I am essentially alive and pay attention. I have many ways to be awake.

And there's Arte Magica, my work with children. I take them into nature, beside a brook, under a big tree; we write and paint and perform rituals. We go on journeys together, and nature is our teacher. It's a creative learning process, different from normal school. These elements of nature are generally so neglected in the classroom. It pains me deeply how children lose contact with Mother Earth and her generous gifts. Children are so tuned into those small electronic devices that they don't even know what they miss out on.

That's how I live. I stretch and develop my skills every day. I have many notebooks and use them to design my dance. I write and plan expression through different media. That's part of my life. My group, Arte Flamenco, is my dance world; Arte Magica is my work with kids. That's how I tie the strands together and offer myself to my community.

I often ask myself the question: Would I want to change my life if I had one year to live? And I say "yes" because I live in a city, and there is a lot of ugliness, industry, and stress in cities today. That's not how I want to live. I'd rather move around, travel widely, experience more of the Earth before I leave.

Examples?

I would like to go to Fez for the sacred music festival, and to Seville in Spain, and to Saintes-Maries-de-la-Mer for the gypsy festival, and to Finland, to Hawaii. I would use the year to go away, and I would always come back to my community here.

MICHAEL BROOME

Creativity is a hard and demanding lover. If you don't devote yourself, she is going to screw you up. "If you don't give me that attention, I am not going to make it work for you. I want your full devotion." That's why it's hard to live a sociable life or have a family as an artist. I never wanted children; my lover and partner is my art.

Yes, that's where the real selfishness of the artist comes in. Can they dare to have that much fun? Fortunately, I've got myself into a place where nobody is watching me! And that's very important. So I can have as much fun as I want, even if there's all this suffering around. Yes, I do watch the world, and I am very well informed. I know the misery of the world and of my friends. Honestly, often I don't even reveal to my close friends how much fun I have with my art objects because they are struggling in their lives. It's a dismal world out there, but I still have fun and joy as an artist.

I saw my doctor recently. We went on a canoe trip many years ago, and we laughed a lot. And when I saw her recently, she asked me, "Do you still laugh as much as you did then?" And I told her that I laugh even more today as I am growing older. I even laugh a lot just by myself. And she said, "I miss that." When I left, we both were laughing together.

Creativity is the willingness to do what is on your mind. Whatever the inspiration, the artist will do it, not only think about it. Thinking about it—that's the philosopher; an artist does the doing of that. Artists make things. I am passionate about that. You get a lot of contentment out of it. Once you start the doing of art, you are in the embrace of change. You are in the real nitty-gritty of life, which is change. Every moment is changing. The artist grabs the moment of change, and then he is changing with it. He is conscious of the change, conscious of building his painting. He is present with great concentration. He is hoping to give that painting some sort of life that continues. That's what art is about. Art is basically movement. It moves with life's energy and contains magic; even found objects can become endowed with magic energy. They carry something inside that moves you when you experience them.

I am glad to live at this time. Yes, even knowing that we are destroying the planet and living very opulent lives. It's the most frustrating development there is today; I am hurting about it. Our small actions do not stop it from going to the edge. I am part of the distractive force—I drive a car. And maybe we all will go over the edge. It does not even really matter where it goes. It will all go off in smoke, just as we all are going naturally some day. The question of whether we survive or not cannot be the point. I think it's more important how we survive, and that's what we need to get a handle on now. I think that I have a bit of a handle on it, but I am a culprit too. I don't know what to do. We are not in control; I feel helpless.

On the other hand, I am excited about living in this time because we are free to live very creative lives. I need a certain amount of freedom from the toil of life. Artists don't really toil in the fields; they put themselves above the toil of life. I see a lot of interest in creativity because people have time to even consider the possibility of creativity. Certainly my parents would not have any notion of being artistic, not even a thought about it. They did not have a clue at their place and time in society. Art was something removed; it was a luxury. But now, our lives are so much easier. People have more spare money and time. They have all those possibilities, and then comes this little nagging feeling: "There's something else; there's something missing in my life." And being an artist looks exciting. But it's really hard work. It's a way of living, not a way out of living. So everybody wants to know: How can I be more creative, how can I make my life more colorful?

Art can be anything, even what Carole creates in the kitchen and serves us dinner: that's art born from creativity and from the delight of food. What counts is what we put into the doing that will make it alive or not. Even sweeping a room can be delightfully creative if you are in a yogic mindset. Everybody thinks you have to paint or so to be creative, but it's much bigger than that. You can live your life as an artist. You need to be conscious of it, then everything carries this magic, this little spark. That's what we are all looking for: the presence of a higher power that is beyond our description, and we are not aware of it unless we concentrate on it. That's where meditation is helpful.

Once you have practiced meditation and you have experienced the magic of it, you are hooked. You can't let it go because it gives you this delicious kiss! The kiss of inspiration! The other peculiar thing is—and it happens in meditation too—that after five years or so of devoted practice, you experience this Wow! moment, and it's the Divine Kiss. And then you go looking for it because after five years, you've almost given up seeking to find it. And after that kiss, you can't stop and keep looking for that magic again and again. And it might take two more years before you ever receive this kiss again.

And art is a bit like that: Just when you were ready to give it up, it will allow you to create a picture or a pot and it will wow you: "I really did that? I am responsible for that?" And it will take another two years before you understand how that happened. You learn that you had to relax and let go of expectations, and how you had to be firmer in your meditation practice and let go of any effort at the same time. And it will bless you many, many times again because the magic enjoys your creation too. It's a mutual attraction.

It's important with art that you've got to get the craft, that you devote yourself to the practice of the craft to really be familiar with it. For example, if you are a writer, you have got to write every, every day, not for any special reason but just to write and get better at the craft. You have to shape your life around that obsession; that's the key. That's why artists don't have good relationships. They have to spend so much time with their art and themselves and the muses. And they have to give their heart and soul for it if they are going to experience this moment and this kiss again.

I live a solitary life, but I am not lonesome. My relationship with Patty is great. She lives at the other end of the compound, and we take our meals together and we go on holidays together. We shape our very personal relationship with each other. It's perfect for us. She has a very deep inner life and needs a lot of solitude, more than me actually. She needs lots of time and space. We are blessed—we live here in the beauty and wilderness of northern New Mexico. It is a place of magic.

Being an artist, being creative is a way of being more alive and involved. Live your life with passion! And if I had only one more year to live? I would go sailing! I love sailing.

I am not an adventurer by choice but by fate.
—Vincent van Gogh

TONY JUNIPER

What I am now is an environmental campaigner and writer. I advise companies on environmental strategies; that's my daily calling. I work in academic circles, and I lecture and write and share ideas. I came to this through quite a long journey, starting with an early childhood fascination with nature, and that led to academic studies in zoology. I needed to choose whether the right way to go was to stay in academia and study the natural world or work through science and the disciplines in conservation, trying to hang on to the natural environment as much as we could, gain awareness through changing policies, teach companies to behave differently. I went down that latter path; it is my calling.

I ended up working in environmental groups, working to conserve endangered habitats and threatened species. Then I went more into campaigning and the political side of it through working with Friends of the Earth for quite a few years. That led me into all sorts of experiences and questions in terms of global development. I have that link to private organizations which are fighting deforestation.

I finished running Friends of the Earth in the U.K. for six years and then became the vice chair of this international organization. I stepped out of that in 2008 to pursue a more flexible life, which I am doing now: lecturing, advising, thinking, contributing, teaching in different places. That's kind of where I am now. I am trying to reconcile these increasing pressures on the natural environment and the increasing aspirations of people to pursue rising standards of living and this endless process of economic growth. What is the drive behind all of those things we accumulate? How do we respond to that pressure for consumption? How can we stop climate change, the resource depletion, the extinction of species?

This morning, for example, I was discussing on the radio the effects of G.M and genetically modified golden rice. There is a tendency just to see this as a scientific, ecological issue. But it has to do with power relations and all the choices we face in agriculture. It has to do with vested interests. Unearthing all of that creatively is for me a really important part of the conversation. These wider questions need to be embraced and made public; they are hidden from view.

I approach it by coming in through the back door. That's an important point.

Friends of the Earth has, over the span of eighteen years, tried to get some political attention to those before-mentioned points. "Coming in through the back door" means you have to reach people where it touches their personal lives. You do have to be quite thoughtful how you tackle those issues. I come through the back door because I have years of experience in how to do this kind of work and know how to approach conflicting interest groups. You don't get very far with regulations until it endangers the interests of the people. If you discuss the birds and the impact of chemicals in the agricultural industry, you meet resistance. But if you come from a different point of view and say, "Actually, your drinking water is contaminated with nitrates from the fertilizers, and this is a health issue for you and your family," then people feel motivated to approach politicians, and they want some answers back. Through the back door is a more literal than rational approach. I suppose that it is creative, inspires new ways of thinking. It's about strategy and how we create plans leading to success.

I devote myself to nature's protection. How do we make that fit with the needs of 8 billion people? That's the center of my work and engagement today.

And if I had only one year to live?

Actually, I would write one more book so as to make a final reflection on what it all meant and where the real solutions may lie. It probably would reveal conclusions for specific actions in different places, with the goal of building a big picture into which they all fit. That might be what I would do. I'd write that and do it in a nice place that supports contemplation, probably by the sea at a beach.

The purpose of my life is to leave the natural world in the best possible state so that people can enjoy it in the future. From a very young age, my inspiration came from nature, and it remains so now. That's why I devote myself and my life to nature's protection. That's my message: Love and respect this earth.

Carole Watanabe

To live the creative life, I would live it as I do now!

I live creatively every day. I cannot think of anything else that I would add to make it more magnificent. I paint in France. I stand in the middle of the field of sunflowers and paint the beauty of it. It heals me. It seems like a very simplistic point of view, but it got me through a lot of trauma and grief. I often wonder how people who don't paint get through their traumas? I assume they are writing or dancing or playing music.

My house has become my art form wherever I live. When I look back, that has always been so: I have always created environments since I was a little kid. I was always the one building the fort. I remember that I had a tepee when I was little. I created the fabric and invited others and held court inside. I said, "I am in my office now and you can come in to ask me questions, like how to make a fortune or live happily." That was my business.

My philosophy is, "You live a brilliant life by creating your environment." I need to create the lifestyle and the environment that stimulates me. And I need to keep it fresh and changing so that I feel continuously inspired. That effect shows itself automatically in my work.

I always found supporters of my art. When I was married to my first husband, he was into astrology, so I found out that I am a triple Scorpio. Astrologers think, "Oh my God, how does she function? She must be so hyper," but I always found it pretty easy to achieve what I need, otherwise my body reacts—I get sick. When I go for a long time in a situation that does not suit me, I get out of whack. Like when I lived in San Francisco, I thought I would get my real estate license and help my husband build this new house. I sold real estate for about three months and was successful but became very depressed. I felt like I was not contributing anything worthwhile to the world. I was just shuffling papers. One day, I slipped out of my chair and fell backward and all the papers in my hands fell all over the floor and on me and I began cracking up and laughing and laughing. When my colleagues rushed in and were concerned, I said, "This was my finale—I quit, I quit! I don't want to be in an office!"

You have to be really clear about what it is that nurtures you. And you know that by practice. Look at this small courtyard outside this window. This morning, when I saw the dead leaves and some dead plants outside my window, I knew I had to drive to the next village and buy some new plants and make my garden beautiful, though I am visiting in France for just one month. That's an example for living creatively: You act on your sense of beauty in your ordinary life daily, without hesitation! You act on what it is your soul needs. That is "making holy," like my urge to plant beautiful flowers in this tiny garden. Now when I look out there, I am happy. Every environment I am in has some beautiful flowers in it. That's Temple Maintenance for me, not only outside but also inside my own psyche. My life is full of beauty. I know the things surrounding me: the hand-painted plates, the French tablecloth, the rich mosaics along the walls, my big paintings inspired by the south of France. I love color; I crave beauty; I am happy.

If I only had one year to live, I would live it exactly as I do now! I live every day the way I want to live it. I cannot think of anything else that I would add to make it more magnificent.

Only do what you really want to do. Don't put up with any advice from the outside, since no one knows what is best for you except you.

> *Surely, all art is the result of*
> *One's having been in danger,*
> *Of having gone through an*
> *Experience all the way to the end,*
> *Where no one can go any further.*
> —Rainer Maria Rilke

CATHY ATEN

Some people think I am in denial, because I seem so happy. I am a survivor. When the doctor told me that I had M.S., he was aghast; he had tears in his eyes. In the beginning, it was easy to hide, but when the weakness got worse, I had to hang on to walls and railings and it became very visible. There came a time when I realized that I could fall and break something and it's not going to be okay, because I live alone and nobody would take care of me. I had to get over the fact that I have to use a walker or wheelchair and I got used to them. Now I can see these helpers as friends.

I cannot hide the M.S. anymore. On the other hand, I realize that everybody I know has something going on that is really challenging—everyone. Mine happens to be very visible, so I had to become transparent and vulnerable. When I tell the truth about what's going on with me, it gives others permission to tell their own stories and be vulnerable too.

How do I make a life with such a challenged body?

You see, being an artist all my life has been a very, very precarious existence. I am not a team player. I live and survive solo as an artist. I am comfortable and familiar with insecurity, with my life's circumstances not being predictable. I am not afraid because I have faced a lot of darkness in my life.

I am fifty-eight years old now and still trying to figure me out. I believe that we humans are probably in some kind of "agreement" with the major events and turns in our lives, the things that shatter us and help our souls to grow. M.S. really transformed me. Sacrifice comes from the Latin *sacrificium*, which means making holy.

People think that being an artist is a really glamorous thing, but it's not. We deal with monsters and angels. And there's the monster of resistance, expressed as procrastination. I discuss this with other artists, and we wonder why we resist and get blocked instead of staying in this nurturing, exciting place of creativity. But there's something scary about creativity. It is The Void, which means it is full of everything, emptiness full, the birthing place of creative vision and expression.

I live my life as art.

I live my illness as art.

How am I changing under the influence of my illness?

I pay attention on a much deeper level than I did when I was healthy, to the people I am with, to what I intuit, to what I eat. I pay attention to my thoughts, to what I write, to the light and to the shadows, to my relationship with everything. Look at this dog sitting on my lap. It's something new for me. I never had a dog, because it was too much responsibility, and then this creature came into my life and taught me how to love. I did not know before what that was. She protects me fiercely. She teaches me how to stay in bed a whole day and rest and be okay with that, without judgment. This small creature is my teacher.

I was a visual artist who painted and created objects out of clay. I was successful. Now my right hand is basically without power, lame. I had to change my creative expression and so I began to write using just my left hand and the keyboard. I keep up my blog on the website and share my insights and struggles in ordinary daily life, and I share openly about my encounters with the monsters in my outer and inner world.

I really want to do public speaking, especially to address kids. That's most interesting to me. I want to talk to kids about not being afraid of those who are different and how good it feels when you help somebody. It's a mutual exchange, heart-warming for both the giver and receiver. I think that I have something to share. People are coming to me and asking, "How are you comfortable doing this restricted life by yourself?" and "How are you okay with these physical limitations?" People want to know, and I share my experiences.

Everybody has some sort of genius. My gift in this lifetime is to be an artist, a voice and a way-shower. My illness has segued into my life as my work of art. My illness has become my artistic path. My whole life has turned into my palette; my whole life has become my art. Every single day is shaped by creativity. It's the same thing as making a sculpture or painting: I create something and see if it works, or I might change it and do something different. It's basically the same process as creating a piece of art, but the canvas is my lived life. The thing that I call God, my creativity, is dependent on my getting out of my own way. When the critical judge relaxes, a channel opens inside me. I feel it in my body, like a charge, something of substance. It's happening right now—palpable energy passing between you and me in this encounter.

In the past, I was so interested in what other people thought about me but not much any more. I have the fierceness of a lioness—I am not afraid to give voice. I honor myself for the choices I have made in life. I was depressed, and now I have some substance, and I worked really hard to get here. I feel like if I can do it, anybody can, and if you are not interested in this intensity of being alive, I don't want to hang out with you.

Look at the piece on that wall over there. I made it from earth-materials, and the seeds and sticks create shadows on the surface when light shines on it. I figured out that when I create a grid, it assuages the fear part; it has order and structure. The shadow and the light hold it together like a net, like blood vessels in the body. These shadows are important parts of the whole piece and bring it fully to life—like the shadows in Santa Fe dancing on the adobe walls.

I can hardly walk, but I have all this space and beauty and time; that's a luxury. People think I am navel-gazing, but I like this contemplative solitude and don't make apologies for it. I live in the space that is shaped by myself and my fate. I live my life how I choose to, and that is true luxury. I am happy most of the time. My handicap is not really anguish; it's rather the experience of intensity, of being in the middle of life and choosing to say, "Yes!" I am always consciously moving toward life.

> *The aim of life is to live, and*
> *To live means to be aware,*
> *Joyously, drunkenly, serenely,*
> *Divinely aware.*
> —Henry Miller

If I had one more year to live? I would devote it to developing a soft heart! We are all so armored. I found out through my own learning that it takes a long time to develop a soft heart.

The richness I feel today is based on the recognition of the shadow and darkness. I had to honor my shadow; I have spent so much time in that realm. I am not afraid anymore of who I am. This inner work is about facing monsters that seem so big and strong and insurmountable. But they are brother and sister; they need each other. Accept your shadow and embrace it like the light. Look at light and shadow in an art object. The shadow is just as important as the actual piece. To me it says something, without having to explain what the object is about.

Look at the shadows in Santa Fe dancing on the adobe walls. They bring life to the houses and transform the sharp light into softness.

Aaron Stern

I cannot *not* be creative; I live it all the time. It penetrates all the things I do inside and outside of this project, the Academy for the Love of Learning. I created a big philanthropic organization, and sit on the board of other philanthropic foundations which are creating all those works in the world, and I have my hands in many of them. And then, oh my God, so many organizations and venues and people I am involved with. I am nurtured and supported by the muses.

You know, this place, the Academy for the Love of Learning, has been the deepest implementation of anything I have ever envisioned in my life. Every decision about it has been exhausting. But I am visionary as well as practical. Same as it happens to a composer: You might be very inspired and also need to decide where you put the next note. You have to write a road map for the music—that's very practical.

When I met Leonard Bernstein, I already had the idea for this institute. So when I left China and came back to the U.S., I had a name for it: the New American School, meaning like the Baja School—a wave, a new style of education. And then Bernstein came up with a new name in 1986. He called me in the middle of the night and said, "I have the name for our thing," as he called it. It was my project; he just believed in it and supported it 100 percent. He offered a lot of time to make it real.

There were moments when I just could not figure out what to do next. I was constantly investing so much energy writing about it and imagining it, dreaming it. There was more dreaming and envisioning than real trial and error. And as I moved into the articulation and experimentation, I would write him these proposals, articles, and notes, and I would say, "Come on, you are the guy who writes all those beautiful melodies. Can't you just write this section for me?" And he said "I can't—it's coming out of you. I am your beloved editor; you write and I edit." And I still have all these printouts. He did not know how to use a computer, so I printed it out and he would slash and cross out and rip.

And then in 1990, he died. The academy did not exist then. And so far, it had been just me functioning as the academy. I would go to institutions and create programs, and implement examples of what is now the basic educational work here. I tested it in different places. That's how I followed through with the plans. But when he died in 1990, I didn't know what to do. I was lost and confused and went into depression: It was my forty years in the desert. It really was. And I kept experimenting and believing; it's basically similar to writing a piece of music. You know that you have something in there that will carry the whole piece. You believe it and you know and feel it. And it's the same thing with this place. I saw it as a vision and I knew I had to build it. I had to carry it through.

I gathered people around me who believed in me and knew my heart and my intention, and also supported me financially through donations. But the first support I got for this project was from Lenny Bernstein. And when he died, I was the only person he dedicated some money to, beside his kids. And it was not huge: $100,000. As long as he was alive, he supported me with $60,000 to $80,000 a year to do my work. I was doing work on behalf of his genius. We were always totally a team.

And if I had one year to live? It's a very touching question to me. Again, I feel faithful to my work. I just turned sixty-five, and I see three distinct chapters. First, I dug into this body of work and honored the call. I built this academy. And music and teaching: I cannot not do it. And I would not want to leave this life having done only that. I need to write about this experience and tell the story of it and what I have learned. And that's how I would spend that last year. And I am even positioning myself now to do that because I have fewer years left than I did yesterday and have to do it now.

So I suggest a call for active creativity: Devote yourself and shut the world out when you focus on your art, especially on writing. It is the most amazing experience to live totally with that dedication. It's close to perfect. It's very erotic and sensual. It's urgent, on the edge of life. You see the angels along your path.

> *We work in the dark—*
> *We do what we can*
> *We give what we have.*
> *Our doubt is our passion,*
> *And our passion is*
> *Our task.*
> *The rest is the*
> *Madness of art.*
> —Henry James

ANYA ACHTENBERG

I am so much with people. I teach and do workshops. I work with youth at risk and others who live a crazy life. I am utterly present and drink them in; they live with me, inside. I love these young people and ache with them. I too grew up in chaos and insecurity.

I trust myself—not in a lot of practical ways like resting enough and cleaning my house and such things, but give me that room full of kids who are lost, and I will be on the ground with them. I understand them. And that is art. That's living a life as art, if you are fully engaged. That helps me trust what I know about life and how I live it. Writing is going it alone. Visiting Cuba, I go also alone. And I am welcome in that culture. It's like home for me.

I need to have community, I love to share art with others, share laughs and talks with others. But writing—you can lock me in a cellar. It might be better if I came out and let others read my writing. But I write alone, because I am not alone when I am writing; I have invisible visitors around me. I never had a close intimate relationship that was truly healthy for my life and art. I believe that some things inside me are not as healthy as my creativity. In my creativity, I am strong. I am a lioness.

Creativity: It surprises me. It rattles me and nurtures me. It offers unexpected gifts, like I found the ending of my book one morning all by surprise.

My mood and energy seem to change a lot. Sometimes I am just sad, feel loneliness and abandonment in this cold Minnesota winter. I ache for sun and music and dance. Sometimes I just break down, exhausted. I don't sleep enough. I overload my schedule and go too far. Sometimes I just have to stop. And then all I can do is watch films, movies.

So I have my special medicine. Cuba recharges me. It is one of the places on this planet that is extraordinarily creative. Art, all the arts, are daily fare everywhere. And there is a general understanding that you've got to make it and have it. In Cuba, you naturally create; without that, you are not present. People know and believe that you have to be cultured to be free! And there are a lot of historical reasons why the arts are so amazingly alive in Cuba. Some of this understanding of culture and creativity mirrors my own philosophy as an artist.

My life is filled with art. I recharge with music and dancing. Or I make direct contact with what I am creating, read about it, explore, go to a museum or galleries, observe beauty. I go out and look at things that I have never seen before, ready to be bewildered and shocked.

I feel drawn to this culture because I have the same sense for esthetics and European influences. I am filled with their kind of life energy, sculpture, music, and dance. I have that same dual influence in me. And I also feel this split between a formal art education and this deep rousing from ancient roots and black culture. In Cuba, these are merging inside me with great force. In the United States, they get suffocated.

You see, I am Jewish; my father was born in the Ukraine. I favor the side of my mother, whose parents were both from Russia. Her mother was part Mongolian and part of the Siberian indigenous culture. My mother's father was from North Africa. That's where my roots are. That's what I favor; that's where I got my wild, curly hair.

The arts are my elixir for life. Without arts, I would wither away.

If I had one year to live I would toss out a whole bunch of stuff or give it away. I would let the people I love know about it and let them choose what they want. .

I would spend some time in Cuba, would write and live there! I would give my total devotion to the writing.

A lively soul is rooted in the creative realm with all the danger and lack of security. Take courage and revel in your urge to manifest the treasures of your soul.

> *When we have listening ears,*
> *God speaks to us in our own*
> *Language,*
> *Whatever that*
> *Language may be.*
> —Mahatma Gandhi

ELIAS RIVERA

Creativity is driven by the need and capacity to express yourself through a specific medium. It chooses you, and you choose it. You have to shape your visions into a specific form: writing or singing or painting or dancing, anything that allows you to communicate your inner self. And usually it is a God-given, specific talent you have. You train your skills in that medium. Discipline is a very important part of this process. If you don't have discipline, you are all over the place. There are so many so-called talented people who don't get anywhere because they lack discipline. Again, that devotional part of your self allows you to take it to a special place. And in the end, it's a gift to yourself. What a gorgeous thing to have: to be able to create something beautiful. It's a gift to the world and to you. I feel so honored to be an artist and, through that, a part of creation, which means I am a force of manifestation.

> *The effort we put into*
> *Our work*
> *Is our gift to God.*
> —Matthew Fox

My most important value is integrity and to honor where my gift comes from. It's being in tune with God—that's the origin of creativity. For me, the delicious part of my relationship with my art is that I know its roots. And because I know that, I don't play around with that source. I have a sense of not letting myself be used for lower purposes. My artistic life has always been focused on that. I never, never forget its Divine origin. I have reverence; that is for me the most important trait. Reverence to the divine source. Without reverence, I could not create art.

The great masters, they knew who they were, and then there was something above and beyond the personality. This world is so crass. We don't need art to be cranked out in a hurry—it has a higher purpose than that. Yes, I have to make money, but my motivation for art comes from a different source.

Art is in the core of my life. I allow lots of time when I am painting; I bless and kiss and stroke the canvas. I thank the universe, I ask for guidance. It's essential to me that I never lose sight of that astounding energy of creativity. I am very, very careful not to be haughty about my talent, or it goes out the window very quickly.

The practical life of an artist is a great challenge. Money and survival—that really depresses me. Sue, my wife, is so strong and reliable, a trooper. If I had her not on my side, I would be dead. She is incredible. She loves me a lot. Aside from that, she is a very smart and no-nonsense person. I need that. And she is a big pain in the rear too. I worry about our finances. I don't have this practical sense for ordinary demands. This has been an issue for me all my life. It seems like art and finances are not friends. They strangle each other, except for the time with Riva Yares Gallery in Santa Fe. With that great gallery, I started earning money.

Depression is the backside of anger. I am angry that I am still in this position of lack and need. I know that I am a very gifted artist, and I am struggling. I want God to know that I am here for Spirit: "Let me be; let me do my thing!" I have a great passion to give and contribute. I am still learning and searching and wanting to know and express the truth, but lack of money cuts me short. And my wife gets very angry with me because I am responsible for the situation we are in. It depresses me. It is what it is: I don't have the talent to deal with money. It's my Achilles heel. I know many artists are in my place. I need to keep my innate sense of hope. I am basically an optimist, but I also have a huge dark side. I know where I want to go artistically. I seek eternal growth. I honor that with gratitude.

I need to watch myself. If I am not mindful, I would be self-destructing! I want to plug into constructive energy. When I paint, I leave this all behind and go to the realm where the soul expresses itself. My studio is my sacred space. I always play classical music as I paint.

When I am involved in my art, I go back and back and deeper and deeper. I try to take the object of my painting to a very deep place so I really see and paint the face of my art objects and the movement of their bodies. I paint mainly women. There's so much beauty. I travel to Mexico and Guatemala and take pictures in those colorful marketplaces. And then I go home and paint from the photographs. Those women and children don't mind the picture-taking; they are so much in the here and now in their lives. They feel that I am honoring them. I hold such respect for them. I have a strong bond to the Mayan culture and their people; that's where my own roots are. I adore those women. Ninety percent of my paintings are of women, and I have a deep connection to them. It makes me really comfortable to enter and portray their world.

It's unbelievable, because I had such a problematic relationship with my mom. When she died, I walked into the room and saw her on the slab and had zero response emotionally. She was such pain in my life. Maybe I am still wanting to heal something in relationship to her when I paint the beauty of women and find a relationship with that feminine world. And I really have tremendous respect for women. They are strong, they are survivors.

And if I had only one year left to live? Would I change? Not really. I would continue to paint and never lose my heart. I know I have a good heart and I am generous. I cherish that in myself—it's the best part of my dad in me. I was always very mindful of that. I have given paintings and drawings away to friends. That's what nurtures the paintings; they want to be with people, desired and admired. I enjoy imagining those pieces as members of families. I give and people still have those gifts in their homes. I want to be part of the good equation; we really create ourselves through our actions. I am mindful of that.

Part of the creative process is
To return to the beginning,
To become childlike again,
Vulnerable to awe and wonder.
—Matthew Fox

YAEL WEISS

I am married to a violinist, and we have a little boy of five years. When I travel a lot, I have to bring back the obligatory present, and he is excited about that. We also travel together sometimes. My husband has two grown sons.

How do I manage all that? How do I live the creative life? I thought I was not really able to do my best as a mother and a musician. But now I have learned through doing and practice, and I am able to keep a very good balance. When you asked me about my source of creativity, I immediately thought about my little son and his smiles and the funny comments he makes. Even just that gives me so much joy.

There's no question that an artist has to be balancing everything carefully. I really feel very content with the time I spend with music, the time I spend with toys and fire trucks and cars, and I don't feel that anything is missing. On the contrary, everything is benefitting.

So how do you care for a family and also live the life of a concert pianist who is touring internationally? It's something that I have given a lot of thought to. And interestingly, the challenge we are facing here is that there are actually not a lot of role models.

Until my boy was born, I could hardly imagine having a child. I was so completely focused on what I did as a musician and could not imagine adding a task like that. And now, somehow having him in my life has raised my music skills to a much higher level. It wasn't something that I forced at all—it happened as a blessing. My boy is a source of creative energy. How beautiful to watch a young child! I have learned so much. Without question, as a mother, I am a different kind of artist now than I was six years ago. I am able to communicate beauty to many more people now.

Motherhood and spending time with a young person, and to realize the way that he sees the world with this sense of discovery, where everything is new—all that is such a source of creativity! And there is that kind of excitement and enthusiasm that is vibrant. It's beautiful; it's like a composer writing a new piece of music. For me personally, it has been a great transformation to learn from my child and to have the experience of being a mother as well as an artist. Both roles hold major parts of my identity.

Whenever I speak with people who are interested in what I do as a musician, I always try to bring others closer to the process first and to inspire them to find their own interest. I am curious and like to communicate with people who are not musicians. Their questions are different, and I learn from that because they have a different perspective.

I was a professor at the University of Indiana for six years. And then it had gotten a little too crazy with the demands of performances and travel. So a year ago, I decided to move back to New York.

I was eager to focus on projects that I wanted to do for some time. I get very involved trying to find that specific sound that communicates to people and reaches their heart. It helps to keep my environment simple and clear, as I tend to lose concentration when I am distracted by projects that are unrelated to what I am rehearsing at the time. I try to keep the setting minimalist, especially around the piano area. I think my sense of order is a personality thing, often different than people expect from an artist.

That's funny because in the paintings of Beethoven's room, there are so many things that one hardly can see the piano. Even my own teacher, Richard Goode, when I came for my first piano lesson, I was amazed about the environment itself, being some kind of chaotic. For me, I actually only need the piano and a bench. I walk on stage and all that is in front of me is the piano and a bench. I need that simplicity and order, and on top of that, I need to play without distraction. That's essential in my life as a pianist.

One year to live? I would pursue two things: I would ask myself whether there are any great masterpieces that I have not yet discovered and I would make it a priority to be with those pieces. I would want to live with them and experience them. I would not stay super-active but possibly just sit down quietly and meditate.

I am highly interested in zen, so I would probably go on retreats and explore silence. Silence is an important part of music. And I would spend a lot of time with my boy.

Talent develops in quiet places,
Character in the full current
Of human life
—Johann Wolfgang von Goethe

Uwe Walter-Nakajima

I studied and lived in Japan in a small village north of Kyoto. I think my purpose is to collect all the new, creative trends and bring them back to Germany, especially for young people. And also to bring European and American creative trends to Japan. Young people here in Japan are hungry, seeking answers, especially after the Fukushima accident. There is a mistrust now, and that's new in Japan. This country is functioning because people trusted each other. It's a society of consensus, and that is lost now. After the Fukushima accident, people felt hurt and cheated, almost paralyzed.

The young people are moving now, many of them leaving Tokyo and coming to the villages, like the one where I live now. The political leaders are lying, and the young folks know that. They look through the web and feel deeply disappointed.

I am just traveling through here in the U.S. I had to borrow money from my sister. I do not have a job right now, but I can live well because I live the simple life in the country, in this small Japanese village north of Kyoto, and I have good survival tools. I bought this old house and fixed it up all by myself. I built my own studio. It did not cost me more than about $1,000 for materials. After one concert, I was paid in building materials for the house instead of cash, like four trees and rocks and mud and windows and so on. We bought the old house, and my wife and I repaired it. She is incredibly good in those things, very skilled, a craftswoman. She repairs kimonos and she bakes German bread. I taught her how, and now she sells it as well.

We live in the countryside and don't need cash. That liberates me in my decisions. I am free. I worked for TV, but there is censorship in Japan now. For example, I was not allowed to perform publicly because I mention Fukushima! It's almost like in China—censorship! I was angry and asked myself why I came to Japan. I am censured here, and in Germany now, I would be free. Germany is changing its history.

So I quit my TV job and moved with my three kids to the countryside. As long as we have a home and food and some gasoline for the car, we don't need much money. It's sometimes hard physical work, like getting the trees for the house building down the mountains with my bare hands. And I carried my child on my back during this work.

I make everything myself, like beer, liquor, wine, cheese, tofu, nuts, pickles. Now I am installing solar energy and biogas. We have a goat to produce goat cheese.

And I have a plan. I will rent an empty house and offer it as a dojo for people who are looking for another lifestyle. We have many futons and mats and a kitchen in the house. We live and work together to awaken the creative kundalini energy. We make music and dance.

I don't have anxiety of not surviving. No! Never! That's not part of me. I am blessed, and maybe I don't deserve it. But I trust—and I am full of music and joy!

The culture in Japan is a matriarchate. Japanese men have their own society, and are very close; they laugh from their hearts and are bonded. I have many close friends there, almost too close. They walk into my home at any time. I am not the white man anymore; people forget my origin because I speak their language fluently, even their dialect. It's like in music: it's not the sound that is important but the aftertaste. There is much said in the in-between spaces, in what is not said but is hanging in the echo of the words. The Japanese are not making it up—you feel it. The silence between the words is important to check out what the other really said. And then the cup of tea—it helps to connect on a deep level. There's an expression that says, "You can read the air." We are connected, not only you and me but throughout the universe. That's the real meaning of a cup of tea. It means, "we are from different cultures but we are connected; we have tea together. We can meet without fighting, so we create peace by having tea together."

These are very sensitive people. They see the universe in a cup of tea. It may take half an hour to have one sip. I love these people. I am at home there.

And here is my message to young people: Find a way to free yourself from worries about yourself; care for others. Move your body; practice aikido, yoga, dance. To be free does not mean that you are selfish; it means that you take responsibility for your freedom. Ask many questions, all the time. Ask why. Ask yourself: What does freedom mean? I escaped from East Germany to the West, and my first experience was that my rich aunt did not allow us to stay in her house—we had to go to the refugee camp. Money is just an abstract idea. Don't let it rule your life. Look at every problem from all different angles to overcome boundaries and separation from others' beliefs. Come together and exchange opinions and insights. Learn from others, constantly. Get rid of fear.

Beauty is an ecstasy;
It is as simple
As hunger.
—W. Somerset Maugham

TIM GOSNELL

One way of living creatively means thinking a lot. I once got a performance report at LANL [Los Alamos National Laboratory] that said, "He is an out-of-the-box-thinker." That was one of those moments where somebody on the outside looking in finds something that I did not really recognize in myself. That's one of the more rewarding things I have been told.

There was never any doubt about my endeavor and interest in science when I started out as a young man. That phase is closed, and I don't think that will be replaced with the stuff young people do and dare today. I don't have the hunger to be a recognizable eccentric. I am now devoted to a quieter way of seeking. Now it's about spending time with my friends, pursuing studies that I find interesting. I have grown into much quieter needs. It's like taking a breath and letting the struggles calm down. Maybe I am now accepting my limitations in the world, like that "life-not-lived business." I can set that aside. It does not have to be burnished. I am looking now for the sanctity of everyday life—engage more in those activities. I have become very interested in cooking. This need is burbling up now, and I find myself kind of surprised about my appreciation of fairly mundane activities, like fixing the faucet or something else way beneath my educational level. I am enjoying the ability to face the physical world and delight in the positive outcome.

When I worked at the lab, the question that occupied me was, "What is the morality of all those weapons around here?" That was very hard for me to answer in a satisfactory way. It was not possible to answer simplistically. I explored history, trying to get some better perspective on the development of the atomic bomb and the end of World War II. Some experts think it was not really necessary to drop the bomb on people, but others do. I don't know if there is ever a truth to be found on that subject. It's hard to ignore that when contemplating morality around those events. At the same time, these things are pretty terrible devices if they can evaporate a whole city. The best I can do is to argue on both sides of the story. Maybe the bombs were necessary, but I would not want to defend that in court. So I mostly invest my inquiry in things I can do something about.

Most of the things I did at LANL had nothing to do with the bomb. I did not really have to confront that personally; I was lucky in this area. But I thought about these questions a lot. I was not really part of it. I was not really troubled by it, and I left the lab for other reasons.

What is my purpose? I get queasy about assigning myself a life purpose. But if that means my contribution to society, I believe I have done my share. I am no longer a public servant. I wrote some papers and books, and they sit now on the library shelves and will be there until the world will end. I think I have evolved. Now I have different needs to fulfill as I get older. One of the reasons I left the lab was that I was getting weary of the battles inside the profession, the endless safety inspections and trainings, the bureaucracy. If a piece of equipment would break, I would have to drive around for miles in my car just to ship it off to be repaired. This is not what I wanted to do for the rest of my life. I listened inside and heard this small voice encouraging me: "What you are really looking around for is to be free, you bastard, free of all this nonsense." It was too annoying to do science under such conditions.

The way I solved the problem is to admit that one doesn't have to work on the big questions of existence. As my thesis adviser once said, "You don't have to solve the existence of the universe." I still would love to if I had the talent to do it, and I might want to try again one day. I think that working on any kind of problem can be fun; it does not have to be earth-shattering, if I can do that in an environment where I am not subject to these bureaucrats. I have some of those creative projects running right now and will see how they are unfolding. Right now, in this stage of development, I don't have an income and live from savings.

It's kind of selfish, but I am not concerned about my fellow men. For me now, it's more about living well and letting go of great ambitions. I enjoy spending time with my friends, my wife, cooking. I want to be doing so many things now which I did not do when young because I was so busy getting an education and building a career. I was so devoted to science but was only making

$10,000 a year until I was twenty-nine years old. I left graduate school with three hundred bucks in my pocket.

My purpose, if I have to design one, is to be as free as I can. I don't have an ambition to be a philanthropist or fix the world. I want to deposit my creative abilities in a container that doesn't push back so much as the working world does in our institutions. I am seeking and probing all the time how to live a creative life. I like to think about myself as creative, but it's not really something I have to worry about; it sort of does what it does by itself. I don't feel like being creative for creativity's sake. On the other hand, I had a creative thought this morning as I was thinking about the difference between artist and scientist, and I thought, "What if we would invent a whole kind of artistic experience where that space between the object and the observer is short?" We have become able to move atoms around and can observe them. What if we made that accessible to the viewer through big machinery and let them build things like a mosaic out of atoms?

Creativity is not something I was seeking. I was pushed more by career requirements, job situations, demands from donors. It's not a burning passion. We talk too much about it. But everyone is creative in some fashion because we are always solving problems. Even newborn babies are solving problems. So there is an everyday experience everybody has got. The one persistent thing in my life is that I have always looked for the funny thing, the absurd, the out-there, the humorous.

And if I had one year to live? I read a quote I liked: "The closer you get to the end of your life, the more risks you should take." I mean life-threatening kinds of things. This notion is carved into the back of my head since years ago. Dr. Kevorkian, who fought for assisted suicide, is such a person for me. He worked all his life in his medical career and then he put himself at existential risk to fight for his beliefs. It's scary to talk about this, which goes back to the question about the dark side of creativity. I sometimes have really black ideas of what I might want to do. This is pretty scary stuff if I imagine it being published. It's pretty black and dark to see how this whole thing could be turned upside down. I see myself descending to the same level to demonstrate the insanity about this point of view. Maybe it could bring some freedom for me so I would not have to care so much for the things that bring me much despair.

On the other hand, I might finally be creating my radio show with the music people love. I want to get to a place of more transcendence. And there is much that I never had a chance to learn in school, connected to the big question of the origin of the universe. I am reading a lot about it now. I want to re-engage in what got me going in the beginning of the scientist's path.

JERRY WENNSTROM

It takes courage to stop and step off the track to watch and just *be*. I decided not to talk for a year. I was tired of social requirements. I wanted to know myself inside silence. It's such a simple act, but there is great social pressure on a silent person. It takes courage to live without spoken words, not using silence as a defense or power trip but just to be quiet when you feel like it.

It takes courage to be what you are. Even when you are annoyed, you are still bouncing off others. It takes courage to do what the moment wants and face the truth of that moment. It says in the Bible, "He who fears to be foolish will never learn to be wise." I have learned to be foolish without fear.

It's about finding the sacred in the moment.

In my daily life, I seek balance. If I write too much or work in my studio to exhaustion, I get up and go into the garden. I love planting and pruning and digging and nurturing. Sometimes so-called mundane activity is more important than our so-called art.

To live with nothingness means that I am available, without interruption, to do anything at any time. Part of giving my belongings away and destroying my art was to come to terms with nothingness. You have to find meaning in emptiness. I discovered that often, it is full of unexpected resources. Exploring nothingness is like learning to dance: It's clumsy at first and you don't know what you are doing. It's even meaningless—what are these steps for? Later, the music comes on and you get in tune and harmony with what you are doing. It's a beautiful experience when you become one with the music.

In my life right now, the music is playing and I am living the dance as my second nature. It's not difficult; I am flowing with it.

But earlier, when I lived in New York, when I decided to give everything up, it was really difficult; I didn't know the territory at all. I didn't know if it would work; I didn't know if I would die. But at this time now, it has become celebratory. It has become my life. If you are so completely available in your daily existence, you learn a lot of practical matters. It's not theoretical but you learn to fix things; you don't go and buy stuff. There is a usefulness that comes with the way I live. You learn to make things, you mow your lawn and don't need to go to exercise class and spend money on that. Simple living is practical. You plant the garden and grow veggies. I have nothing, but I have everything I might need, and beyond.

I have become conscious and see that there is no victim. We can change our field of action any time if we want to; we have choices how we live in this world. One of the benefits of living with nothing, as I did for thirteen years, is that I can always go back to nothing if my life changes and I don't have money or relationships. There's great freedom in that. It's almost like going back to an old romance.

The hardest thing to do after destroying my art was doing nothing. It's good to know how to do that because we all have to finally let go and do nothing. Daily life keeps us busy, is holding us in its routine, but doing nothing creates an ultimate challenge.

How to discern between creativity and just living my life? There's no difference. Even you are not always being creative. Just be alert to what the next moment might bring.

One year to live?

Death is the ultimate limitation. Life is to die again and again. We cannot even let go of our ideas about ourselves—how are we supposed to let go of everything in the moment of death? It's going to require creativity and inspiration. If you live your authentic self, don't worry too much if you hurt somebody. Your example could be the best thing to teach courage. You just follow your intuitive self. When you do what really inspires you, everybody gains.

I think we should deal with death as early as possible so to live fully in life. If we are running from death, we will never be free. The only way to deal with that bogey-man is to look him in the face.

God dwells within the heart of the artist
And the artist draws God
Out of her heart
When she is at work.
—Matthew Fox

Vijali Hamilton

My journey to travel with the World Wheel around the world started in 1986 and has been growing over twenty-five years now. At the onset of it, I didn't have any base in the U.S. and considered every country my home and my family. And now I have a base here in Santa Fe, and that is a different situation. In the past, I had a home in Utah on a five-acre place in the most beautiful wilderness in the Canyonlands area. After I had finished the first Wheel journey around the world, I built a straw bale hogan and used all natural materials. I felt I needed to be grounded on earth. I surprise myself as I sit here in this apartment in Santa Fe and wonder about it. Yes, I am missing my raw place out there where I lived for seventeen years in the wilderness in utter beauty and solitude.

That's where I wrote my book *World Wheel, One Woman's Quest for Peace*, and I wrote poetry. I have a cave on the land for meditation. There's a very profound depth that comes with such a solitary life connected to the earth. I lived there for five years before I started my World Wheel, and then I had a dream that called me out of my solo retreat and guided me to go into the world and enact the World Wheel. That's how I stretched mightily beyond myself and started the global work. It was initiated by a dream. I was called and I followed the call. In the fields of life, I have made myself as strong as a lion.

And how do I deal with ordinary daily life beside such a big vision? That's really the most important thing: how you do your daily chores. Everything that comes your way needs you and is more important than turning your back to the world and isolating yourself for your art. Ultimately, to live an ordinary life is the greatest task. You have this longing inside of you, and no matter what happens in your life, to hear and follow that calling is what it's about.

So I decided to enjoy it, all those little practical tasks of ordinary life. I scrubbed my kitchen floor this morning, and wow—it looks so good and I enjoy it so much that I think it is practical spirituality, how it's lived and integrated into everyday life. I think it's important to keep your life as simple as possible. I have always done that, have always lived my life in modest ways. For me, that is now all integrated: the day-to-day demands and the big vision of global work. A lot of my time is involved in responding to the demands of the practical life around the art itself.

For so many years, I have concentrated on environmental work and the Wheel. That includes all the emails and contacts I make, my response to people I met along the road or maybe my financial support of them. That takes up much time, and instead of that being a nuisance, I see it as part of my artwork.

Action may not always bring happiness
But there is no happiness
Without action.
—Henry James

WESLEY WEST AND AMANDA MCPHAIL

Amanda: I don't think I always focus on my art 100 percent because I like doing too many things, such as gardening, the kids, family, and friends. To be really creative, you have to be almost one-sided. And very selfish! And for a woman, that can be difficult. I run the home in an organizational style, so my time is always eaten into. I envy people who can just do creative endeavors because there is nothing else to disturb them. Yes, I do my artistic work, but I am grabbing time from other things. And that is hard for me as a woman and mother. When my children were young, I tried hard to do both, my work and my duties as a mother, and it did not come out well, neither with my children—I was grumpy—nor with my ceramic work, where I felt hurried. So I decided to structure that better: When they were out of the house, I worked in my studio, and when they were at home, I was with them. I heard that women don't concentrate like men because we think about all the stuff of our lives, like, "Did I take that fish out of the freezer?" I am preoccupied with family things while Wesley does not worry what's for supper!

Wesley: Yes, that's true. I remember once in Lincoln, we had drinks with dear friends and we talked about her father, the painter A.J. She had written a book about him, and she said to both of us, "In one relationship, there is only room for *one* creative person if you want the relationship to be together and work well. If both are equally creative, then other things might be neglected."

Amanda has been wonderful and always supported my creative life. But I must admit, sadly, that—yes—I have supported her creative life but not like she did mine. She was all the time devoted to me. We had two friends who lived in Cornwall. They are both creative people, but their marriage got less attention than their art. They live together, she does her work and he does his work, and when you go there, there is no social engagement and atmosphere. They are both individual artists. They are husband and wife but only by name. They are very together, and they live the creative life totally, but their couple-ship is in the shadow of their creativity.

We are together as a couple, but when the family needs feeding or our aunt needs help when she was sick, Amanda is the one who is engaged.

I think to live a truly creative life, one has to be 100 percent selfish. When you walk through a famous artist's exhibition, like Picasso's, you see the impossibility to be devoted to art and also do other things, like organizing kids and caring for a social life and so on.

Does the relationship suffer when you have an artist's career, or does your art suffer when you live in a relationship and have children?

I think we have a fantastic marriage, but there are compromises in our creativity. You have to compromise. I am fairly selfish, but I still don't get the 100 percent of devotion to my art, because Amanda would not let me. But she also gives me space, allows time to support me. We compromise. I think every creative person needs the other person to do the everyday things, especially when there are children. I think I failed sometimes.

My children look through the photo albums and say, "Where were you, Dad, during those holidays? First, I don't like holidays, and second, I was always working, day and night, with the pressure of deadlines. I was a very successful creative person in the '80s and '90s. And you couldn't be that successful and creative if you had a full family life.

Amanda: Sometimes I envy people with nine-to-five jobs. We had to cancel so many weekends. In those years, it was full-on non-stop work. Wesley was in London, in New York. He was so busy; the work was just coming in and coming in. Sometimes he had to do three jobs in a day. He worked for advertising and short movies on TV, created the props and settings.

Wesley: And when we were done, my co-workers and I would sit together and plan the next pieces. It was a wonderful, wonderful time. But it was also a selfish time because I had a family and was sitting there with this group of creative people being engaged and inspired and doing things, having much fun. And when I came home, I was often angry because I didn't really want to be there—I wanted to be back in the studio with these interesting people. But we made it through and I was bringing money back home, got the children through school.

Amanda: Is that a creative life?

My favorite days are those when I put on my red hat and go into my studio and do my work undisrupted. A creative day is wonderful. I am doing what I love doing. And there are so many different things I wished I could do, like organizing an art show that's coming up for me. But, you see, I can't just be doing that without half an ear to the world outside, to my aunt who is in the hospital or a friend who is in distress and needs me.

Wesley: Maybe creativity is defined by the act of actually doing something and producing an object. It's not just life lived creatively. Or maybe, creativity does apply to everything we do. Even if you work in a factory, making serial things, you created them with your own hands.

Amanda: Or maybe your raised your children as pacifists and they care for you and other people and they are politically active. Isn't that creative too? Or you stroke your cat and look outside and see that the sun is shining—you recognize what's happening around you. Is that a creative life? I think that we are producing not just out of ourselves but we always integrate inspiration and new ideas from the people around us. We are not totally original in what we create.

Wesley: So we take all those ideas from others or from nature and put them together in a very personal way, or make them out of different material, and that's our creativity.

Amanda: I think there is a difference between the modes of art. I always thought that painters are more serious about their art. They would probably define creativity much more eloquently. We have never been good in artistic verbiage. I don't care much for it. I want to look at it and get a feel for it. I don't want it all explained in art-speak. Art-speak annoys the hell out of me because you can pass off bad work with clever words.

Wesley: I hate everything that makes me feel ignorant. It upsets me. You have been to art school and someone is telling you why you don't understand this piece. Once we visited a beautiful art space where they had set out twenty chairs in a circle, and we thought it was a conference room. But then I said that might not be a conference; this might be "art." So we read about it, and it was "art;" it was a visual vocalization of a space without the people so your own imagination could visualize the conversations. But in reality, there were just those bloody chairs!

Beauty is an ecstasy;
It is as simple
As hunger.

Amanda: If we had only one year to live, I would not change anything. We don't have a bucket list. Maybe people would become more important than my work. I would not shut myself away for the arts; I would be with people. Definitely, family and friends would be more important than any art object.

Wes: I don't know, and I often wonder what is the purpose of my life? It's the people who count, whom you met and connected with—they give purpose. They make life worth living. Our home has always had an open door, a place where people can come. We welcome people. People who had cancer or are ill in some way, people who are happy, they find an open house. I think that's our achievement. We have always been generous; even if sometimes we haven't had anything to share, we share ourselves.

It is not the language of painters
But the language of nature
Which one should listen to.
—Vincent van Gogh

Sara Warber

Creativity is like food or breathing; it's so essential that it makes life vibrant and worth living. I think that in our country, art is seen as non-essential, yet I believe that it is indispensible for our soul, personal or collective. It's essential for health and well-being. I wonder how we can build community that honors that, so that the artist has food on their table. This is a fundamental question that has bothered me for a long time in my life. One of the things that drove me to be a doctor is my need to contribute to the basic values of a culture.

I would have been very happy not to be a physician. I would have been very happy to not be anything other than an artist. When I was younger, I wanted to stay with theater—that's what I studied. All its aspects enchanted me, not only the acting but also the creative activities around that: the environment, costumes, and lighting. I think that now, I would choose two- and three-dimensional fabric art.

Yes, I am a doctor now, but you cannot look from the back end of your life and say I could have been this or that or the other. When I engaged with healing and medicine, I knew that I was truly on my path. When I registered for that first class in med school, I knew it was right. I knew that I was stepping onto my path.

Today I have learned to be expressive and artistic as a physician. That's the way I have chosen to integrate and live my creativity now. In the latter half of my life, there's always the draw toward a more personal engagement of my artistic skills. I need the joy of color, absolutely. In my profession, I miss the artistic and playful aspects of the arts. Yes, there's something like sacrifice in this. I had a dream in which I was in a powerful way ordered to "Sacrifice!" and I answered: "I am willing to sacrifice for the people."

I am a physician and see the work of a doctor as the halfway place between science and art. The scientist and the artist are both required to create out of thin air. The physician creates on the spot. In interaction with the patient, she draws on what she knows and on her intuition. If I am truly involved, I am allowing something new to emerge in that moment of encounter with the patient.

When I need to solve a problem, it usually shows itself in the physical world, and I need a practical solution. Our work is often on the physical level, down to earth, in the body, and it is rooted in science and in spirit. So I sit quietly and draw pictures. I figure out how to see the full circle of the problem. These drawings help me to be wholly engaged in bringing the idea out into reality. The process is rewarding in itself. I enjoy this inner doodling. I am a visual person. That is for me where my art and science meet.

The routine that supports this process is journal writing on white paper, where I can draw and write without lines and order on the page. That is problem solving at its best, free and relaxed. The source of solutions is the connectivity in my brain that has built up over many years of work with the human body and mind. They suddenly inspire each other in new ways and allow different ways of relating. My metaphysical self knows that it's all Spirit. This kind of work opens up the connection to the Universe. So the physician is an artist who works with the science of medicine.

Place is essential for me. My home is such a haven, where I can be in a creative environment as I am right now: in my creative spot on the couch, looking outside over a pond, with the trees around. I track the sun as it moves across and changes from summer to winter. It's a quiet house. My husband plays music and we talk occasionally; otherwise, it's quiet. All my creative work comes from this place in my home; it's like a nest. To do my demanding work, I need a life in which I get nurtured and energized, where I can focus on my self. Otherwise, in the clinic, I am very, very available and present in my relationship with the patients. I need this balance between self and other, inner and outer.

One year to live? I would quit my job, wander around, do only what I want to do. I would make and build things, always new ones. Wild stuff. Or I would probably work harder, because I had a deadline, and I love deadlines. I am actually hoping to have more than one year left, because I have a lot on my list. I am looking forward to the freedom of retirement.

Ruth Bamford

I am a scientist—physics and mathematics. I live my life creatively and bring science and math into my everyday activity all the time. Here's an example: The other day, my "out-laws" were visiting. They wanted to go on a boat trip. We had two cars, six people in each of them, three drivers. I wanted to arrange it so that we had a minimum amount of driving back and forth for each driver. It was very clear to me what the pattern was. I repeated it to them, but they did not get it.

I use my creativity in daily life, naturally, and sometimes I don't understand what's mysterious about it. I am practical. I make a chicken coop out of an old wardrobe and it gets converted easily and without struggle. I hate it to be messy. I like esthetics, especially in daily life. In our home, we have a rabbit that walks around the house. I don't want him to be in the bedroom, so I invented an automatically closing door with weights on ropes; it gently closes the bedroom door after one walks through so the rabbit cannot get in. And it can be used for Halloween, with stuff going up and down as the door moves. I love when things around me work logically and smoothly. Science should help to make life easier.

My work is focused on that cosmic realm out there. I am fascinated with space and its rules and conditions. Its mystery fascinates me. I developed a deflector shield. a protective umbrella, a force field that will keep humans in space safe from cosmic rays when they are outside the atmosphere that protects us. This active magnetic shield is an ingenious and portable protection outside the spacecraft. We are using its own nature and energy against its possibly destructive force.

Yes, I think often about my children, who are twelve and ten. My daughter has her own alert perceptions and can very quickly follow what I am saying. So I know how her mind works in the same way as mine. She is often my audience, and what I appreciate in her is her lively and curious approach to physical reality. She is very creative, and often she thinks differently than others do. So she calls our house rabbit a cabbit, because the rabbit thinks he is a cat. Our son loves to have fun with whatever he does. He is my critical audience, and he challenges me when we work on something together. My children have alert and lively minds.

I think it's important not to just exist but to think. I observe and feel amazed just by the fact that anybody is alive. Look at flowers or other creations and be amazed; be awake and conscious. Be amazed even by machines; they are complicated and well constructed. And watch the moon up there. I want to keep a sense of that awe, even in the darkest times. This universe is amazing even if you don't like the circumstances in which we live right now.

If I had only one year to live, I would devote it to my children. I would make sure that there's some continuity when I can't come back. Professionally, I would continue to do the same research. I think that considering the ending of all would change my perspective on what's important and what's not. I always had a sense of urgency, which means I keep that thought in mind: It could happen to you; don't waste the time.

If I would be offered the same choices again, I might study psychology this time. I always wanted to study the nature of the universe, and physics is the motivating factor to do that, to determine the truth. You find it by living life, actually being involved with it, and a lot of that truth is found in how you look at life, your attitude. So the greater sense of discovery is to understand yourself.

Follow Shakespeare's advice: To thine own self, be true. Always.

Creativity is our birthright; it's inherent in us.
It's not a lazy game. Surrender is the end product of a whole lot of hard work.
—Jerry Wennstrom

Peggy O'Kelly

I turn my life into art when I nurture myself. When I eat, spend slow time, light candles, appreciate my environment, my life becomes art. What kills it is time pressure, administrative demands. I fill up my days with those business demands and have no time to reflect and just be. I need to create specific islands of time to think and imagine and appreciate. Like today, when I got my new products from Morocco, I slowed down to unpack them and be alert and relaxed with them.

I am learning that I need to restrict my business expansion for the sake of my personal peace. I do not have to live the bigger and better thing. It is so tempting, but I had to ask myself for whom I would do that. This is new for me: to observe that I am changing. That is my new way of living a creative professional life. I always headed toward a goal, and if I wanted something and it felt right, I went for it and usually reached it. It feeds the ego but not my spirit. I am now building and following new values and visions. I have not been able to think that way before. I am in new territory. Before, my basic vision said, "Being successful is having multiple stores, creating a national brand." Now, I shape that path differently. I build only one store in the way that it feeds me and brings income. And I am an accountant by trade, so I see that can be done. Why would I not follow that more peaceful direction? Is it because from the outside, it looks less successful? And the people around me got nervous, asking how will you do this or that, will you not lose when you shrink instead of expanding?

Oh, I had to calm myself down. Yes I knew how I would do that. I live and breathe that stuff and understand business very well. I usually have a solid plan. I reflected and realized that the first step would be to prepare a sacred space. This reduction of business space and demand would be a big move for me. The space needs to support the flow of energy in my business. So much of flow in creativity is dependent on the space where it can live and unfold, where we are available.

My purpose in life is to develop and live my trust in spirit and to follow my heart more than my head, to walk the path that allows expansion. And by doing so, I influence people whom I touch. It does not matter if I have a multimillion-dollar business or just one store. I want to bring light to what I do. I have so much left to do. All is quickly unfolding in front of me, like this whole business cooperation with Morocco for olive oil and rose water production. Bringing that into the villages and empowering the women who live and work there means a lot to me.

I have this idea that I am going to do something completely out of the norm. And it will be out of most people's comfort level. And it will be right in mine, without me knowing yet what that will be. I have impact, but I feel like I have so much more to offer to the planet than what I am doing now. I trust that I will manifest it.

One more year to live? I would travel to sacred places all over the world, and I would also seek closeness with my children. My message to them: Find your connection to the Earth; first and foremost, honor the Earth.

I made wrong decisions and will continue to make wrong decisions,
That's part of a creative life.
—Chrissie Orr

CHRISSIE ORR

My whole life changed when I stepped off the usual path and became part of a group in which we actually used the creative process in a different and more connected way, away from the art college and the gallery and the art market. This was the way the arts should work, I thought. It was more than creating an object of art. I was actually using that spirit of creativity as they did in tribal societies—that's what art is about. It needs to have a function inside the community to tell the story, to hold the story, to hold the culture. It's taken me many years to do that, and it's what

I am still doing today. This weaves like a thread through my whole life—community involvement.

In my world, before that awakening, I had a sense of innocence. I loved studying the arts; it was wonderful. And after college, I was living in a tiny apartment on Royal Mile in Edinburgh and working in the evening as a barmaid. I was creating my art in this small space. I was a successful artist. I had a couple of one-woman shows, and people were collecting my work. And then everything changed for me when I had this epiphany. One of the collectors asked me if I would want to come and visit his apartment to see how he had placed my work, and did I want to look at his other works that he had collected? "Yes," I said, "I would be delighted to do that," and I remember how I came to his flat. In Edinburgh, most people live in very small apartments on the fifth or sixth floor. I got to his door and knocked and he opened it, and I looked at his apartment, and then I got this huge hit; it hit me in the center as I realized: "This guy has the worst taste in the universe!"

My mouth just dropped open and I was speechless, did not know what to say or do! I remember leaving and going back to my little flat and asking: "What is this world about, the one I was trained for as an artist?" I realized that the artist's work has no connection to anything around it. It might be exhibited in a gallery but is not bonded to real life. And somebody buys it and hangs it—and I can't see the threat that's coming from my soul to them. I mean, if you are a creative being in this world, a really creative being, this work comes from your deepest self, exposing your naked inner depth—oh, I thought, I do not want to do this art this way anymore. I don't want to create any more art where the work went out and I have no connection to it anymore.

That put me into a huge dilemma. I had finished art college and was doing well, but this experience pulled the rug out from under me. I remember going into the bar where I worked and speaking to my colleague and saying, "I don't know what I am going to do! I am really lost now." My colleague said, "I heard about this workshop just around the corner. There are lots of different artists working there, and they go out to communities with their work. I don't know much about it, have just a gut feeling, so go and look."

That happened to me, and it started the next stage in my life as a creative person. I did go around to this place. I met the director, and basically, we chatted for two hours. He told me that they had theater people and musicians, visual artists and writers working there together. And they would go out into the street and work with community and community issues, building community, using the arts as a way of expression and connection with people and real life. He said, "Why don't you go and dream up something?" He took me on. There was no money in the beginning. I just went and joined. One of the first things I did with him was that we went to work at a school for the blind. That was a new beginning, and I have never looked back.

My art has taken many, many different forms. I tried to give it up, but I stuck with it and basically gave up any kind of work in the studio. And today it has shifted so that my work straddles a bit of both sides. I feel now that you really need that—you need that reflection time in the quiet of the studio in addition to the work in teams. I can't do the community work all the time as I did when I was younger. That time had a sense of urgency that drove us to be activists. I learned a lot on my feet, but it took several years for me to look back and reflect. That's where I am now—one foot in community, the other in my reflective space. I have integrated the two, and I am still seeking and changing.

> *Every moment of one's existence*
> *One is growing into more*
> *Or retreating into less.*
> *One is always living*
> *A little more—*
> *Or dying a little bit.*
> —Norman Mailer

One year to live? I would definitely pick one project and be out there doing that. I often think I would have loved to live my life like John Muir and take off with my tools and be in nature and bring the story home. When I stood at the crossroads between scientist and artist, I made the decision to study art instead of becoming a botanist. I long for the outside territory, want to take off with my plant press, my camera, and a backpack, wandering, immersing myself during that last year of my life.

I live my creativity most truly in community. If you are creative and alert, you find your work along the streets, in the city. There is a hunger for the arts: Listen, involve yourself! Live your art in your daily life.

> *Now I become myself. It's taken time, many years and places;*
> *I have been dissolved and shaken—worn other people's faces.*
> *My work, my love, my time,*
> *My face now gathered into one song.*
> —May Sarton

THEODORA CAPALDO

I live my life as art as I surround myself with my personal sense of beauty, and also when I appreciate creativity in others. I am creative in my daily life when I write, when I use metaphors, when I cook. Oh, let's not forget cooking. I love food. I am Italian. Cooking is so imaginative! Cooking is art. I never follow a recipe. Food is such a beautiful way of enjoying life and nurturing the body at the same time. I got more tomatoes this year than ever before because my cousin planted them and taught me how to do it right. Oh, those red tomatoes!

Living creatively means being reminded of the intensity that is you, and marveling how amazing life is. That's when you are motivated and have the energy to make something happen in a proactive way, not in a reactive way. We spend in general much too much time reacting to the outer world. Creativity is proactive. And in our ordinary daily life, we often come not from a creative place but from routine and habit and caring and planning.

Somebody asked me years ago, "Why do you do this animal work?" And I said, "Because the moment when people get it is like nothing else!" Watching that is the creative aspect of my endeavor. That's the product you are searching for. It's not about, "You have to think like I do." It's much deeper, a deep understanding emerging.

Here's a recent example, a film of an amazing whale whose fin was trapped by a fisher's net, and the fisher was in a tiny boat, and the whale had to bring herself up and again up to breathe, and they realized on the boat that she was in trouble, that she was held down by this net in which she was caught. It would have killed her. So they freed her from the net, and you can watch how she is celebrating and full of joy, having her freedom back, and the viewers see it and they are transformed in that moment. That's social activism. It's bigger than mankind. It's what everything is made of, and we have to constantly figure out how we relate to that in ways that do not destroy it. McCarthy says in his book about the wolf, "It is that which mankind cannot afford to lose." That relationship is what I see as the core of my animal work, the creative transformation of this relationship to the Other, the creature world. This is social activism that helps people to see this universe in new ways.

I have some rituals in my life that intensify my joy.

Yes—French roast expensive coffee! If I try another, I am miserable. This is for me a very sacred drug that I take every morning! And I look forward to this ritual.

My home is my ritual, my coffee and three or four different places to sit and look outside into my trees. One morning, I saw a little pack of coyotes in my back yard; other times, there may be deer, or there may be just silence, or the Parker River, and I am twenty minutes from the ocean—I go there and delight in the salty air. Every day, my yard and my home are my comfort and a reminder how important beauty is, and nature and calm. My friends call my home a sanctuary,

I surround myself with what I love. As Rumi says, "Let the beauty you love be what you do." Beauty is so important for me that I admit that when I go to a hotel, I might take pictures off the wall in my room because they don't delight me, or rather distract me and make me unhappy.

What sets me on fire? Beauty, and music—a lot of music. It affects my energy level and my joy of life, totally.

To celebrate and protect life in all its richness, I cannot celebrate being alive while I know so many suffer. I have helped humans for decades, and my last twenty-five years or more have been dedicated to celebrating the beauty of animals and working to protect the many ways in which they are vulnerable to the dark sides of humans. For me, no prayer is truer than that of the bodhisattva Kuan Yin who lived a life devoted to helping all beings be happy.

My passion for animal work is at once both a drive toward beauty as much as it is a drive to fight evil. I do believe that some people delight in hurting animals. Others do so out of a blindness caused by their own self-interest, and some because they are simply unaware and do not care. I am moved to tears by the natural beauty that animals of all species hold: the magnificence of a silverback gorilla—handsome, powerful—or the strength and genius of the matriarch of an elephant herd of her sisters and aunts and children and grandchildren, or the leaping agility of a golden red fox in the field hunting for dinner, in perfect balance with her natural world.

I left my life as a psychotherapist to fully pursue animal advocacy. My own consciousness reached a pitch where I could not sit back anymore and allow what I saw and knew was happening to continue without my fight, my voice raised clear and wise and loud for them. I had to turn my sight and work to penetrate the abuse and suffering. I had to find ways to end their cruel and senseless man-made suffering and deaths. This day and to my final day, I am committed, every cell in me is committed to this work. My life's purpose is to be one who helps to restore the balance and respect humans are meant to have with the natural world. My work is dedicated to life so that the intricate, fierce and vulnerable life system can remain whole and as nature planned.

I see my rage, my sadness in the face of the atrocities as simply one more proof of how much I love it all. To me, nothing is as grand or holy as nature—her beauty, her violence and storms. I can so understand how native people, indigenous people, worship the gods and goddesses of nature. It is where for me too everything is right, my lessons learned. The delicate wild flowers and the speed with which a cheetah hunts and kills are part of a plan, a divine plan that humans have not only not contributed to but to our own demise have acted counter to. We cannot save ourselves if we do not save the animals. Their beauty is our beauty. And so I work now, every day, for the animals. It is my gift to them, to me and to every human that walks on Mother Earth, even those who do not realize this.

As I am reminded of the intensity that this all stirs in me, I am most in touch with my marveling at how amazing life is. This is when I am truly motivated and have the energy to make something new or fresh happen in a proactive way. I am fortunate to be born under the sign of the archer, allowing me to see and aim ahead while both my feet are firmly planted beneath me. Creativity is this same vision. It is proactive, looking firmly at what is and at the same time at what might be out there beyond the here and now.

I suspect we all need a passion and mission to help where needed, the comfort of being surrounded by our personal sense of beauty, and the sustenance of food that was loved when prepared and turned into the fuel for your life so you could love and be loved.

If I had one year to live, there is one thing I would do: I would fulfill the fantasy of living in Europe for a while. I would go to Italy and live there for at least six months. *Dolce far niente*! Other than that, no, I wouldn't do anything differently. It's kind of a nice thing to realize that I don't have a bucket list. There are things to do, but I don't have to, have no big urge. I am enjoying life but don't have a list of desired things not yet lived.

One more experience of creativity: She is an exciting and sometimes terrifying goddess because she helps you to stretch beyond the edge of the map on which you are living your life. That's possibly new for you and will shine its light bright and stunningly on your actions. If you want to sit on your couch undisturbed, don't get involved with her.

Shanti's Muse

Her feet are heavy and large; there's sand and mud between her crusty toes. Where she walks, grass bows down to earth and stones press into the ground. She is brown-skinned, and her hair moves like a lazy river in waves and circles. There is no sweetness in her fierce eyes. Her laughter is the roar of a lion, and she cries into the wind with the croaking sound of raven. She smells like piñon and fur. Her sweat is spicy; her eyes flicker like ambers. She is wounded; flowers and young birch trees grow out of the crack in her heart. She loves this earth like a mother bear her cubs; she strikes with claws at any intruder in her den. At the end of the day, she pulls darkness from the sky so all creatures may sleep and dream. She spreads her arms, and owls settle on her shoulders, night birds nestle in her furry hair and in her bearded armpits. She is the sister I meet when I walk through forests. She approaches me and reaches with her arms around my waist to lift my body toward the moon.

She is protectress and challenger. She is the muse of wind and hail, of thunder and earthquakes. She tears holes into the clouds to open them for inspiration so that the unknown will be known to me. Don't anger her, don't hurt her, or she might strike you and rip you apart to feed you to the foxes and ferrets or to her own children. But if you gently reach toward her, comb her muddy hair and hold her big feet in your lap, she will smile. She will dance until the ground shakes under her toes and heels and her heavy steps will crack stones and branches.

I love her with fear, and I fear her with love. I trust her. She has planted seeds in my heart, seeds that want to grow into art and songs and poems of the night and day.

> *We must become ignorant*
> *Of all we've been taught,*
> *And be, instead, bewildered.*
> *Run from what's profitable and comfortable.*
> *If you drink those liqueurs, you'll spill*
> *The spring water of your real life.*
> *Forget safety.*
> *Live where you fear to live,*
> *Destroy your reputation.*
> *Be notorious.*
> *I have tried notorious planning*
> *Long enough; from now on,*
> *I'll live wild.*
> —Rumi

The Interview Questions

(Numbers indicate the chapters related to those questions.)

- What are the first memories about a creative object for you as a child?
- Did you have supporters of your creativity in your youth?

* * *

1. How do you define creativity?
2. Do you know your creative process?
3. Talk about profound encounters with the art/science of somebody else.
4. What role do time, place, and location play in your creative endeavors?
5. What is the source of your creativity?
6. Is there a dark side to creativity? How does it manifest?
7. What triggers your resistance to the process of creating?
8. Do you work in community or do you prefer solitude?
9. Creativity and money?
10. Is there a difference between an artist and a scientist?
11. What is the healing power of creativity?
12. How do you live your life as art?

* * *

Other questions to contemplate:
- Do you think suffering is part of creativity, or even a source of it?
- Do creative people have to sacrifice to create their art?
- How do you charge your creative batteries?

- What sets you on fire?
- Are you sometimes bored or blocked? How do you deal with it?
- Does the recipient, the reader/viewer/listener/buyer of your art/work mean to you?
- If you had only one more year to live, would you change your life and lifestyle?

About the Author

Shanti Elke Bannwart was born in Hamburg, Germany, at the onset of World War II, and moved to the United States in 1983.

She is a life-coach and psychotherapist in private practice in Santa Fe, New Mexico, as well as a clay artist educated at the Institute of American Indian Arts, with a focus on indigenous mythology and art. She also has a master's degree in Expressive Arts Therapies from Lesley University in Cambridge, Massachusetts, and received an MFA in creative writing from Goddard College in 2009.

She has traveled worldwide and led national and international workshops and educational training. Her writing includes literary competition prize-winners and essays in national and international magazines.

Made in the USA
Monee, IL
07 July 2020